D1569622

The Elements of Computing Systems

Waubonsee Community College
Libraries
Aurora - Sugar Grove - Plano

Noam Nisan and Shimon Schocken

The Elements of Computing Systems

Building a Modern Computer from First Principles

The MIT Press
Cambridge, Massachusetts
London, England

First MIT Press paperback edition, 2008
© 2005 Massachusetts Institute of Technology

All rights reserved. No part of this book may be reproduced in any form by any electronic or mechanical means (including photocopying, recording, or information storage and retrieval) without permission in writing from the publisher.

This book was set in Times New Roman on 3B2 by Asco Typesetters, Hong Kong.
Printed and bound in the United States of America.

Library of Congress Cataloging-in-Publication Data

Nisan, Noam.
The elements of computing systems: building a modern computer from first principles /
Noam Nisan and Shimon Schocken.
    p.   cm.
Includes bibliographical references and index.
ISBN 978-0-262-14087-4 (hc : alk. paper)—978-0-262-64068-8 (pb)
1. Electronic digital computers. I. Schocken, Shimon. II. Title.
TK7888.3.N57   2005
004.16—dc22   2005042807

10   9   8

Note on Software

The book's web site (http://www.nand2tetris.org) provides the tools and materials necessary to build all the hardware and software systems described in the book. These include a hardware simulator, a CPU emulator, a VM emulator, and executable versions of the assembler, virtual machine, compiler, and operating system described in the book. The Web site also includes all the project materials—about 200 test programs and test scripts, allowing incremental development and unit-testing of each one of the 12 projects. All the supplied software tools and project materials can be used as is on any computer equipped with either Windows or Linux.

To our parents,
For teaching us that less is more.

Contents

Preface

What I hear, I forget; What I see, I remember; What I do, I understand.
—Confucius, 551–479 BC

Once upon a time, every computer specialist had a gestalt understanding of how computers worked. The overall interactions among hardware, software, compilers, and the operating system were simple and transparent enough to produce a coherent picture of the computer's operations. As modern computer technologies have become increasingly more complex, this clarity is all but lost: the most fundamental ideas and techniques in computer science—the very essence of the field—are now hidden under many layers of obscure interfaces and proprietary implementations. An inevitable consequence of this complexity has been specialization, leading to computer science curricula of many courses, each covering a single aspect of the field.

We wrote this book because we felt that many computer science students are missing the forest for the trees. The typical student is marshaled through a series of courses in programming, theory, and engineering, without pausing to appreciate the beauty of the picture at large. And the picture at large is such that hardware and software systems are tightly interrelated through a hidden web of abstractions, interfaces, and contract-based implementations. Failure to see this intricate enterprise in the flesh leaves many students and professionals with an uneasy feeling that, well, they don't fully understand what's going on inside computers.

We believe that the best way to understand how computers work is to build one from scratch. With that in mind, we came up with the following concept. Let's specify a simple but sufficiently powerful computer system, and have the students build its hardware platform and software hierarchy from the ground up, starting with nothing more than elementary logic gates. And while we are at it, let's do it right. We say this because building a general-purpose computer from first principles is a huge undertaking. Therefore, we identified a unique educational opportunity not only to build the thing, but also to illustrate, in a hands-on fashion, how to effectively plan and manage large-scale hardware and software development projects. In addition, we sought to demonstrate the ability to construct, through recursive ascent and human reasoning, fantastically complex and useful systems from nothing more than a few primitive building blocks.

Scope

The book exposes students to a significant body of computer science knowledge, gained through a series of hardware and software construction tasks. These tasks demonstrate how theoretical and applied techniques taught in other computer science courses are used in practice. In particular, the following topics are illustrated in a hands-on fashion:

- *Hardware:* Logic gates, Boolean arithmetic, multiplexors, flip-flops, registers, RAM units, counters, Hardware Description Language (HDL), chip simulation and testing.

- *Architecture:* ALU/CPU design and implementation, machine code, assembly language programming, addressing modes, memory-mapped input/output (I/O).

- *Operating systems:* Memory management, math library, basic I/O drivers, screen management, file I/O, high-level language support.

- *Programming languages:* Object-based design and programming, abstract data types, scoping rules, syntax and semantics, references.

- *Compilers:* Lexical analysis, top-down parsing, symbol tables, virtual stack-based machine, code generation, implementation of arrays and objects.

- *Data structures and algorithms:* Stacks, hash tables, lists, recursion, arithmetic algorithms, geometric algorithms, running time considerations.

- *Software engineering:* Modular design, the interface/implementation paradigm, API design and documentation, proactive test planning, programming at the large, quality assurance.

All these topics are presented with a very clear purpose: building a modern computer from the ground up. In fact, this has been our topic selection rule: The book focuses on the minimal set of topics necessary for building a fully functioning computer system. As it turns out, this set includes many fundamental ideas in applied computer science.

Courses

The book's web site (www.idc.ac.il/tecs) features a complete set of lectures—one lecture per book chapter—that support a full semester course on applied computer science. Variants of this course are offered by universities and colleges, where they are titled *Elements of Computing Systems*, *Digital Systems Construction*, *Computer Construction Workshop*, *Let's Build a Computer*, and the like, and are typically open to both undergraduate and graduate students. Generally speaking, courses based on the book are "perpendicular" to the normal computer science curriculum, and can be taken at almost any point during the program. Two natural slots are "CS-2"—an introductory post-programming course, and "CS-199"—an elective or capstone course coming at the end of the program. The former course entails a systems-oriented introduction to computer science, and the latter an integrative, project-oriented systems building course.

The book is completely self-contained, requiring only programming (in any language) as a prerequisite. In particular, all the CS knowledge required to build the computer is given in the book. Thus, the book lends itself not only to CS majors, but also to non-majors and computer-savvy students (including high schools) seeking a hands-on view of hardware architectures, compilation, operating systems, and modern software engineering in the framework of one course. The book is also popular among self-learners who read the text and build the computer off the web, following our project specifications, as we explain below.

Structure

The introduction chapter presents our approach and previews the main hardware and software abstractions discussed in the book. This sets the stage for chapters 1–12, each dedicated to a key hardware or software abstraction, a proposed implementation, and an actual project that builds and tests it. The first five chapters focus on constructing the hardware platform of a simple modern computer. The remaining seven chapters describe the design and implementation of a typical multi-tier software hierarchy, culminating in the construction of an object-based programming language and a simple operating system. The complete game plan is depicted in figure P.1.

The book is based on an *abstraction-implementation* paradigm. Each chapter starts with a Background section, describing relevant concepts and a generic hardware or software system. The next section is always Specification, which provides a clear

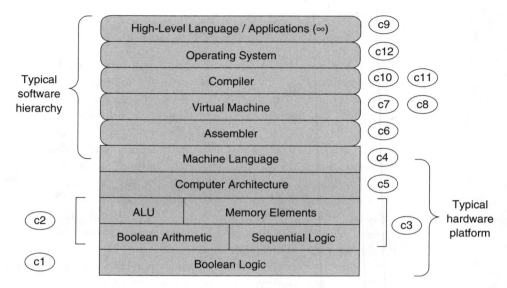

Figure P.1　Book and proposed course map, with chapter numbers in circles.

statement of the system's abstraction—namely, the various services that it is expected to deliver. Having presented the *what*, each chapter proceeds to discuss *how* the abstraction can be implemented, leading to a (proposed) Implementation section. The next section is always Perspective, in which we highlight noteworthy issues left out from the chapter. Each chapter ends with a Project section that provides step-by-step building instructions, testing materials, and software tools for actually building and unit-testing the system described in the chapter.

Projects

The computer system described in the book is *for real*—it can actually be built, and it works! A reader who takes the time and effort to gradually build this computer will gain a level of intimate understanding unmatched by mere reading. Hence, the book is geared toward active readers who are willing to roll up their sleeves and build a computer from the ground up.

Each chapter includes a complete description of a stand-alone hardware or software development project. The four projects that construct the computer platform are built using a simple Hardware Description Language (HDL) and simulated on a hardware simulator supplied with the book. Five of the subsequent software projects (assembler, virtual machine I and II, and compiler I and II) can be written in any modern programming language. The remaining three projects (low-level programming, high-level programming, and the operating system) are written in the assembly language and high-level language implemented in previous projects.

Project Tips   There are twelve projects altogether. On average, each project entails a weekly homework load in a typical, rigorous university-level course. The projects are completely self-contained and can be done (or skipped) in any desired order. Of course the "full experience" package requires doing all the projects in their order of appearance, but this is just one option.

When we teach courses based on this book, we normally make two significant concessions. First, except for obvious cases, we pay no attention to optimization, leaving this very important subject to other, more specific courses. Second, when developing the translators suite (assembler, VM implementation, and compiler), we supply error-free test files (source programs), allowing the students to assume that the inputs of these translators are error-free. This eliminates the need to write code for handling errors and exceptions, making the software projects significantly more manageable. Dealing with incorrect input is of course critically important, but once again we assume that students can hone this skill elsewhere, for example, in dedicated programming and software design courses.

Software

The book's web site (www.nand2tetris.org) provides the tools and materials necessary to build all the hardware and software systems described in the book. These include a hardware simulator, a CPU emulator, a VM emulator, and executable versions of the assembler, virtual machine, compiler, and operating system described in the book. The Web site also includes all the project materials—about two hundred test programs and test scripts, allowing incremental development and unit-testing of each one of the twelve projects. All the supplied software tools and project materials can be used as is on any computer equipped with either Windows or Linux.

Acknowledgments

All the software that accompanies the book was developed by our students at the Efi Arazi School of Computer Science at IDC Herzliya, a new Israeli university, and at the Hebrew University of Jerusalem. The chief software architects were Yaron Ukrainitz and Yannai Gonczarowski, and the developers included Iftach Amit, Nir Rozen, Assaf Gad, and Hadar Rosen-Sior. Working with these student-developers has been a great pleasure, and we feel proud and fortunate to have had the opportunity to play a role in their education. We also thank our teaching assistants, Muawyah Akash, David Rabinowitz, Ran Navok, and Yaron Ukrainitz, who helped run early versions of the course that led to this book. Thanks also to Jonathan Gross and Oren Baranes, who worked on related projects under the excellent supervision of Dr. Danny Seidner, to Uri Zeira and Oren Cohen, for designing an integrated development environment for the Jack language, to Tal Achituv, for useful advice on open source issues, and to Aryeh Schnall and Zdzislaw Ploski, for careful reading and meticulous editing suggestions.

Writing the book without taking any reduction in our regular professional duties was not simple, and so we wish to thank Esti Romem, administrative director of the Efi Arazi School of Computer Science, for holding the fort in difficult times. Finally, we are indebted to the many students who endured early versions of this book and helped polish it through numerous bug reports. In the process, we hope, they have learned first-hand that insight of James Joyce, that *mistakes are the portals of discovery*.

Noam Nisan

Shimon Schocken

The Elements of Computing Systems

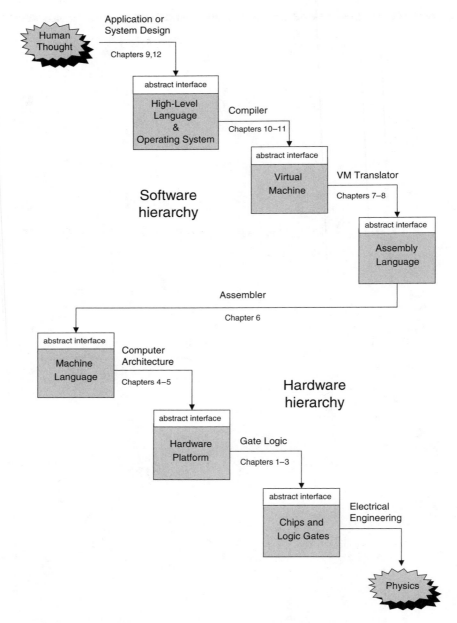

Figure I.1 The major abstractions underlying the design of a typical computing system. The implementation of each level is accomplished using abstract services and building blocks from the level below.

Introduction: Hello, World Below

The true voyage of discovery consists not of going to new places, but of having a new pair of eyes.
—Marcel Proust (1871–1922)

This book is a voyage of discovery. You are about to learn three things: how computers work, how to break complex problems into manageable modules, and how to develop large-scale hardware and software systems. This will be a hands-on process as you create a complete and working computer system from the ground up. The lessons you will learn, which are far more important and general than the computer itself, will be gained as side effects of this activity. According to the psychologist Carl Rogers, "the only kind of learning which significantly influences behavior is self-discovered or self-appropriated—truth that has been assimilated in experience." This chapter sketches some of the discoveries, truths, and experiences that lie ahead.

The World Above

If you have taken any programming course, you've probably encountered something like the program below early in your education. This particular program is written in *Jack*—a simple high-level language that has a conventional object-based syntax.

```
// First example in Programming 101:
class Main {
  function void main() {
    do Output.printString("Hello World");
    do Output.println(); // New line.
    return;
  }
}
```

Trivial programs like Hello World are deceptively simple. Did you ever think about what it takes to *actually run* such a program on a computer? Let's look under the hood. For starters, note that the program is nothing more than a bunch of dead characters stored in a text file. Thus, the first thing we must do is parse this text, uncover its semantics, and reexpress it in some low-level language understood by our computer. The result of this elaborate translation process, known as *compilation*, will be yet another text file, containing machine-level code.

Of course machine language is also an abstraction—an agreed upon set of binary codes. In order to make this abstract formalism concrete, it must be realized by some *hardware architecture*. And this architecture, in turn, is implemented by a certain *chip set*—registers, memory units, ALU, and so on. Now, every one of these hardware devices is constructed from an integrated package of *elementary logic gates*. And these gates, in turn, can be built from primitive gates like *Nand* and *Nor*. Of course every one of these gates consists of several *switching devices*, typically implemented by transistors. And each transistor is made of— Well, we won't go further than that, because that's where computer science ends and physics starts.

You may be thinking: "On *my* computer, compiling and running a program is much easier—all I have to do is click some icons or write some commands!" Indeed, a modern computer system is like a huge iceberg, and most people get to see only the top. Their knowledge of computing systems is sketchy and superficial. If, however, you wish to explore beneath the surface, then lucky you! There's a fascinating world down there, made of some of the most beautiful stuff in computer science. An intimate understanding of this underworld is one of the things that separate naïve programmers from sophisticated developers—people who can create not only application programs, but also complex hardware and software technologies. And the best way to understand how these technologies work—and we mean understand them in the marrow of your bones—is to build a complete computer system from scratch.

Abstractions

You may wonder how it is humanly possible to construct a complete computer system from the ground up, starting with nothing more than elementary logic gates. This must be an enormously complex enterprise! We deal with this complexity by breaking the project into *modules*, and treating each module separately, in a stand-alone chapter. You might then wonder, how is it possible to describe and construct these modules in isolation? Obviously they are all interrelated! As we will show throughout the book, a good modular design implies just that: You can work on the individual modules independently, while completely ignoring the rest of the system. In fact, you can even build these modules in any desired order!

It turns out that this strategy works well thanks to a special gift unique to humans: our ability to create and use *abstractions*. The notion of abstraction, central to many arts and sciences, is normally taken to be a mental expression that seeks to separate in thought, and capture in some concise manner, the essence of some entity. In computer science, we take the notion of abstraction very concretely, defining it to be a statement of "what the entity does" and ignoring the details of "how it does it." This functional description must capture all that needs to be known in order to use the entity's services, and nothing more. All the work, cleverness, information, and drama that went into the entity's implementation are concealed from the client who is supposed to use it, since they are simply irrelevant. The articulation, use, and implementation of such abstractions are the bread and butter of our profession: Every hardware and software developer is routinely defining abstractions (also called "interfaces") and then implementing them, or asking other people to implement them. The abstractions are often built layer upon layer, resulting in higher and higher levels of capabilities.

Designing good abstractions is a practical art, and one that is best acquired by seeing many examples. Therefore, this book is based on an abstraction-implementation paradigm. Each book chapter presents a key hardware or software abstraction, and a project designed to actually implement it. Thanks to the modular nature of these abstractions, each chapter also entails a stand-alone intellectual unit, inviting the reader to focus on two things only: understanding the given abstraction (a rich world of its own), and then implementing it using abstract services and building blocks from the level below. As you push ahead in this journey, it will be rather thrilling to look back and appreciate the computer that is gradually taking shape in the wake of your efforts.

The World Below

The multi-tier collection of abstractions underlying the design of a computing system can be described *top-down*, showing how high-level abstractions can be reduced into, or expressed by, simpler ones. This structure can also be described *bottom-up*, focusing on how lower-level abstractions can be used to construct more complex ones. This book takes the latter approach: We begin with the most basic elements—

primitive logic gates—and work our way upward, culminating in the construction of a general-purpose computer system. And if building such a computer is like climbing Mount Everest, then planting a flag on the mountaintop is like having the computer run a program written in some high-level language. Since we are going to ascend this mountain from the ground up, let us survey the book plan in the opposite direction—from the top down—starting in the familiar territory of high-level programming.

Our tour consists of three main legs. We start at the top, where people write and run high-level programs (chapters 9 and 12). We then survey the road down to hardware land, tracking the fascinating twists and turns of translating high-level programs into machine language (chapters 6, 7, 8, 10, 11). Finally, we reach the low grounds of our journey, describing how a typical hardware platform is actually constructed (chapters 1–5).

High-Level Language Land

The topmost abstraction in our journey is the art of programming, where entrepreneurs and programmers dream up applications and write software that implements them. In doing so, they blissfully take for granted the two key tools of their trade: the high-level language in which they work, and the rich library of services that supports it. For example, consider the statement do `Output.printString("Hello World")`. This code invokes an abstract service for printing strings—a service that must be implemented *somewhere*. Indeed, a bit of drilling reveals that this service is usually supplied jointly by the host operating system and the standard language library.

What then is a *standard language library*? And how does an *operating system* (OS) work? These questions are taken up in chapter 12. We start by presenting key algorithms relevant to OS services, and then use them to implement various mathematical functions, string operations, memory allocation tasks, and input/output (I/O) routines. The result is a simple operating system, written in the Jack programming language, just like Unix is written in the C language.

Jack is a simple object-based language, designed for a single purpose: to illustrate the key software engineering principles underlying the design and implementation of modern programming languages like Java and C#. Jack is presented in chapter 9, which also illustrates how to build Jack-based applications, for example, computer games. If you have any programming experience with a modern object-oriented language, you can start writing Jack programs right away and watch them execute on the computer platform developed in previous chapters. However, the goal of chapter

9 is not to turn you into a Jack programmer, but rather to prepare you to develop the compiler and operating system described in subsequent chapters.

The Road Down to Hardware Land

Before any program can actually run and do something for real, it must be translated into the machine language of some target computer platform. This *compilation* process is sufficiently complex to be broken into several layers of abstraction, and these usually involve three translators: a compiler, a virtual machine implementation, and an assembler. We devote five book chapters to this trio, as follows.

The translation task of the *compiler* is performed in two conceptual stages: syntax analysis and code generation. First, the source text is analyzed and grouped into meaningful language constructs that can be kept in a data structure called a "parse tree." These parsing tasks, collectively known as *syntax analysis*, are described in chapter 10. This sets the stage for chapter 11, which shows how the parse tree can be recursively processed to yield a program written in an intermediate language. As with Java and C#, the intermediate code generated by the Jack compiler describes a sequence of generic steps operating on a stack-based virtual machine (VM). This classical model, as well as a VM implementation that realizes it on an actual computer, are elaborated in chapters 7–8. Since the output of our VM implementation is a large assembly program, we have to translate it further into binary code. Writing an assembler is a relatively simple task, taken up in chapter 6.

Hardware Land

We have reached the most profound step in our journey—the descent from machine language to the machine itself—the point where software finally meets hardware. This is also the point where *Hack* enters the picture. Hack is a general-purpose computer system, designed to strike a balance between simplicity and power. On the one hand, the Hack architecture can be built in just a few hours of work, using the guidelines and chip set presented in chapters 1–3. At the same time, Hack is sufficiently general to illustrate the key operating principles and hardware elements underlying the design of any digital computer.

The machine language of the Hack platform is specified in chapter 4, and the computer design itself is discussed and specified in chapter 5. Readers can build this computer as well as all the chips and gates mentioned in the book on their home computers, using the software-based hardware simulator supplied with the book and the Hardware Description Language (HDL) documented in appendix A. All the developed hardware modules can be tested using supplied test scripts, written in a scripting language documented in appendix B.

The computer that emerges from this construction is based on typical components like CPU, RAM, ROM, and simulated screen and keyboard. The computer's registers and memory systems are built in chapter 3, following a brief discussion of sequential logic. The computer's combinational logic, culminating in the Arithmetic Logic Unit (ALU) chip, is built in chapter 2, following a brief discussion of Boolean arithmetic. All the chips presented in these chapters are based on a suite of elementary logic gates, presented and built in chapter 1.

Of course the layers of abstraction don't stop here. Elementary logic gates are built from transistors, using technologies based on solid-state physics and ultimately quantum mechanics. Indeed, this is where the abstractions of the *natural world*, as studied and formulated by physicists, become the building blocks of the abstractions of the *synthetic worlds* built and studied by computer scientists.

This marks the end of our grand tour preview—the descent from the high-level peaks of object-based software, all the way down to the bricks and mortar of the hardware platform. This typical modular rendition of a multi-tier system represents not only a powerful engineering paradigm, but also a central dogma in human reasoning, going back at least 2,500 years:

We deliberate not about ends, but about means. For a doctor does not deliberate whether he shall heal, nor an orator whether he shall persuade ... They assume the end and consider how and by what means it is attained, and if it seems easily and best produced thereby; while if it is achieved by other means, *they consider how* it *will be achieved and by what means* this *will be achieved, until they come to the first cause ... and what is last in the order of analysis seems to be first in the order of becoming.* (Aristotles, *Nicomachean Ethics*, Book III, 3, 1112b)

So here's the plan, in the order of becoming. Starting with the construction of elementary logic gates (chapter 1), we go bottom-up to combinational and sequential chips (chapters 2–3), through the design of a typical computer architecture (chapters 4–5) and a typical software hierarchy (chapters 6–8), all the way to implementing a compiler (chapters 10–11) for a modern object-based language (chapter 9), ending with the design and implementation of a simple operating system (chapter 12). We hope that the reader has gained a general idea of what lies ahead and is eager to push forward on this grand tour of discovery. So, assuming that you are ready and set, let the countdown start: 1, 0, Go!

1   Boolean Logic

Such simple things, And we make of them something so complex it defeats us, Almost.
—John Ashbery (b. 1927), American poet

Every digital device—be it a personal computer, a cellular telephone, or a network router—is based on a set of chips designed to store and process information. Although these chips come in different shapes and forms, they are all made from the same building blocks: Elementary *logic gates*. The gates can be physically implemented in many different materials and fabrication technologies, but their logical behavior, or interface, is consistent across all computers. In this chapter we start out with one primitive logic gate—Nand—and build all the other logic gates from it. The result is a rather standard set of gates, which will be later used to construct our computer's processing and storage chips. This will be done in chapters 2 and 3, respectively.

All the hardware chapters in the book, beginning with this one, have the same structure. Each chapter focuses on a well-defined task, designed to construct or integrate a certain family of chips. The prerequisite knowledge needed to approach this task is provided in a brief Background section. The next section provides a complete Specification of the chips' abstractions, namely, the various services that they should deliver, one way or another. Having presented the *what*, a subsequent Implementation section proposes guidelines and hints about *how* the chips can be actually implemented. A Perspective section rounds up the chapter with concluding comments about important topics that were left out from the discussion. Each chapter ends with a technical Project section. This section gives step-by-step instructions for actually building the chips on a personal computer, using the hardware simulator supplied with the book.

This being the first hardware chapter in the book, the Background section is somewhat lengthy, featuring a special section on *hardware description and simulation tools*.

1.1   Background

This chapter focuses on the construction of a family of simple chips called *Boolean gates*. Since Boolean gates are physical implementations of *Boolean functions*, we start with a brief treatment of Boolean algebra. We then show how Boolean gates implementing simple Boolean functions can be interconnected to deliver the functionality of more complex chips. We conclude the background section with a description of how hardware design is actually done in practice, using software simulation tools.

1.1.1   Boolean Algebra

Boolean algebra deals with Boolean (also called binary) values that are typically labeled true/false, 1/0, yes/no, on/off, and so forth. We will use 1 and 0. A Boolean function is a function that operates on binary inputs and returns binary outputs. Since computer hardware is based on the representation and manipulation of binary values, Boolean functions play a central role in the specification, construction, and optimization of hardware architectures. Hence, the ability to formulate and analyze Boolean functions is the first step toward constructing computer architectures.

Truth Table Representation   The simplest way to specify a Boolean function is to enumerate all the possible values of the function's input variables, along with the function's output for each set of inputs. This is called the *truth table* representation of the function, illustrated in figure 1.1.

The first three columns of figure 1.1 enumerate all the possible binary values of the function's variables. For each one of the 2^n possible tuples $v_1 \ldots v_n$ (here $n = 3$), the last column gives the value of $f(v_1 \ldots v_n)$.

Boolean Expressions   In addition to the truth table specification, a Boolean function can also be specified using Boolean operations over its input variables. The basic Boolean operators that are typically used are "And" (x And y is 1 exactly when both x and y are 1) "Or" (x Or y is 1 exactly when either x or y or both are 1), and "Not" (Not x is 1 exactly when x is 0). We will use a common arithmetic-like notation for these operations: $x \cdot y$ (or xy) means x And y, $x + y$ means x Or y, and $\bar{x}$ means Not x.

To illustrate, it turns out that the function defined in figure 1.1 is equivalently given by the Boolean expression $f(x, y, z) = (x + y) \cdot \bar{z}$. For example, let us evaluate

x	y	z	$f(x, y, z)$
0	0	0	0
0	0	1	0
0	1	0	1
0	1	1	0
1	0	0	1
1	0	1	0
1	1	0	1
1	1	1	0

Figure 1.1   Truth table representation of a Boolean function (example).

this expression on the inputs $x = 0$, $y = 1$, $z = 0$ (third row in the table). Since y is 1, it follows that $x + y = 1$ and thus $1 \cdot \bar{0} = 1 \cdot 1 = 1$. The complete verification of the equivalence between the expression and the truth table is achieved by evaluating the functional expression on each of the eight possible input combinations, verifying that it yields the same value listed in the table's right column.

Canonical Representation   As it turns out, every Boolean function can be expressed using at least one Boolean expression called the *canonical representation*. Starting with the function's truth table, we focus on all the rows in which the function has value 1. For each such row, we construct a term created by And-ing together *literals* (variables or their negations) that fix the values of all the row's inputs. For example, let us focus on the third row in figure 1.1, where the function's value is 1. Since the variable values in this row are $x = 0$, $y = 1$, $z = 0$, we construct the term $\bar{x}y\bar{z}$. Following the same procedure, we construct the terms $x\bar{y}\bar{z}$ and $xy\bar{z}$ for rows 5 and 7. Now, if we Or-together all these terms (for all the rows where the function has value 1), we get a Boolean expression that is equivalent to the given truth table. Thus the canonical representation of the Boolean function shown in figure 1.1 is $f(x, y, z) = \bar{x}y\bar{z} + x\bar{y}\bar{z} + xy\bar{z}$. This construction leads to an important conclusion: Every Boolean function, no matter how complex, can be expressed using three Boolean operators only: And, Or, and Not.

Two-Input Boolean Functions   An inspection of figure 1.1 reveals that the number of Boolean functions that can be defined over n binary variables is 2^{2^n}. For example, the sixteen Boolean functions spanned by two variables are listed in figure 1.2. These functions were constructed systematically, by enumerating all the possible 4-wise combinations of binary values in the four right columns. Each function has a conventional

Function		x	0	0	1	1
		y	0	1	0	1
Constant 0	0		0	0	0	0
And	$x \cdot y$		0	0	0	1
x And Not y	$x \cdot \bar{y}$		0	0	1	0
x	x		0	0	1	1
Not x And y	$\bar{x} \cdot y$		0	1	0	0
y	y		0	1	0	1
Xor	$x \cdot \bar{y} + \bar{x} \cdot y$		0	1	1	0
Or	$x + y$		0	1	1	1
Nor	$\overline{x + y}$		1	0	0	0
Equivalence	$x \cdot y + \bar{x} \cdot \bar{y}$		1	0	0	1
Not y	$\bar{y}$		1	0	1	0
If y then x	$x + \bar{y}$		1	0	1	1
Not x	$\bar{x}$		1	1	0	0
If x then y	$\bar{x} + y$		1	1	0	1
Nand	$\overline{x \cdot y}$		1	1	1	0
Constant 1	1		1	1	1	1

Figure 1.2   All the Boolean functions of two variables.

name that seeks to describe its underlying operation. Here are some examples: The name of the Nor function is shorthand for Not-Or: Take the Or of x and y, then negate the result. The Xor function—shorthand for "exclusive or"—returns 1 when its two variables have opposing truth-values and 0 otherwise. Conversely, the Equivalence function returns 1 when the two variables have identical truth-values. The If-x-then-y function (also known as $x \rightarrow y$, or "x Implies y") returns 1 when x is 0 or when both x and y are 1. The other functions are self-explanatory.

The Nand function (as well as the Nor function) has an interesting theoretical property: Each one of the operations And, Or, and Not can be constructed from it, and it alone (e.g., x Or $y = (x$ Nand $x)$ Nand $(y$ Nand $y))$. And since every Boolean function can be constructed from And, Or, and Not operations using the canonical representation method, it follows that every Boolean function can be constructed from Nand operations alone. This result has far-reaching practical implications: Once we have in our disposal a physical device that implements Nand, we can use many copies of this device (wired in a certain way) to implement in hardware any Boolean function. All we have to do is come up with the right pattern of connectivity.

1.1.2   Gate Logic

A *gate* is a physical device that implements a Boolean function. If a Boolean function *f* operates on *n* variables and returns *m* binary results (in all our examples so far, *m* was 1), the gate that implements *f* will have *n* *input pins* and *m* *output pins*. When we put some values $v_1 \ldots v_n$ in the gate's input pins, the gate's "logic"—its internal structure—should compute and output $f(v_1 \ldots v_n)$. And just like complex Boolean functions can be expressed in terms of simpler functions, complex gates are composed from more elementary gates. The simplest gates of all are made from tiny switching devices, called *transistors*, wired in a certain topology designed to effect the overall gate functionality.

Although most digital computers today use electricity to represent and transmit binary data from one gate to another, any alternative technology permitting switching and conducting capabilities can be employed. Indeed, during the last fifty years, researchers have built many hardware implementations of Boolean functions, including magnetic, optical, biological, hydraulic, and pneumatic mechanisms. Today, most gates are implemented as transistors etched in silicon, packaged as *chips*. In this book we use the words *chip* and *gate* interchangeably, tending to use the term *gates* for simple chips.

The availability of alternative switching technology options, on the one hand, and the observation that Boolean algebra can be used to abstract the behavior of *any* such technology, on the other, is extremely important. Basically, it implies that computer scientists don't have to worry about physical things like electricity, circuits, switches, relays, and power supply. Instead, computer scientists can be content with the abstract notions of Boolean algebra and gate logic, trusting that someone else (the physicists and electrical engineers—bless their souls) will figure out how to actually realize them in hardware. Hence, a *primitive gate* (see figure 1.3) can be viewed as a black box device that implements an elementary logical operation in one way or another—we don't care how. A hardware designer starts from such primitive gates and designs more complicated functionality by interconnecting them, leading to the construction of *composite* gates.

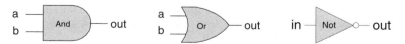

Figure 1.3   Standard symbolic notation of some elementary logic gates.

Gate interface   **Gate implementation**

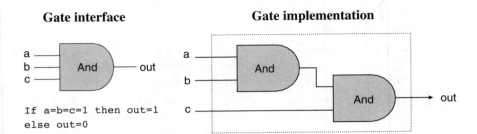

If a=b=c=1 then out=1
else out=0

Figure 1.4 Composite implementation of a three-way And gate. The rectangle on the right defines the conceptual boundaries of the gate interface.

Primitive and Composite Gates   Since all logic gates have the same input and output semantics (0's and 1's), they can be chained together, creating *composite gates* of arbitrary complexity. For example, suppose we are asked to implement the 3-way Boolean function And(a, b, c). Using Boolean algebra, we can begin by observing that $a \cdot b \cdot c = (a \cdot b) \cdot c$, or, using prefix notation, And$(a, b, c) =$ And$($And$(a, b), c)$. Next, we can use this result to construct the composite gate depicted in figure 1.4.

The construction described in figure 1.4 is a simple example of *gate logic*, also called *logic design*. Simply put, logic design is the art of interconnecting gates in order to implement more complex functionality, leading to the notion of *composite gates*. Since composite gates are themselves realizations of (possibly complex) Boolean functions, their "outside appearance" (e.g., left side of figure 1.4) looks just like that of primitive gates. At the same time, their internal structure can be rather complex.

We see that any given logic gate can be viewed from two different perspectives: external and internal. The right-hand side of figure 1.4 gives the gate's internal architecture, or *implementation*, whereas the left side shows only the gate *interface*, namely, the input and output pins that it exposes to the outside world. The former is relevant only to the gate designer, whereas the latter is the right level of detail for other designers who wish to use the gate as an abstract off-the-shelf component, without paying attention to its internal structure.

Let us consider another logic design example—that of a Xor gate. As discussed before, Xor(a, b) is 1 exactly when either a is 1 and b is 0, or when a is 0 and b is 1. Said otherwise, Xor$(a, b) =$ Or$($And$(a,$ Not$(b))$, And$($Not$(a), b))$. This definition leads to the logic design shown in figure 1.5.

Note that the gate *interface* is unique: There is only one way to describe it, and this is normally done using a truth table, a Boolean expression, or some verbal specifica-

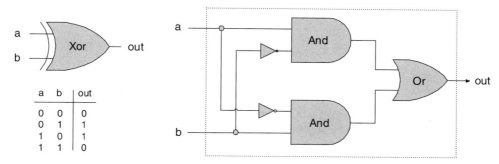

a	b	out
0	0	0
0	1	1
1	0	1
1	1	0

Figure 1.5   Xor gate, along with a possible implementation.

tion. This interface, however, can be realized using many different *implementations*, some of which will be better than others in terms of cost, speed, efficiency, simplicity, and elegance. For example, the Xor function can be implemented using four, rather than five, And, Or, and Not gates. Thus, from a functional standpoint, the fundamental requirement of logic design is that *the gate implementation will realize its stated interface, in one way or another.* From an efficiency standpoint, the general rule is to try to *do more with less*, that is, use as few gates as possible.

To sum up, the art of logic design can be described as follows: Given a gate specification (interface), find an efficient way to implement it using other gates that were already implemented. This, in a nutshell, is what we will do in the rest of this chapter.

1.1.3   Actual Hardware Construction

Having described the logic of composing complex gates from simpler ones, we are now in a position to discuss how gates are actually built. Let us start with an intentionally naïve example.

Suppose we open a chip fabrication shop in our home garage. Our first contract is to build a hundred Xor gates. Using the order's downpayment, we purchase a soldering gun, a roll of copper wire, and three bins labeled "And gates," "Or gates," and "Not gates," each containing many identical copies of these elementary logic gates. Each of these gates is sealed in a plastic casing that exposes some input and output pins, as well as a power supply plug. To get started, we pin figure 1.5 to our garage wall and proceed to realize it using our hardware. First, we take two And gates, two Not gates, and one Or gate, and mount them on a board according to the figure's layout. Next, we connect the chips to one another by running copper wires among them and by soldering the wire ends to the respective input/output pins. Now, if we follow the gate diagram carefully, we will end up having three exposed wire ends. We then solder a pin to each one of these wire ends, seal the entire device (except for the three pins) in a plastic casing, and label it "Xor." We can repeat this assembly process many times over. At the end of the day, we can store all the chips that we've built in a new bin and label it "Xor gates." If we (or other people) are asked to construct some other chips in the future, we'll be able to use these Xor gates as elementary building blocks, just as we used the And, Or, and Not gates before.

As the reader has probably sensed, the garage approach to chip production leaves much to be desired. For starters, there is no guarantee that the given chip diagram is correct. Although we can prove correctness in simple cases like Xor, we cannot do so in many realistically complex chips. Thus, we must settle for empirical testing: Build the chip, connect it to a power supply, activate and deactivate the input pins in various configurations, and hope that the chip outputs will agree with its specifications. If the chip fails to deliver the desired outputs, we will have to tinker with its physical structure—a rather messy affair. Further, even if we will come up with the right design, replicating the chip assembly process many times over will be a time-consuming and error-prone affair. There must be a better way!

1.1.4   Hardware Description Language (HDL)

Today, hardware designers no longer build anything with their bare hands. Instead, they plan and optimize the chip architecture on a computer workstation, using structured modeling formalisms like *Hardware Description Language*, or HDL (also known as VHDL, where V stands for *Virtual*). The designer specifies the chip structure by writing an *HDL program*, which is then subjected to a rigorous battery of tests. These tests are carried out virtually, using computer simulation: A special software tool, called a *hardware simulator*, takes the HDL program as input and builds an image of the modeled chip in memory. Next, the designer can instruct the simulator to test the virtual chip on various sets of inputs, generating simulated chip outputs. The outputs can then be compared to the desired results, as mandated by the client who ordered the chip built.

In addition to testing the chip's correctness, the hardware designer will typically be interested in a variety of parameters such as speed of computation, energy consumption, and the overall cost implied by the chip design. All these parameters can be simulated and quantified by the hardware simulator, helping the designer optimize the design until the simulated chip delivers desired cost/performance levels.

Thus, using HDL, one can completely plan, debug, and optimize the entire chip before a single penny is spent on actual production. When the HDL program is deemed complete, that is, when the performance of the simulated chip satisfies the client who ordered it, the HDL program can become the blueprint from which many copies of the physical chip can be stamped in silicon. This final step in the chip life cycle—from an optimized HDL program to mass production—is typically outsourced to companies that specialize in chip fabrication, using one switching technology or another.

Example: Building a Xor Gate   As we have seen in figures 1.2 and 1.5, one way to define *exclusive or* is $\mathrm{Xor}(a,b) = \mathrm{Or}(\mathrm{And}(a, \mathrm{Not}(b)), \mathrm{And}(\mathrm{Not}(a), b))$. This logic can be expressed either graphically, as a gate diagram, or textually, as an HDL program. The latter program is written in the HDL variant used throughout this book, defined in appendix A. See figure 1.6 for the details.

Explanation   An HDL definition of a chip consists of a *header* section and a *parts* section. The header section specifies the chip *interface*, namely the chip name and the names of its input and output pins. The parts section describes the names and topology of all the lower-level parts (other chips) from which this chip is constructed. Each part is represented by a *statement* that specifies the part name and the way it is connected to other parts in the design. Note that in order to write such statements legibly, the HDL programmer must have a complete documentation of the underlying parts' *interfaces*. For example, figure 1.6 assumes that the input and output pins of the Not gate are labeled `in` and `out`, and those of And and Or are labeled `a`, `b` and `out`. This API-type information is not obvious, and one must have access to it before one can plug the chip parts into the present code.

Inter-part connections are described by creating and connecting *internal pins*, as needed. For example, consider the bottom of the gate diagram, where the output of a Not gate is piped into the input of a subsequent And gate. The HDL code describes this connection by the pair of statements `Not(...,out=nota)` and `And(a=nota,...)`. The first statement creates an internal pin (outbound wire) named `nota`, feeding `out` into it. The second statement feeds the value of `nota` into the `a` input of an And gate. Note that pins may have an unlimited fan out. For example, in figure 1.6, each input is simultaneously fed into two gates. In gate

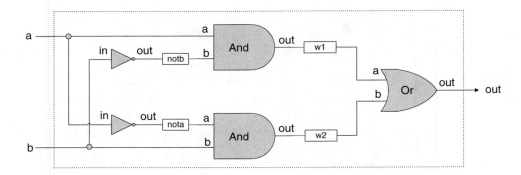

HDL program (Xor.hdl)	*Test script* (Xor.tst)	*Output file* (Xor.out)

```
/* Xor (exclusive or) gate:        load Xor.hdl,
   If a<>b out=1 else out=0. */    output-list a, b, out;
CHIP Xor {                         set a 0, set b 0,
   IN a, b;                        eval, output;
   OUT out;                        set a 0, set b 1,
   PARTS:                          eval, output;
   Not(in=a, out=nota);           set a 1, set b 0,
   Not(in=b, out=notb);           eval, output;
   And(a=a, b=notb, out=w1);      set a 1, set b 1,
   And(a=nota, b=b, out=w2);      eval, output;
   Or(a=w1, b=w2, out=out);
}
```

a	b	out
0	0	0
0	1	1
1	0	1
1	1	0

Figure 1.6   HDL implementation of a Xor gate.

diagrams, multiple connections are described using forks. In HDL, the existence of forks is implied by the code.

Testing   Rigorous quality assurance mandates that chips be tested in a specific, replicable, and well-documented fashion. With that in mind, hardware simulators are usually designed to run *test scripts*, written in some scripting language. For example, the test script in figure 1.6 is written in the scripting language understood by the hardware simulator supplied with the book. This scripting language is described fully in appendix B.

Let us give a brief description of the test script from figure 1.6. The first two lines of the test script instruct the simulator to load the Xor.hdl program and get ready to print the values of selected variables. Next, the script lists a series of testing scenarios, designed to simulate the various contingencies under which the Xor chip will have to operate in "real-life" situations. In each scenario, the script instructs the simulator to bind the chip inputs to certain data values, compute the resulting output, and record the test results in a designated output file. In the case of simple gates like Xor, one can write an exhaustive test script that enumerates all the possible input values of the gate. The resulting output file (right side of figure 1.6) can then be viewed as a complete empirical proof that the chip is well designed. The luxury of such certitude is not feasible in more complex chips, as we will see later.

1.1.5   Hardware Simulation

Since HDL is a hardware construction *language*, the process of writing and debugging HDL programs is quite similar to software development. The main difference is that instead of writing code in a language like Java, we write it in HDL, and instead of using a compiler to translate and test the code, we use a *hardware simulator*. The hardware simulator is a computer program that knows how to parse and interpret HDL code, turn it into an executable representation, and test it according to the specifications of a given test script. There exist many commercial hardware simulators on the market, and these vary greatly in terms of cost, complexity, and ease of use. Together with this book we provide a simple (and free!) hardware simulator that is sufficiently powerful to support sophisticated hardware design projects. In particular, the simulator provides all the necessary tools for building, testing, and integrating all the chips presented in the book, leading to the construction of a general-purpose computer. Figure 1.7 illustrates a typical chip simulation session.

1.2   Specification

This section specifies a typical set of gates, each designed to carry out a common Boolean operation. These gates will be used in the chapters that follow to construct the full architecture of a typical modern computer. Our starting point is a single primitive Nand gate, from which all other gates will be derived recursively. Note that we provide only the gates' specifications, or interfaces, delaying implementation details until a subsequent section. Readers who wish to construct the specified gates in HDL are encouraged to do so, referring to appendix A as needed. All the gates can be built and simulated on a personal computer, using the hardware simulator supplied with the book.

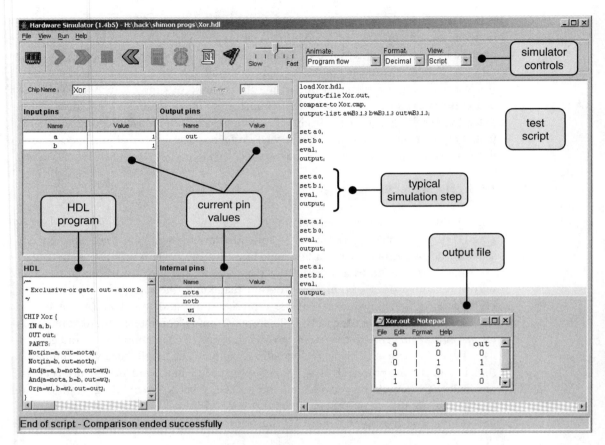

Figure 1.7 A screen shot of simulating an Xor chip on the hardware simulator. The simulator state is shown just after the test script has completed running. The pin values correspond to the last simulation step ($a = b = 1$). Note that the *output file* generated by the simulation is consistent with the Xor truth table, indicating that the loaded HDL program delivers a correct Xor functionality. The *compare file*, not shown in the figure and typically specified by the chip's client, has exactly the same structure and contents as that of the output file. The fact that the two files agree with each other is evident from the status message displayed at the bottom of the screen.

1.2.1   The Nand Gate

The starting point of our computer architecture is the Nand gate, from which all other gates and chips are built. The Nand gate is designed to compute the following Boolean function:

a	b	$\text{Nand}(a, b)$
0	0	1
0	1	1
1	0	1
1	1	0

Throughout the book, we use "chip API boxes" to specify chips. For each chip, the API specifies the chip name, the names of its input and output pins, the function or operation that the chip effects, and an optional comment.

```
Chip name:  Nand
Inputs:     a, b
Outputs:    out
Function:   If a=b=1 then out=0 else out=1
Comment:    This gate is considered primitive and thus there is
            no need to implement it.
```

1.2.2   Basic Logic Gates

Some of the logic gates presented here are typically referred to as "elementary" or "basic." At the same time, every one of them can be composed from Nand gates alone. Therefore, they need not be viewed as primitive.

Not   The single-input Not gate, also known as "converter," converts its input from 0 to 1 and vice versa. The gate API is as follows:

```
Chip name:  Not
Inputs:     in
Outputs:    out
Function:   If in=0 then out=1 else out=0.
```

And   The And function returns 1 when both its inputs are 1, and 0 otherwise.

```
Chip name: And
Inputs:    a, b
Outputs:   out
Function:  If a=b=1 then out=1 else out=0.
```

Or   The Or function returns 1 when at least one of its inputs is 1, and 0 otherwise.

```
Chip name: Or
Inputs:    a, b
Outputs:   out
Function:  If a=b=0 then out=0 else out=1.
```

Xor   The Xor function, also known as "exclusive or," returns 1 when its two inputs have opposing values, and 0 otherwise.

```
Chip name: Xor
Inputs:    a, b
Outputs:   out
Function:  If a!=b then out=1 else out=0.
```

Multiplexor   A multiplexor (figure 1.8) is a three-input gate that uses one of the inputs, called "selection bit," to select and output one of the other two inputs, called "data bits." Thus, a better name for this device might have been *selector*. The name *multiplexor* was adopted from communications systems, where similar clocked devices are used to serialize (multiplex) several input signals over a single output wire.

```
Chip name: Mux
Inputs:    a, b, sel
Outputs:   out
Function:  If sel=0 then out=a else out=b.
```

a	b	sel	out
0	0	0	0
0	1	0	0
1	0	0	1
1	1	0	1
0	0	1	0
0	1	1	1
1	0	1	0
1	1	1	1

sel	out
0	a
1	b

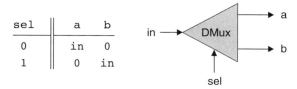

Figure 1.8 Multiplexor. The table at the top right is an abbreviated version of the truth table on the left.

sel	a	b
0	in	0
1	0	in

Figure 1.9 Demultiplexor.

Demultiplexor   A demultiplexor (figure 1.9) performs the opposite function of a multiplexor: It takes a single input and channels it to one of two possible outputs according to a selector bit that specifies which output to chose.

```
Chip name:  DMux
Inputs:     in, sel
Outputs:    a, b
Function:   If sel=0 then {a=in, b=0} else {a=0, b=in}.
```

1.2.3   Multi-Bit Versions of Basic Gates

Computer hardware is typically designed to operate on multi-bit arrays called "buses." For example, a basic requirement of a 32-bit computer is to be able to compute (bit-wise) an And function on two given 32-bit buses. To implement this operation, we can build an array of 32 binary And gates, each operating separately on a pair of bits. In order to enclose all this logic in one package, we can encapsulate the gates array in a single chip interface consisting of two 32-bit input buses and one 32-bit output bus.

This section describes a typical set of such multi-bit logic gates, as needed for the construction of a typical 16-bit computer. We note in passing that the architecture of n-bit logic gates is basically the same irrespective of n's value.

When referring to individual bits in a bus, it is common to use an array syntax. For example, to refer to individual bits in a 16-bit bus named `data`, we use the notation `data[0]`, `data[1]`,..., `data[15]`.

Multi-Bit Not   An n-bit Not gate applies the Boolean operation Not to every one of the bits in its n-bit input bus:

```
Chip name:  Not16
Inputs:     in[16] // a 16-bit pin
Outputs:    out[16]
Function:   For i=0..15 out[i]=Not(in[i]).
```

Multi-Bit And   An n-bit And gate applies the Boolean operation And to every one of the n bit-pairs arrayed in its two n-bit input buses:

```
Chip name:  And16
Inputs:     a[16], b[16]
Outputs:    out[16]
Function:   For i=0..15 out[i]=And(a[i],b[i]).
```

Multi-Bit Or   An n-bit Or gate applies the Boolean operation Or to every one of the n bit-pairs arrayed in its two n-bit input buses:

```
Chip name:  Or16
Inputs:     a[16], b[16]
Outputs:    out[16]
Function:   For i=0..15 out[i]=Or(a[i],b[i]).
```

Multi-Bit Multiplexor   An *n*-bit multiplexor is exactly the same as the binary multi-plexor described in figure 1.8, except that the two inputs are each *n*-bit wide; the selector is a single bit.

```
Chip name: Mux16
Inputs:    a[16], b[16], sel
Outputs:   out[16]
Function:  If sel=0 then for i=0..15 out[i]=a[i]
           else for i=0..15 out[i]=b[i].
```

1.2.4   Multi-Way Versions of Basic Gates

Many 2-way logic gates that accept two inputs have natural generalization to multi-way variants that accept an arbitrary number of inputs. This section describes a set of multi-way gates that will be used subsequently in various chips in our computer architecture. Similar generalizations can be developed for other architectures, as needed.

Multi-Way Or   An *n*-way Or gate outputs 1 when at least one of its *n* bit inputs is 1, and 0 otherwise. Here is the 8-way variant of this gate:

```
Chip name: Or8Way
Inputs:    in[8]
Outputs:   out
Function:  out=Or(in[0],in[1],...,in[7]).
```

Multi-Way/Multi-Bit Multiplexor   An *m*-way *n*-bit multiplexor selects one of *m n*-bit input buses and outputs it to a single *n*-bit output bus. The selection is speci-fied by a set of *k* control bits, where $k = \log_2 m$. Figure 1.10 depicts a typical example.

   The computer platform that we develop in this book requires two variations of this chip: A 4-way 16-bit multiplexor and an 8-way 16-bit multiplexor:

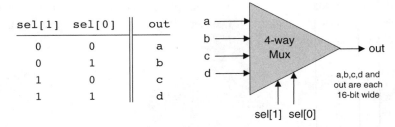

sel[1]	sel[0] || out
0	0	a
0	1	b
1	0	c
1	1	d

Figure 1.10   4-way multiplexor. The width of the input and output buses may vary.

```
Chip name:  Mux4Way16
Inputs:     a[16], b[16], c[16], d[16], sel[2]
Outputs:    out[16]
Function:   If sel=00 then out=a else if sel=01 then out=b
            else if sel=10 then out=c else if sel=11 then out=d
Comment:    The assignment operations mentioned above are all
            16-bit. For example, "out=a" means "for i=0..15
            out[i]=a[i]".
```

```
Chip name:  Mux8Way16
Inputs:     a[16],b[16],c[16],d[16],e[16],f[16],g[16],h[16],
            sel[3]
Outputs:    out[16]
Function:   If sel=000 then out=a else if sel=001 then out=b
            else if sel=010 out=c ... else if sel=111 then out=h
Comment:    The assignment operations mentioned above are all
            16-bit. For example, "out=a" means "for i=0..15
            out[i]=a[i]".
```

Multi-Way/Multi-Bit Demultiplexor   An m-way n-bit demultiplexor (figure 1.11) channels a single n-bit input into one of m possible n-bit outputs. The selection is specified by a set of k control bits, where $k = \log_2 m$.

The specific computer platform that we will build requires two variations of this chip: A 4-way 1-bit demultiplexor and an 8-way 1-bit demultiplexor, as follows.

sel[1]	sel[0]	a	b	c	d
0	0	in	0	0	0
0	1	0	in	0	0
1	0	0	0	in	0
1	1	0	0	0	in

Figure 1.11   4-way demultiplexor.

```
Chip name:  DMux4Way
Inputs:     in, sel[2]
Outputs:    a, b, c, d
Function:   If sel=00 then      {a=in, b=c=d=0}
            else if sel=01 then {b=in, a=c=d=0}
            else if sel=10 then {c=in, a=b=d=0}
            else if sel=11 then {d=in, a=b=c=0}.
```

```
Chip name:  DMux8Way
Inputs:     in, sel[3]
Outputs:    a, b, c, d, e, f, g, h
Function:   If sel=000 then      {a=in, b=c=d=e=f=g=h=0}
            else if sel=001 then {b=in, a=c=d=e=f=g=h=0}
            else if sel=010 ...
            ...
            else if sel=111 then {h=in, a=b=c=d=e=f=g=0}.
```

1.3   Implementation

Similar to the role of *axioms* in mathematics, *primitive gates* provide a set of elementary building blocks from which everything else can be built. Operationally, primitive gates have an "off-the-shelf" implementation that is supplied externally. Thus, they can be used in the construction of other gates and chips without worrying about their internal design. In the computer architecture that we are now beginning to build, we have chosen to base all the hardware on one primitive gate only: Nand. We now turn to outlining the first stage of this bottom-up hardware construction project, one gate at a time.

Our implementation guidelines are intentionally partial, since we want you to discover the actual gate architectures yourself. We reiterate that each gate can be implemented in more than one way; the simpler the implementation, the better.

Not: The implementation of a unary Not gate from a binary Nand gate is simple. Tip: Think positive.

And: Once again, the gate implementation is simple. Tip: Think negative.

Or/Xor: These functions can be defined in terms of some of the Boolean functions implemented previously, using some simple Boolean manipulations. Thus, the respective gates can be built using previously built gates.

Multiplexor/Demultiplexor: Likewise, these gates can be built using previously built gates.

Multi-Bit Not/And/Or Gates: Since we already know how to implement the elementary versions of these gates, the implementation of their n-ary versions is simply a matter of constructing arrays of n elementary gates, having each gate operate separately on its bit inputs. This implementation task is rather boring, but it will carry its weight when these multi-bit gates are used in more complex chips, as described in subsequent chapters.

Multi-Bit Multiplexor: The implementation of an n-ary multiplexor is simply a matter of feeding the same selection bit to every one of n binary multiplexors. Again, a boring task resulting in a very useful chip.

Multi-Way Gates: Implementation tip: Think forks.

1.4   Perspective

This chapter described the first steps taken in an applied digital design project. In the next chapter we will build more complicated functionality using the gates built here.

Although we have chosen to use Nand as our basic building block, other approaches are possible. For example, one can build a complete computer platform using Nor gates alone, or, alternatively, a combination of And, Or, and Not gates. These constructive approaches to logic design are theoretically equivalent, just as all the theorems in the same geometry can be founded on different sets of axioms as alternative points of departure. The theory and practice of such constructions are covered in standard textbooks about *digital design* or *logic design*.

Throughout the chapter, we paid no attention to efficiency considerations such as the number of elementary gates used in constructing a composite gate or the number of wire crossovers implied by the design. Such considerations are critically important in practice, and a great deal of computer science and electrical engineering expertise focuses on optimizing them. Another issue we did not address at all is the physical implementation of gates and chips using the laws of physics, for example, the role of transistors embedded in silicon. There are of course several such implementation options, each having its own characteristics (speed, power requirements, production cost, etc.). Any nontrivial coverage of these issues requires some background in electronics and physics.

1.5   Project

Objective   Implement all the logic gates presented in the chapter. The only building blocks that you can use are primitive Nand gates and the composite gates that you will gradually build on top of them.

Resources   The only tool that you need for this project is the hardware simulator supplied with the book. All the chips should be implemented in the HDL language specified in appendix A. For each one of the chips mentioned in the chapter, we provide a skeletal `.hdl` program (text file) with a missing implementation part. In addition, for each chip we provide a `.tst` script file that tells the hardware simulator how to test it, along with the correct output file that this script should generate, called `.cmp` or "compare file." Your job is to complete the missing implementation parts of the supplied `.hdl` programs.

Contract   When loaded into the hardware simulator, your chip design (modified `.hdl` program), tested on the supplied `.tst` file, should produce the outputs listed in the supplied `.cmp` file. If that is not the case, the simulator will let you know.

Tips   The Nand gate is considered primitive and thus there is no need to build it: Whenever you use Nand in one of your HDL programs, the simulator will automatically invoke its built-in `tools/builtIn/Nand.hdl` implementation. We recommend implementing the other gates in this project in the order in which they appear in the chapter. However, since the `builtIn` directory features working versions of all the chips described in the book, you can always use these chips without defining them first: The simulator will automatically use their built-in versions.

For example, consider the skeletal `Mux.hdl` program supplied in this project. Suppose that for one reason or another you did not complete this program's implementation, but you still want to use Mux gates as internal parts in other chip designs. This is not a problem, thanks to the following convention. If our simulator fails to find a `Mux.hdl` file in the current directory, it automatically invokes a built-in Mux implementation, pre-supplied with the simulator's software. This built-in implementation—a Java class stored in the `builtIn` directory—has the same interface and functionality as those of the Mux gate described in the book. Thus, if you want the simulator to ignore one or more of your chip implementations, simply move the corresponding `.hdl` files out of the current directory.

Steps   We recommend proceeding in the following order:

0.   The *hardware simulator* needed for this project is available in the `tools` directory of the book's software suite.

1.   Read appendix A, sections A1–A6 only.

2.   Go through the *hardware simulator tutorial*, parts I, II, and III only.

3.   Build and simulate all the chips specified in the `projects/01` directory.

2   Boolean Arithmetic

Counting is the religion of this generation, its hope and salvation.
—Gertrude Stein (1874–1946)

In this chapter we build gate logic designs that represent numbers and perform arithmetic operations on them. Our starting point is the set of logic gates built in chapter 1, and our ending point is a fully functional Arithmetic Logical Unit. The ALU is the centerpiece chip that executes all the arithmetic and logical operations performed by the computer. Hence, building the ALU functionality is an important step toward understanding how the Central Processing Unit (CPU) and the overall computer work.

As usual, we approach this task gradually. The first section gives a brief Background on how binary codes and Boolean arithmetic can be used, respectively, to represent and add signed numbers. The Specification section describes a succession of *adder chips*, designed to add two bits, three bits, and pairs of n-bit binary numbers. This sets the stage for the ALU specification, which is based on a sophisticated yet simple logic design. The Implementation and Project sections provide tips and guidelines on how to build the adder chips and the ALU on a personal computer, using the hardware simulator supplied with the book.

Binary addition is a simple operation that runs deep. Remarkably, most of the operations performed by digital computers can be reduced to elementary additions of binary numbers. Therefore, constructive understanding of binary addition holds the key to the implementation of numerous computer operations that depend on it, one way or another.

2.1 Background

Binary Numbers   Unlike the decimal system, which is founded on base 10, the binary system is founded on base 2. When we are given a certain binary pattern, say "10011," and we are told that this pattern is supposed to represent an integer number, the equivalent decimal value of this number is computed by convention as follows:

$$(10011)_{two} = 1 \cdot 2^4 + 0 \cdot 2^3 + 0 \cdot 2^2 + 1 \cdot 2^1 + 1 \cdot 2^0 = 19 \tag{1}$$

In general, let $x = x_n x_{n-1} \ldots x_0$ be a string of digits. The *value* of x in base b, denoted $(x)_b$, is defined as follows:

$$(x_n x_{n-1} \ldots x_0)_b = \sum_{i=0}^{n} x_i \cdot b^i \tag{2}$$

The reader can verify that in the case of $(10011)_{two}$, rule (2) reduces to calculation (1).

The result of calculation (1) happens to be 19. Thus, when we press the keyboard keys labeled '1', '9' and ENTER while running, say, a spreadsheet program, what ends up in some register in the computer's memory is the binary code 10011. More precisely, if the computer happens to be a 32-bit machine, what gets stored in the register is the bit pattern 00000000000000000000000000010011.

Binary Addition   A pair of binary numbers can be added digit by digit from right to left, according to the same elementary school method used in decimal addition. First, we add the two right-most digits, also called the *least significant bits* (LSB) of the two binary numbers. Next, we add the resulting carry bit (which is either 0 or 1) to the sum of the next pair of bits up the significance ladder. We continue the process until the two *most significant bits* (MSB) are added. If the last bit-wise addition generates a carry of 1, we can report overflow; otherwise, the addition completes successfully:

0	0	0	1		(carry)	1	1	1	1	
	1	**0**	**0**	**1**	x		**1**	**0**	**1**	**1**
+	**0**	**1**	**0**	**1**	y	+	**0**	**1**	**1**	**1**
0	1	1	1	0	$x + y$	1	0	0	1	0
	no overflow						overflow			

We see that computer hardware for binary addition of two n-bit numbers can be built from logic gates designed to calculate the sum of three bits (pair of bits plus carry bit). The transfer of the resulting carry bit forward to the addition of the next significant pair of bits can be easily accomplished by proper wiring of the 3-bit adder gates.

Signed Binary Numbers   A binary system with n digits can generate a set of 2^n different bit patterns. If we have to represent signed numbers in binary code, a natural solution is to split this space into two equal subsets. One subset of codes is assigned to represent positive numbers, and the other negative numbers. Ideally, the coding scheme should be chosen in such a way that the introduction of signed numbers would complicate the hardware implementation as little as possible.

This challenge has led to the development of several coding schemes for representing signed numbers in binary code. The method used today by almost all computers is called the *2's complement* method, also known as *radix complement*. In a binary system with n digits, the 2's complement of the number x is defined as follows:

$$\bar{x} = \begin{cases} 2^n - x & \text{if } x \neq 0 \\ 0 & \text{otherwise} \end{cases}$$

For example, in a 5-bit binary system, the 2's complement representation of -2 or "minus$(00010)_{two}$" is $2^5 - (00010)_{two} = (32)_{ten} - (2)_{ten} = (30)_{ten} = (11110)_{two}$. To check the calculation, the reader can verify that $(00010)_{two} + (11110)_{two} = (00000)_{two}$. Note that in the latter computation, the sum is actually $(100000)_{two}$, but since we are dealing with a 5-bit binary system, the left-most sixth bit is simply ignored. As a rule, when the 2's complement method is applied to n-bit numbers, $x + (-x)$ always sums up to 2^n (i.e., 1 followed by n 0's)—a property that gives the method its name. Figure 2.1 illustrates a 4-bit binary system with the 2's complement method.

An inspection of figure 2.1 suggests that an n-bit binary system with 2's complement representation has the following properties:

Positive numbers		Negative numbers	
0	0000		
1	0001	1111	-1
2	0010	1110	-2
3	0011	1101	-3
4	0100	1100	-4
5	0101	1011	-5
6	0110	1010	-6
7	0111	1001	-7
		1000	-8

Figure 2.1   2's complement representation of signed numbers in a 4-bit binary system.

- The system can code a total of 2^n signed numbers, of which the maximal and minimal numbers are $2^{n-1} - 1$ and -2^{n-1}, respectively.
- The codes of all positive numbers begin with a 0.
- The codes of all negative numbers begin with a 1.
- To obtain the code of $-x$ from the code of x, leave all the trailing (least significant) 0's and the first least significant 1 intact, and flip all the remaining bits (convert 0's to 1's and vice versa). An equivalent shortcut, which is easier to implement in hardware, is to flip all the bits of x and add 1 to the result.

A particularly attractive feature of this representation is that addition of any two signed numbers in 2's complement is exactly the same as addition of positive numbers. Consider, for example, the addition operation $(-2) + (-3)$. Using 2's complement (in a 4-bit representation), we have to add, in binary, $(1110)_{two} + (1101)_{two}$. Without paying any attention to which numbers (positive or negative) these codes represent, bit-wise addition will yield 1011 (after throwing away the overflow bit). As figure 2.1 shows, this indeed is the 2's complement representation of -5.

In short, we see that the 2's complement method facilitates the addition of any two signed numbers without requiring special hardware beyond that needed for simple bit-wise addition. What about subtraction? Recall that in the 2's complement method, the arithmetic negation of a signed number x, that is, computing $-x$, is achieved by negating all the bits of x and adding 1 to the result. Thus subtraction can be easily handled by $x - y = x + (-y)$. Once again, hardware complexity is kept to a minimum.

The material implications of these theoretical results are significant. Basically, they imply that a single chip, called *Arithmetic Logical Unit*, can be used to encapsulate all the basic arithmetic and logical operators performed in hardware. We now turn to specify one such ALU, beginning with the specification of an *adder* chip.

2.2 Specification

2.2.1 Adders

We present a hierarchy of three adders, leading to a multi-bit adder chip:

- *Half-adder:* designed to add two bits
- *Full-adder:* designed to add three bits
- *Adder:* designed to add two n-bit numbers

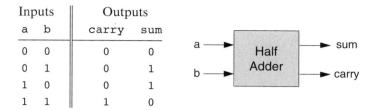

Inputs		Outputs	
a	b	carry	sum
0	0	0	0
0	1	0	1
1	0	0	1
1	1	1	0

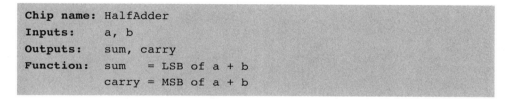

```
Chip name: HalfAdder
Inputs:    a, b
Outputs:   sum, carry
Function:  sum   = LSB of a + b
           carry = MSB of a + b
```

Figure 2.2   Half-adder, designed to add 2 bits.

We also present a special-purpose adder, called *incrementer*, designed to add 1 to a given number. We intentionally focus on the abstract/functional description of these chips, delaying implementation details to a later section.

Half-Adder   The first step on our way to adding binary numbers is to be able to add two bits. Let us call the least significant bit of the addition sum, and the most significant bit carry. Figure 2.2 presents a chip, called half-adder, designed to carry out this operation.

Full-Adder   Now that we know how to add two bits, figure 2.3 presents a *full-adder* chip, designed to add three bits. Like the half-adder case, the full-adder chip produces two outputs: the least significant bit of the addition, and the carry bit.

Adder   Memory and register chips represent integer numbers by n-bit patterns, n being 16, 32, 64, and so forth—depending on the computer platform. The chip whose job is to add such numbers is called a multi-bit adder, or simply *adder*. Figure 2.4 presents a 16-bit adder, noting that the same logic and specifications scale up as is to any n-bit adder.

Incrementer   It is convenient to have a special-purpose chip dedicated to adding the constant 1 to a given number. Here is the specification of a 16-bit incrementer:

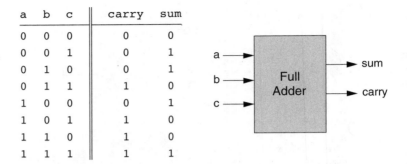

a	b	c	carry	sum
0	0	0	0	0
0	0	1	0	1
0	1	0	0	1
0	1	1	1	0
1	0	0	0	1
1	0	1	1	0
1	1	0	1	0
1	1	1	1	1

```
Chip name:  FullAdder
Inputs:     a, b, c
Outputs:    sum, carry
Function:   sum = LSB of a + b + c
            carry = MSB of a + b + c
```

Figure 2.3 Full-adder, designed to add 3 bits.

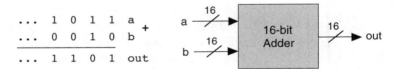

```
Chip name:  Add16
Inputs:     a[16], b[16]
Outputs:    out[16]
Function:   out = a + b
Comment:    Integer 2's complement addition.
            Overflow is neither detected nor handled.
```

Figure 2.4 16-bit adder. Addition of two *n*-bit binary numbers for any *n* is "more of the same."

```
Chip name:  Inc16
Inputs:     in[16]
Outputs:    out[16]
Function:   out=in+1
Comment:    Integer 2's complement addition.
            Overflow is neither detected nor handled.
```

2.2.2 The Arithmetic Logic Unit (ALU)

The specifications of the adder chips presented so far were generic, meaning that they hold for any computer. In contrast, this section describes an ALU that will later become the centerpiece of a specific computer platform called *Hack*. At the same time, the principles underlying the design of our ALU are rather general. Further, our ALU architecture achieves a great deal of functionality using a minimal set of internal parts. In that respect, it provides a good example of an efficient and elegant logic design.

The Hack ALU computes a fixed set of functions $out = f_i(x, y)$ where x and y are the chip's two 16-bit inputs, *out* is the chip's 16-bit output, and f_i is an arithmetic or logical function selected from a fixed repertoire of eighteen possible functions. We instruct the ALU which function to compute by setting six input bits, called *control bits*, to selected binary values. The exact input-output specification is given in figure 2.5, using pseudo-code.

Note that each one of the six control bits instructs the ALU to carry out a certain elementary operation. Taken together, the combined effects of these operations cause the ALU to compute a variety of useful functions. Since the overall operation is driven by six control bits, the ALU can potentially compute $2^6 = 64$ different functions. Eighteen of these functions are documented in figure 2.6.

We see that programming our ALU to compute a certain function $f(x, y)$ is done by setting the six control bits to the code of the desired function. From this point on, the internal ALU logic specified in figure 2.5 should cause the ALU to output the value $f(x, y)$ specified in figure 2.6. Of course, this does not happen miraculously, it's the result of careful design.

For example, let us consider the twelfth row of figure 2.6, where the ALU is instructed to compute the function x-1. The zx and nx bits are 0, so the x input is neither zeroed nor negated. The zy and ny bits are 1, so the y input is first zeroed, and then negated bit-wise. Bit-wise negation of zero, $(000\ldots00)_{two}$, gives $(111\ldots11)_{two}$, the 2's complement code of -1. Thus the ALU inputs end up being x

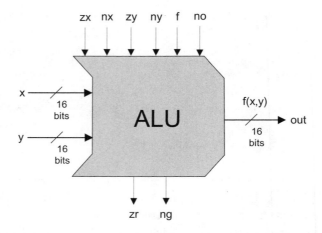

```
Chip name: ALU
Inputs:    x[16], y[16],    // Two 16-bit data inputs
           zx,              // Zero the x input
           nx,              // Negate the x input
           zy,              // Zero the y input
           ny,              // Negate the y input
           f,               // Function code: 1 for Add, 0 for And
           no               // Negate the out output
Outputs:   out[16],         // 16-bit output
           zr,              // True iff out=0
           ng               // True iff out<0
Function:  if zx then x = 0       // 16-bit zero constant
           if nx then x = !x      // Bit-wise negation
           if zy then y = 0       // 16-bit zero constant
           if ny then y = !y      // Bit-wise negation
           if f then out = x + y  // Integer 2's complement addition
                else out = x & y  // Bit-wise And
           if no then out = !out  // Bit-wise negation
           if out=0 then zr = 1 else zr = 0   // 16-bit eq. comparison
           if out<0 then ng = 1 else ng = 0   // 16-bit neg. comparison
Comment:   Overflow is neither detected nor handled.
```

Figure 2.5   The Arithmetic Logic Unit.

These bits instruct how to preset the x input		These bits instruct how to preset the y input		This bit selects between + / And	This bit inst. how to postset out	Resulting ALU output
zx	nx	zy	ny	f	no	out=
if zx then x=0	if nx then x=!x	if zy then y=0	if ny then y=!y	if f then out=x+y else out=x&y	if no then out=!out	f(x,y)=
1	0	1	0	1	0	0
1	1	1	1	1	1	1
1	1	1	0	1	0	-1
0	0	1	1	0	0	x
1	1	0	0	0	0	y
0	0	1	1	0	1	!x
1	1	0	0	0	1	!y
0	0	1	1	1	1	-x
1	1	0	0	1	1	-y
0	1	1	1	1	1	x+1
1	1	0	1	1	1	y+1
0	0	1	1	1	0	x-1
1	1	0	0	1	0	y-1
0	0	0	0	1	0	x+y
0	1	0	0	1	1	x-y
0	0	0	1	1	1	y-x
0	0	0	0	0	0	x&y
0	1	0	1	0	1	x|y

Figure 2.6 The ALU truth table. Taken together, the binary operations coded by the first six columns effect the function listed in the right column (we use the symbols !, &, and | to represent the operators Not, And, and Or, respectively, performed bit-wise). The complete ALU truth table consists of sixty-four rows, of which only the eighteen presented here are of interest.

and -1. Since the f-bit is 1, the selected operation is *arithmetic addition*, causing the ALU to calculate x+(-1). Finally, since the no bit is 0, the output is not negated but rather left as is. To conclude, the ALU ends up computing x-1, which was our goal.

Does the ALU logic described in figure 2.6 compute every one of the other seventeen functions listed in the figure's right column? To verify that this is indeed the case, the reader can pick up some other rows in the table and prove their respective ALU operation. We note that some of these computations, beginning with the function $f(x, y) = 1$, are not trivial. We also note that there are some other useful functions computed by the ALU but not listed in the figure.

It may be instructive to describe the thought process that led to the design of this particular ALU. First, we made a list of all the primitive operations that we wanted our computer to be able to perform (right column in figure 2.6). Next, we used backward reasoning to figure out how x, y, and out can be manipulated in binary fashion in order to carry out the desired operations. These processing requirements, along with our objective to keep the ALU logic as simple as possible, have led to the design decision to use six control bits, each associated with a straightforward binary operation. The resulting ALU is simple and elegant. And in the hardware business, simplicity and elegance imply inexpensive and powerful computer systems.

2.3   Implementation

Our implementation guidelines are intentionally partial, since we want you to discover the actual chip architectures yourself. As usual, each chip can be implemented in more than one way; the simpler the implementation, the better.

Half-Adder   An inspection of figure 2.2 reveals that the functions $sum(a, b)$ and $carry(a, b)$ happen to be identical to the standard $Xor(a, b)$ and $And(a, b)$ Boolean functions. Thus, the implementation of this adder is straightforward, using previously built gates.

Full-Adder   A full adder chip can be implemented from two half adder chips and one additional simple gate. A direct implementation is also possible, without using half-adder chips.

Adder   The addition of two signed numbers represented by the 2's complement method as two n-bit buses can be done bit-wise, from right to left, in n steps. In step 0, the least significant pair of bits is added, and the carry bit is fed into the addition of the next significant pair of bits. The process continues until in step $n - 1$ the most significant pair of bits is added. Note that each step involves the addition of three bits. Hence, an n-bit adder can be implemented by creating an array of n full-adder chips and propagating the carry bits up the significance ladder.

Incrementer   An n-bit incrementer can be implemented trivially from an n-bit adder.

ALU   Note that our ALU was carefully planned to effect all the desired ALU operations *logically*, using simple Boolean operations. Therefore, the *physical* implementation of the ALU is reduced to implementing these simple Boolean operations, following their pseudo-code specifications. Your first step will likely be to create a logic circuit that manipulates a 16-bit input according to the nx and zx control bits (i.e., the circuit should conditionally zero and negate the 16-bit input). This logic can be used to manipulate the x and y inputs, as well as the out output. Chips for bitwise And-ing and addition have already been built in this and in the previous chapter. Thus, what remains is to build logic that chooses between them according to the f control bit. Finally, you will need to build logic that integrates all the other chips into the overall ALU. (When we say "build logic," we mean "write HDL code").

2.4   Perspective

The construction of the multi-bit adder presented in this chapter was standard, although no attention was paid to efficiency. In fact, our suggested adder implementation is rather inefficient, due to the long delays incurred while the carry bit propagates from the least significant bit pair to the most significant bit pair. This problem can be alleviated using logic circuits that effect so-called carry look-ahead techniques. Since addition is one of the most prevalent operations in any given hardware platform, any such low-level improvement can result in dramatic and global performance gains throughout the computer.

In any given computer, the overall functionality of the hardware/software platform is delivered jointly by the ALU and the operating system that runs on top of it. Thus, when designing a new computer system, the question of how much functionality the ALU should deliver is essentially a cost/performance issue. The general rule is that hardware implementations of arithmetic and logical operations are usually more costly, but achieve better performance. The design trade-off that we have chosen in this book is to specify an ALU hardware with a limited functionality and then implement as many operations as possible in software. For example, our ALU features neither multiplication nor division nor floating point arithmetic. We will implement some of these operations (as well as more mathematical functions) at the operating system level, described in chapter 12.

Detailed treatments of Boolean arithmetic and ALU design can be found in most computer architecture textbooks.

2.5   Project

Objective   Implement all the chips presented in this chapter. The only building blocks that you can use are the chips that you will gradually build and the chips described in the previous chapter.

Tip   When your HDL programs invoke chips that you may have built in the previous project, we recommend that you use the built-in versions of these chips instead. This will ensure correctness and speed up the operation of the hardware simulator. There is a simple way to accomplish this convention: Make sure that your project directory includes only the `.hdl` files that belong to the present project.

The remaining instructions for this project are identical to those of the project from the previous chapter, except that the last step should be replaced with "Build and simulate all the chips specified in the `projects/02` directory."

3 Sequential Logic

It's a poor sort of memory that only works backward.
—Lewis Carroll (1832–1898)

All the Boolean and arithmetic chips that we built in chapters 1 and 2 were *combinational*. Combinational chips compute functions that depend solely on *combinations* of their input values. These relatively simple chips provide many important processing functions (like the ALU), but they cannot *maintain state*. Since computers must be able to not only compute values but also store and recall values, they must be equipped with memory elements that can preserve data over time. These memory elements are built from *sequential chips*.

The implementation of memory elements is an intricate art involving synchronization, clocking, and feedback loops. Conveniently, most of this complexity can be embedded in the operating logic of very low-level sequential gates called *flip-flops*. Using these flip-flops as elementary building blocks, we will specify and build all the memory devices employed by typical modern computers, from binary cells to registers to memory banks and counters. This effort will complete the construction of the chip set needed to build an entire computer—a challenge that we take up in the chapter 5.

Following a brief overview of clocks and flip-flops, the Background section introduces all the memory chips that we will build on top of them. The next two sections describe the chips Specification and Implementation, respectively. As usual, all the chips mentioned in the chapter can be built and tested using the hardware simulator supplied with the book, following the instructions given in the final Project section.

3.1   Background

The act of "remembering something" is inherently time-dependent: You remember *now* what has been committed to memory *before*. Thus, in order to build chips that "remember" information, we must first develop some standard means for representing the progression of time.

The Clock   In most computers, the passage of time is represented by a master clock that delivers a continuous train of alternating signals. The exact hardware implementation is usually based on an oscillator that alternates continuously between two phases labeled 0–1, *low-high, tick-tock*, etc. The elapsed time between the beginning of a "tick" and the end of the subsequent "tock" is called *cycle*, and each clock cycle is taken to model one discrete time unit. The current clock phase (*tick* or *tock*) is represented by a binary signal. Using the hardware's circuitry, this signal is simultaneously broadcast to every sequential chip throughout the computer platform.

Flip-Flops   The most elementary sequential element in the computer is a device called a *flip-flop*, of which there are several variants. In this book we use a variant called a *data flip-flop*, or DFF, whose interface consists of a single-bit data input and a single-bit data output. In addition, the DFF has a *clock* input that continuously changes according to the master clock's signal. Taken together, the data and the clock inputs enable the DFF to implement the time-based behavior $out(t) = in(t-1)$, where *in* and *out* are the gate's input and output values and t is the current clock cycle. In other words, the DFF simply outputs the input value from the previous time unit.

As we now show, this elementary behavior can form the basis of all the hardware devices that computers use to *maintain state*, from binary cells to registers to arbitrarily large random access memory (RAM) units.

Registers   A *register* is a storage device that can "store," or "remember," a value over time, implementing the classical storage behavior $out(t) = out(t-1)$. A DFF, on the other hand, can only output its previous input, namely, $out(t) = in(t-1)$. This suggests that a register can be implemented from a DFF by simply feeding the output of the latter back into its input, creating the device shown in the middle of figure 3.1. Presumably, the output of this device at any time t will echo its output at time $t-1$, yielding the classical function expected from a storage unit.

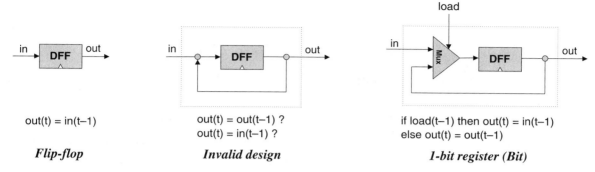

Figure 3.1 From a DFF to a single-bit register. The small triangle represents the clock input. This icon is used to state that the marked chip, as well as the overall chip that encapsulates it, is time-dependent.

Well, not so. The device shown in the middle of figure 3.1 is invalid. First, it is not clear how we'll ever be able to load this device with a new data value, since there are no means to tell the DFF when to draw its input from the `in` wire and when from the `out` wire. More generally, the rules of chip design dictate that internal pins must have a fan-in of 1, meaning that they can be fed from a single source only.

The good thing about this thought experiment is that it leads us to the correct and elegant solution shown in the right side of figure 3.1. In particular, a natural way to resolve our input ambiguity is to introduce a multiplexor into the design. Further, the "select bit" of this multiplexor can become the "load bit" of the overall register chip: If we want the register to start storing a new value, we can put this value in the `in` input and set the `load` bit to 1; if we want the register to keep storing its internal value until further notice, we can set the `load` bit to 0.

Once we have developed the basic mechanism for remembering a single bit over time, we can easily construct arbitrarily wide registers. This can be achieved by forming an array of as many single-bit registers as needed, creating a register that holds multi-bit values (figure 3.2). The basic design parameter of such a register is its *width*—the number of bits that it holds—e.g., 16, 32, or 64. The multi-bit contents of such registers are typically referred to as *words*.

Memories   Once we have the basic ability to represent words, we can proceed to build memory banks of arbitrary length. As figure 3.3 shows, this can be done by stacking together many registers to form a *Random Access Memory* RAM unit. The term *random access memory* derives from the requirement that read/write operations

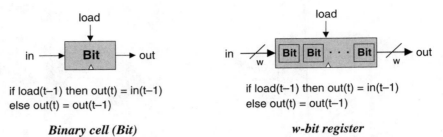

if load(t−1) then out(t) = in(t−1)   if load(t−1) then out(t) = in(t−1)
else out(t) = out(t−1)   else out(t) = out(t−1)

Binary cell (Bit)   **w-bit register**

Figure 3.2   From single-bit to multi-bit registers. A multi-bit register of width *w* can be constructed from an array of *w* 1-bit chips. The operating functions of both chips is exactly the same, except that the "=" assignments are single-bit and multi-bit, respectively.

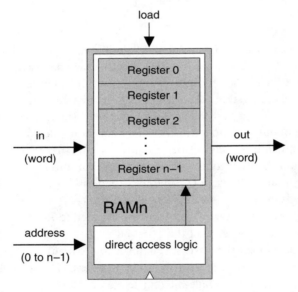

Figure 3.3   RAM chip (conceptual). The width and length of the RAM can vary.

on a RAM should be able to access randomly chosen words, with no restrictions on the order in which they are accessed. That is to say, we require that any word in the memory—irrespective of its physical location—be accessed directly, in equal speed.

This requirement can be satisfied as follows. First, we assign each word in the *n*-register RAM a unique *address* (an integer between 0 to $n-1$), according to which it will be accessed. Second, in addition to building an array of *n* registers, we build a gate logic design that, given an address *j*, is capable of selecting the individual register whose address is *j*. Note however that the notion of an "address" is not an explicit part of the RAM design, since the registers are not "marked" with addresses in any physical sense. Rather, as we will see later, the chip is equipped with direct access logic that implements the notion of addressing using logical means.

In sum, a classical RAM device accepts three inputs: a data input, an address input, and a load bit. The *address* specifies which RAM register should be accessed in the current time unit. In the case of a read operation (`load=0`), the RAM's output immediately emits the value of the selected register. In the case of a write operation (`load=1`), the selected memory register commits to the input value in the next time unit, at which point the RAM's output will start emitting it.

The basic design parameters of a RAM device are its data *width*—the width of each one of its words, and its *size*—the number of words in the RAM. Modern computers typically employ 32- or 64-bit-wide RAMs whose sizes are up to billions of words.

Counters   A counter is a sequential chip whose state is an integer number that increments every time unit, effecting the function $out(t) = out(t-1) + c$, where *c* is typically 1. Counters play an important role in digital architectures. For example, a typical CPU includes a *program counter* whose output is interpreted as the address of the instruction that should be executed next in the current program.

A counter chip can be implemented by combining the input/output logic of a standard register with the combinatorial logic for adding a constant. Typically, the counter will have to be equipped with some additional functionality, such as possibilities for resetting the count to zero, loading a new counting base, or decrementing instead of incrementing.

Time Matters   All the chips described so far in this chapter are *sequential*. Simply stated, a sequential chip is a chip that embeds one or more DFF gates, either directly or indirectly. Functionally speaking, the DFF gates endow sequential chips with the ability to either maintain state (as in memory units) or operate on state (as in

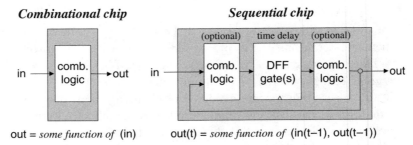

Figure 3.4   Combinational versus sequential logic (in and out stand for one or more input and output variables). Sequential chips always consist of a layer of DFFs sandwiched between optional combinational logic layers.

counters). Technically speaking, this is done by forming feedback loops inside the sequential chip (see figure 3.4). In combinational chips, where time is neither modeled nor recognized, the introduction of feedback loops is problematic: The output would depend on the input, which itself would depend on the output, and thus the output would depend on itself. On the other hand, there is no difficulty in feeding the output of a sequential chip back into itself, since the DFFs introduce an inherent time delay: The output at time t does not depend on itself, but rather on the output at time $t - 1$. This property guards against the uncontrolled "data races" that would occur in combinational chips with feedback loops.

Recall that the outputs of combinational chips change when their inputs change, irrespective of time. In contrast, the inclusion of the DFFs in the sequential architecture ensures that their outputs change only at the point of transition from one clock cycle to the next, and not within the cycle itself. In fact, we allow sequential chips to be in unstable states *during* clock cycles, requiring only that at the beginning of the next cycle they output correct values.

This "discretization" of the sequential chips' outputs has an important side effect: It can be used to synchronize the overall computer architecture. To illustrate, suppose we instruct the arithmetic logic unit (ALU) to compute $x + y$ where x is the value of a nearby register and y is the value of a remote RAM register. Because of various physical constraints (distance, resistance, interference, random noise, etc.) the electric signals representing x and y will likely arrive at the ALU at different times. However, being a *combinational chip*, the ALU is insensitive to the concept of time— it continuously adds up whichever data values happen to lodge in its inputs. Thus, it will take some time before the ALU's output stabilizes to the correct $x + y$ result. Until then, the ALU will generate garbage.

How can we overcome this difficulty? Well, since the output of the ALU is always routed to some sort of a sequential chip (a register, a RAM location, etc.), *we don't really care*. All we have to do is ensure, when we build the computer's clock, that the length of the clock cycle will be slightly longer that the time it takes a bit to travel the longest distance from one chip in the architecture to another. This way, we are guaranteed that by the time the sequential chip updates its state (at the beginning of the next clock cycle), the inputs that it receives from the ALU will be valid. This, in a nutshell, is the trick that synchronizes a set of stand-alone hardware components into a well-coordinated system, as we shall see in chapter 5.

3.2   Specification

This section specifies a hierarchy of sequential chips:

- Data-flip-flops (DFFs)
- Registers (based on DFFs)
- Memory banks (based on registers)
- Counter chips (also based on registers)

3.2.1   Data-Flip-Flop

The most elementary sequential device that we present—the basic component from which all memory elements will be designed—is the *data flip-flop* gate. A DFF gate has a single-bit input and a single-bit output, as follows:

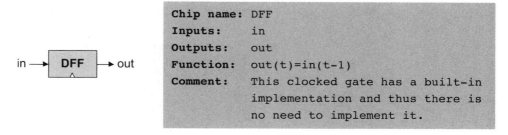

Like Nand gates, DFF gates enter our computer architecture at a very low level. Specifically, all the sequential chips in the computer (registers, memory, and counters) are based on numerous DFF gates. All these DFFs are connected to the same master clock, forming a huge distributed "chorus line." At the beginning of each clock cycle, the outputs of *all* the DFFs in the computer commit to their inputs during the previous time unit. At all other times, the DFFs are "latched," meaning that changes in their inputs have no immediate effect on their outputs. This conduction operation effects any one of the billions of DFF gates that make up the system, about a billion times per second (depending on the computer's clock frequency).

Hardware implementations achieve this time dependency by simultaneously feeding the master clock signal to all the DFF gates in the platform. Hardware simulators emulate the same effect in software. As far as the computer architect is concerned, the end result is the same: The inclusion of a DFF gate in the design of any chip ensures that the overall chip, as well as all the chips up the hardware hierarchy that depend on it, will be inherently time-dependent. These chips are called *sequential*, by definition.

The physical implementation of a DFF is an intricate task, and is based on connecting several elementary logic gates using feedback loops (one classic design is based on Nand gates alone). In this book we have chosen to abstract away this complexity, treating DFFs as primitive building blocks. Thus, our hardware simulator provides a built-in DFF implementation that can be readily used by other chips.

3.2.2   Registers

A single-bit register, which we call Bit, or *binary cell*, is designed to store a single bit of information (0 or 1). The chip interface consists of an input pin that carries a data bit, a `load` pin that enables the cell for writes, and an output pin that emits the current state of the cell. The interface diagram and API of a binary cell are as follows:

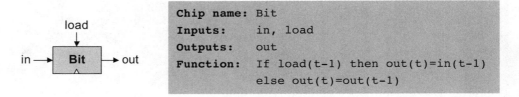

The API of the Register chip is essentially the same, except that the input and output pins are designed to handle multi-bit values:

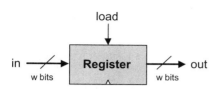

```
Chip name:  Register
Inputs:     in[16], load
Outputs:    out[16]
Function:   If load(t-1) then out(t)=in(t-1)
            else out(t)=out(t-1)
Comment:    "=" is a 16-bit operation.
```

The Bit and Register chips have exactly the same read/write behavior:

Read: To read the contents of a register, we simply probe its output.

Write: To write a new data value *d* into a register, we put *d* in the `in` input and assert (set to 1) the `load` input. In the next clock cycle, the register commits to the new data value, and its output starts emitting *d*.

3.2.3 Memory

A direct-access memory unit, also called RAM, is an array of *n* *w*-bit registers, equipped with direct access circuitry. The number of registers (*n*) and the width of each register (*w*) are called the memory's *size* and *width*, respectively. We will now set out to build a hierarchy of such memory devices, all 16 bits wide, but with varying sizes: RAM8, RAM64, RAM512, RAM4K, and RAM16K units. All these memory chips have precisely the same API, and thus we describe them in one parametric diagram:

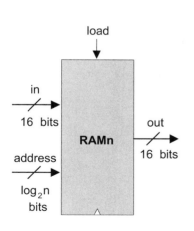

```
Chip name:  RAMn // n and k are listed below
Inputs:     in[16], address[k], load
Outputs:    out[16]
Function:   out(t)=RAM[address(t)](t)
            If load(t-1) then
                RAM[address(t-1)](t)=in(t-1)
Comment:    "=" is a 16-bit operation.
```

The specific RAM chips needed for the Hack platform are:

Chip name	n	k
RAM8	8	3
RAM64	64	6
RAM512	512	9
RAM4K	4096	12
RAM16K	16384	14

Read: To read the contents of register number m, we put m in the `address` input. The RAM's direct-access logic will select register number m, which will then emit its output value to the RAM's output pin. This is a combinational operation, independent of the clock.

Write: To write a new data value d into register number m, we put m in the `address` input, d in the `in` input, and assert the `load` input bit. This causes the RAM's direct-access logic to select register number m, and the `load` bit to enable it. In the next clock cycle, the selected register will commit to the new value (d), and the RAM's output will start emitting it.

3.2.4 Counter

Although a *counter* is a stand-alone abstraction in its own right, it is convenient to motivate its specification by saying a few words about the context in which it is normally used. For example, consider a counter chip designed to contain the address of the instruction that the computer should fetch and execute next. In most cases, the counter has to simply increment itself by 1 in each clock cycle, thus causing the computer to fetch the next instruction in the program. In other cases, for example, in "jump to execute instruction number n," we want to be able to set the counter to n, then have it continue its default counting behavior with $n+1$, $n+2$, and so forth. Finally, the program's execution can be restarted anytime by resetting the counter to 0, assuming that that's the address of the program's first instruction. In short, we need a loadable and resettable counter.

With that in mind, the interface of our Counter chip is similar to that of a register, except that it has two additional control bits labeled `reset` and `inc`. When `inc=1`, the counter increments its state in every clock cycle, emitting the value `out(t)=` `out(t-1)+1`. If we want to reset the counter to 0, we assert the `reset` bit; if we want to initialize it to some other counting base d, we put d in the `in` input and assert the `load` bit. The details are given in the counter API, and an example of its operation is depicted in figure 3.5.

3.3 Implementation

Flip-Flop DFF gates can be implemented from lower-level logic gates like those built in chapter 1. However, in this book we treat DFFs as primitive gates, and thus they can be used in hardware construction projects without worrying about their internal implementation.

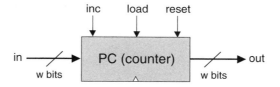

```
Chip name: PC   // 16-bit counter
Inputs:    in[16], inc, load, reset
Outputs:   out[16]
Function:  If reset(t-1) then out(t)=0
              else if load(t-1) then out(t)=in(t-1)
                    else if inc(t-1) then out(t)=out(t-1)+1
                          else out(t)=out(t-1)
Comment:   "=" is 16-bit assignment.
           "+" is 16-bit arithmetic addition.
```

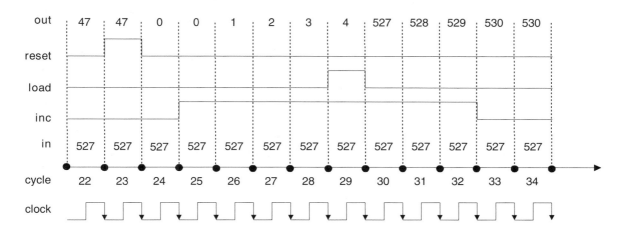

We assume that we start tracking the counter in time unit 22, when its input and output happen to be 527 and 47, respectively. We also assume that the counter's control bits (reset, load, inc) start at 0—all arbitrary assumptions.

Figure 3.5 Counter simulation. At time 23 a *reset* signal is issued, causing the counter to emit 0 in the following time unit. The 0 persists until an *inc* signal is issued at time 25, causing the counter to start incrementing, one time unit later. The counting continues until, at time 29, the load bit is asserted. Since the counter's input holds the number 527, the counter is reset to that value in the next time unit. Since inc is still asserted, the counter continues incrementing until time 33, when inc is de-asserted.

1-Bit Register (Bit)   The implementation of this chip was given in figure 3.1.

Register   The construction of a w-bit Register chip from 1-bit registers is straight-forward. All we have to do is construct an array of w Bit gates and feed the register's load input to every one of them.

8-Register Memory (RAM8)   An inspection of figure 3.3 may be useful here. To implement a RAM8 chip, we line up an array of eight registers. Next, we have to build combinational logic that, given a certain address value, takes the RAM8's in input and loads it into the selected register. In a similar fashion, we have to build combinational logic that, given a certain address value, selects the right register and pipes its out value to the RAM8's out output. Tip: This combinational logic was already implemented in chapter 1.

n-Register Memory   A memory bank of arbitrary length (a power of 2) can be built recursively from smaller memory units, all the way down to the single register level. This view is depicted in figure 3.6. Focusing on the right-hand side of the figure, we note that a 64-register RAM can be built from an array of eight 8-register RAM chips. To select a particular register from the RAM64 memory, we use a 6-bit address, say $xxxyyy$. The MSB xxx bits select one of the RAM8 chips, and the LSB yyy bits select one of the registers within the selected RAM8. The RAM64 chip should be equipped with logic circuits that effect this hierarchical addressing scheme.

Counter   A w-bit counter consists of two main elements: a regular w-bit register, and combinational logic. The combinational logic is designed to (a) compute the counting function, and (b) put the counter in the right operating mode, as mandated by the values of its three control bits. Tip: Most of this logic was already built in chapter 2.

3.4   Perspective

The cornerstone of all the memory systems described in this chapter is the flip-flop—a gate that we treated here as an atomic, or primitive, building block. The usual approach in hardware textbooks is to construct flip-flops from elementary combinatorial gates (e.g., Nand gates) using appropriate feedback loops. The standard con-

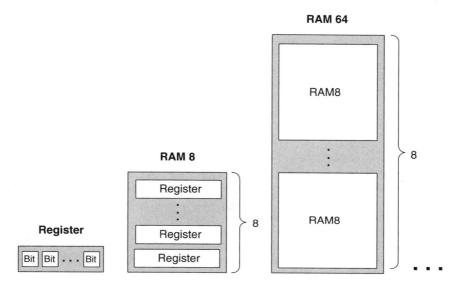

Figure 3.6 Gradual construction of memory banks by recursive ascent. A *w*-bit register is an array of *w* binary cells, an 8-register RAM is an array of eight *w*-bit registers, a 64-register RAM is an array of eight RAM8 chips, and so on. Only three more similar construction steps are necessary to build a 16K RAM chip.

struction begins by building a simple (non-clocked) flip-flop that is bi-stable, namely, that can be set to be in one of two states. Then a clocked flip-flop is obtained by cascading two such simple flip-flops, the first being set when the clock *ticks* and the second when the clock *tocks*. This "master-slave" design endows the overall flip-flop with the desired clocked synchronization functionality.

These constructions are rather elaborate, requiring an understating of delicate issues like the effect of feedback loops on combinatorial circuits, as well as the implementation of clock cycles using a two-phase binary clock signal. In this book we have chosen to abstract away these low-level considerations by treating the flip-flop as an atomic gate. Readers who wish to explore the internal structure of flip-flop gates can find detailed descriptions in most logic design and computer architecture textbooks.

In closing, we should mention that memory devices of modern computers are not always constructed from standard flip-flops. Instead, modern memory chips are usually very carefully optimized, exploiting the unique physical properties of the underlying storage technology. Many such alternative technologies are available today to computer designers; as usual, which technology to use is a cost-performance issue.

Aside from these low-level considerations, all the other chip constructions in this chapter—the registers and memory chips that were built on top of the flip-flop gates—were standard.

3.5   Project

Objective   Build all the chips described in the chapter. The only building blocks that you can use are primitive DFF gates, chips that you will build on top of them, and chips described in previous chapters.

Resources   The only tool that you need for this project is the hardware simulator supplied with the book. All the chips should be implemented in the HDL language specified in appendix A. As usual, for each chip we supply a skeletal `.hdl` program with a missing implementation part, a `.tst` script file that tells the hardware simulator how to test it, and a `.cmp` compare file. Your job is to complete the missing implementation parts of the supplied `.hdl` programs.

Contract   When loaded into the hardware simulator, your chip design (modified `.hdl` program), tested on the supplied `.tst` file, should produce the outputs listed in the supplied `.cmp` file. If that is not the case, the simulator will let you know.

Tip   The Data Flip-Flop (DFF) gate is considered primitive and thus there is no need to build it: When the simulator encounters a DFF gate in an HDL program, it automatically invokes the built-in `tools/builtIn/DFF.hdl` implementation.

The Directory Structure of This Project   When constructing RAM chips from smaller ones, we recommend using built-in versions of the latter. Otherwise, the simulator may run very slowly or even out of (real) memory space, since large RAM chips contain tens of thousands of lower-level chips, and all these chips are kept in memory (as software objects) by the simulator. For this reason, we have placed the `RAM512.hdl`, `RAM4K.hdl`, and `RAM16K.hdl` programs in a separate directory. This way, the recursive descent construction of the RAM4K and RAM16K chips stops with the RAM512 chip, whereas the lower-level chips from which the latter chip is made are bound to be built-in (since the simulator does not find them in this directory).

Steps   We recommend proceeding in the following order:

0.   The hardware simulator needed for this project is available in the `tools` directory of the book's software suite.

1.   Read appendix A, focusing on sections A.6 and A.7.

2.   Go through the *hardware simulator tutorial*, focusing on parts IV and V.

3.   Build and simulate all the chips specified in the `projects/03` directory.

4   Machine Language

Make everything as simple as possible, but not simpler.
—Albert Einstein (1879–1955)

A computer can be described *constructively*, by laying out its hardware platform and explaining how it is built from low-level chips. A computer can also be described *abstractly*, by specifying and demonstrating its machine language capabilities. And indeed, it is convenient to get acquainted with a new computer system by first seeing some low-level programs written in its machine language. This helps us understand not only how to program the computer to do useful things, but also why its hardware was designed in a certain way. With that in mind, this chapter focuses on low-level programming in machine language. This sets the stage for chapter 5, where we complete the construction of a general-purpose computer designed to run machine language programs. This computer will be constructed from the chip set built in chapters 1–3.

A machine language is an agreed-upon formalism, designed to code low-level programs as series of machine instructions. Using these instructions, the programmer can command the processor to perform arithmetic and logic operations, fetch and store values from and to the memory, move values from one register to another, test Boolean conditions, and so on. As opposed to high-level languages, whose basic design goals are generality and power of expression, the goal of machine language's design is direct execution in, and total control of, a given hardware platform. Of course, generality, power, and elegance are still desired, but only to the extent that they support the basic requirement of direct execution in hardware.

Machine language is the most profound interface in the overall computer enterprise—the fine line where hardware and software meet. This is the point where the abstract thoughts of the programmer, as manifested in symbolic instructions, are turned into physical operations performed in silicon. Thus, machine language can be construed as both a programming tool and an integral part of the hardware platform. In fact, just as we say that the machine language is designed to exploit a given hardware platform, we can say that the hardware platform is designed to fetch, interpret, and execute instructions written in the given machine language.

The chapter begins with a general introduction to machine language programming. Next, we give a detailed specification of the Hack machine language, covering both its binary and its symbolic assembly versions. The project that ends the chapter engages you in writing a couple of machine language programs. This project offers a hands-on appreciation of low-level programming and prepares you for building the computer itself in the next chapter.

Although most people will never write programs directly in machine language, the study of low-level programming is a prerequisite to a complete understanding of computer architectures. Also, it is rather fascinating to realize how the most sophisticated software systems are, at bottom, long series of elementary instructions, each specifying a very simple and primitive operation on the underlying hardware. As usual, this understanding is best achieved constructively, by writing some low-level code and running it directly on the hardware platform.

4.1   Background

This chapter is language-oriented. Therefore, we can abstract away most of the details of the underlying hardware platform, deferring its description to the next chapter. Indeed, to give a general description of machine languages, it is sufficient to focus on three main abstractions only: a *processor*, a *memory*, and a set of *registers*.

4.1.1   Machines

A *machine language* can be viewed as an agreed-upon formalism, designed to manipulate a *memory* using a *processor* and a set of *registers*.

Memory   The term *memory* refers loosely to the collection of hardware devices that store data and instructions in a computer. From the programmer's standpoint, all memories have the same structure: A continuous array of cells of some fixed width, also called *words* or *locations*, each having a unique *address*. Hence, an individual word (representing either a data item or an instruction) is specified by supplying its address. In what follows we will refer to such individual words using the equivalent notation Memory[address], RAM[address], or M[address] for brevity.

Processor   The processor, normally called *Central Processing Unit* or *CPU*, is a device capable of performing a fixed set of elementary operations. These typically include arithmetic and logic operations, memory access operations, and control (also called *branching*) operations. The operands of these operations are binary values that come from registers and selected memory locations. Likewise, the results of the operations (the processor's output) can be stored either in registers or in selected memory locations.

Registers   Memory access is a relatively slow operation, requiring long instruction formats (an address may require 32 bits). For this reason, most processors are equipped with several registers, each capable of holding a single value. Located in the processor's immediate proximity, the registers serve as a high-speed local memory, allowing the processor to manipulate data and instructions quickly. This setting enables the programmer to minimize the use of memory access commands, thus speeding up the program's execution.

4.1.2   Languages

A machine language program is a series of coded instructions. For example, a typical instruction in a 16-bit computer may be 1010001100011001. In order to figure out what this instruction means, we have to know the rules of the game, namely, the instruction set of the underlying hardware platform. For example, the language may be such that each instruction consists of four 4-bit fields: The left-most field codes a CPU operation, and the remaining three fields represent the operation's operands. Thus the previous command may code the operation *set R3 to R1 + R9*, depending of course on the hardware specification and the machine language syntax.

   Since binary codes are rather cryptic, machine languages are normally specified using both binary codes and symbolic mnemonics (a *mnemonic* is a symbolic label whose name hints at what it stands for—in our case hardware elements and binary operations). For example, the language designer can decide that the operation code 1010 will be represented by the mnemonic add and that the registers of the machine will be symbolically referred to using the symbols R0, R1, R2, and so forth. Using these conventions, one can specify machine language instructions either directly, as 1010001100011001, or symbolically, as, say, ADD R3,R1,R9.

Taking this symbolic abstraction one step further, we can allow ourselves not only to *read* symbolic notation, but to actually *write* programs using symbolic commands rather than binary instructions. Next, we can use a text processing program to parse the symbolic commands into their underlying fields (mnemonics and operands), translate each field into its equivalent binary representation, and assemble the resulting codes into binary machine instructions. The symbolic notation is called *assembly language*, or simply *assembly*, and the program that translates from assembly to binary is called *assembler*.

Since different computers vary in terms of CPU operations, number and type of registers, and assembly syntax rules, there is a Tower of Babel of machine languages, each with its own obscure syntax. Yet irrespective of this variety, all machine languages support similar sets of generic commands, which we now describe.

4.1.3   Commands

Arithmetic and Logic Operations   Every computer is required to perform basic arithmetic operations like addition and subtraction as well as basic Boolean operations like bit-wise negation, bit shifting, and so forth. Here are some examples, written in typical machine language syntax:

```
ADD R2,R1,R3   // R2←R1+R3 where R1,R2,R3 are registers

ADD R2,R1,foo  // R2←R1+foo where foo stands for the
               // value of the memory location pointed
               // at by the user-defined label foo.

AND R1,R1,R2   // R1←bit wise And of R1 and R2
```

Memory Access   Memory access commands fall into two categories. First, as we have just seen, arithmetic and logical commands are allowed to operate not only on registers, but also on selected memory locations. Second, all computers feature explicit *load* and *store* commands, designed to move data between registers and memory. These memory access commands may use several types of *addressing modes*—ways of specifying the address of the required memory word. As usual, different computers offer different possibilities and different notations, but the following three memory access modes are almost always supported:

■ *Direct addressing*   The most common way to address the memory is to express a specific address or use a symbol that refers to a specific address, as follows:

```
LOAD R1,67      //  R1←Memory[67]

// Or, assuming that bar refers to memory address 67:

LOAD R1,bar     //  R1←Memory[67]
```

■ *Immediate addressing* This form of addressing is used to load constants—namely, load values that appear in the instruction code: Instead of treating the numeric field that appears in the instruction as an address, we simply load the value of the field itself into the register, as follows:

```
LOADI R1,67     //  R1←67
```

■ *Indirect addressing* In this addressing mode the address of the required memory location is not hard-coded into the instruction; instead, the instruction specifies a memory location that holds the required address. This addressing mode is used to handle *pointers*. For example, consider the high-level command x=foo[j], where foo is an array variable and x and j are integer variables. What is the machine language equivalent of this command? Well, when the array foo is declared and initialized in the high-level program, the compiler allocates a memory segment to hold the array data and makes the symbol foo refer to the *base address* of that segment.

Now, when the compiler later encounters references to array cells like foo[j], it translates them as follows. First, note that the *j*th array entry should be physically located in a memory location that is at a displacement *j* from the array's base address (assuming, for simplicity, that each array element uses a single word). Hence the address corresponding to the expression foo[j] can be easily calculated by adding the value of j to the value of foo. Thus in the C programming language, for example, a command like x=foo[j] can be also expressed as x=*(foo+j), where the notation "*n" stands for "the value of Memory[n]". When translated into machine language, such commands typically generate the following code (depending on the assembly language syntax):

```
// Translation of x=foo[j] or x=*(foo+j):
ADD R1,foo,j    // R1←foo+j
LOAD* R2,R1     // R2←Memory[R1]
STR R2,x        // x←R2
```

Flow of Control While programs normally execute in a linear fashion, one command after the other, they also include occasional branches to locations other than the next command. Branching serves several purposes including *repetition* (jump

```
High-level                 Low-level

// A while loop:           // Typical translation:
while (R1>=0) {            beginWhile:
    code segment 1            JNG R1,endWhile // If R1<0 goto endWhile
}                            // Translation of code segment 1 comes here
code segment 2               JMP beginWhile  // Goto beginWhile
                           endWhile:
                             // Translation of code segment 2 comes here
```

Figure 4.1 High- and low-level branching logic. The syntax of *goto commands* varies from one language to another, but the basic idea is the same.

backward to the beginning of a loop), *conditional execution* (if a Boolean condition is false, jump forward to the location after the "if-then" clause), and *subroutine calling* (jump to the first command of some other code segment). In order to support these programming constructs, every machine language features the means to jump to selected locations in the program, both conditionally and unconditionally. In assembly languages, locations in the program can also be given symbolic names, using some syntax for specifying labels. Figure 4.1 illustrates a typical example.

Unconditional jump commands like JMP beginWhile specify only the address of the target location. *Conditional jump* commands like JNG R1,endWhile must also specify a Boolean condition, expressed in some way. In some languages the condition is an explicit part of the command, while in others it is a by-product of executing a previous command.

This ends our informal introduction to machine languages and the generic operations that they normally support. The next section gives a formal description of one specific machine language—the native code of the computer that we will build in chapter 5.

4.2   Hack Machine Language Specification

4.2.1   Overview

The Hack computer is a von Neumann platform. It is a 16-bit machine, consisting of a CPU, two separate memory modules serving as instruction memory and data memory, and two memory-mapped I/O devices: a screen and a keyboard.

Memory Address Spaces   The Hack programmer is aware of two distinct address spaces: an *instruction memory* and a *data memory*. Both memories are 16-bit wide and have a 15-bit address space, meaning that the maximum addressable size of each memory is 32K 16-bit words.

The CPU can only execute programs that reside in the instruction memory. The instruction memory is a read-only device, and programs are loaded into it using some exogenous means. For example, the instruction memory can be implemented in a ROM chip that is pre-burned with the required program. Loading a new program is done by replacing the entire ROM chip, similar to replacing a cartridge in a game console. In order to simulate this operation, hardware simulators of the Hack platform provide a means to load the instruction memory from a text file containing a machine language program.

Registers   The Hack programmer is aware of two 16-bit registers called D and A. These registers can be manipulated explicitly by arithmetic and logical instructions like A=D-1 or D=!A (where "!" means a 16-bit Not operation). While D is used solely to store data values, A doubles as both a data register and an address register. That is to say, depending on the instruction context, the contents of A can be interpreted either as a data value, or as an address in the data memory, or as an address in the instruction memory, as we now explain.

First, the A register can be used to facilitate direct access to the data memory (which, from now on, will be often referred to as "memory"). Since Hack instructions are 16-bit wide, and since addresses are specified using 15 bits, it is impossible to pack both an operation code and an address in one instruction. Thus, the syntax of the Hack language mandates that memory access instructions operate on an implicit memory location labeled "M", for example, D=M+1. In order to resolve this address, the convention is that M always refers to the memory word whose address is the current value of the A register. For example, if we want to effect the operation $D = \text{Memory}[516] - 1$, we have to use one instruction to set the A register to 516, and a subsequent instruction to specify D=M-1.

In addition, the hardworking A register is also used to facilitate direct access to the instruction memory. Similar to the memory access convention, Hack jump instructions do not specify a particular address. Instead, the convention is that any jump operation always effects a jump to the instruction located in the memory word addressed by A. Thus, if we want to effect the operation *goto 35*, we use one instruction to set A to 35, and a second instruction to code a *goto* command, without specifying an address. This sequence causes the computer to fetch the instruction located in InstructionMemory[35] in the next clock cycle.

Example   Since the Hack language is self-explanatory, we start with an example. The only non-obvious command in the language is *@value*, where *value* is either a number or a symbol representing a number. This command simply stores the specified value in the A register. For example, if sum refers to memory location 17, then both @17 and @sum will have the same effect: A←17.

And now to the example: Suppose we want to add the integers 1 to 100, using repetitive addition. Figure 4.2 gives a C language solution and a possible compilation into the Hack language.

Although the Hack syntax is more accessible than that of most machine languages, it may still look obscure to readers who are not familiar with low-level programming. In particular, note that every operation involving a memory location requires two Hack commands: one for fixing the address on which we want to operate, and one for specifying the desired operation. Indeed, the Hack language consists of two generic instructions: an *address instruction*, also called *A*-instruction, and a *compute instruction*, also called *C*-instruction. Each instruction has a binary representation, a symbolic representation, and an effect on the computer, as we now specify.

4.2.2   The *A*-Instruction

The *A*-instruction is used to set the A register to a 15-bit value:

A-instruction: *@value*   // Where *value* is either a non-negative decimal number
                                // or a symbol referring to such number.

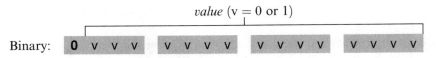

Binary:

This instruction causes the computer to store the specified value in the A register. For example, the instruction @5, which is equivalent to 0000000000000101, causes the computer to store the binary representation of 5 in the A register.

The *A*-instruction is used for three different purposes. First, it provides the only way to enter a constant into the computer under program control. Second, it sets the stage for a subsequent *C*-instruction designed to manipulate a certain data memory location, by first setting A to the address of that location. Third, it sets the stage for a subsequent *C*-instruction that specifies a jump, by first loading the address of the jump destination to the A register. All these use cases are demonstrated in figure 4.2.

C language

```
// Adds 1+...+100.
   int i = 1;
   int sum = 0;
   while (i <= 100){
      sum += i;
      i++;
   }
```

Hack machine language

```
// Adds 1+...+100.
        @i         // i refers to some mem. location.
        M=1        // i=1
        @sum       // sum refers to some mem. location.
        M=0        // sum=0
(LOOP)
        @i
        D=M        // D=i
        @100
        D=D-A      // D=i-100
        @END
        D;JGT      // If (i-100)>0 goto END
        @i
        D=M        // D=i
        @sum
        M=D+M      // sum=sum+i
        @i
        M=M+1      // i=i+1
        @LOOP
        0;JMP      // Goto LOOP
(END)
        @END
        0;JMP      // Infinite loop
```

Figure 4.2   C and assembly versions of the same program. The infinite loop at the program's end is our standard way to "terminate" the execution of Hack programs. As a convention, we use upper-case symbols to represent labels and lower-case symbols to represent variables. All these symbols are resolved to physical memory addresses as part of the program's translation process from assembly language to machine language, as we describe later in the book.

4.2.3   The *C*-Instruction

The *C*-instruction is the programming workhorse of the Hack platform—the instruction that gets almost everything done. The instruction code is a specification that answers three questions: (a) what to compute, (b) where to store the computed value, and (c) what to do next? Along with the *A*-instruction, these specifications determine all the possible operations of the computer.

C-instruction: *dest=comp;jump*   // Either the *dest* or *jump* fields may be empty.
                                          // If *dest* is empty, the "=" is omitted;
                                          // If *jump* is empty, the ";" is omitted.

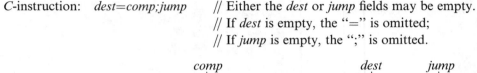

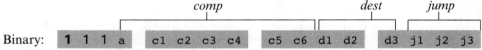

The leftmost bit is the *C*-instruction code, which is 1. The next two bits are not used. The remaining bits form three fields that correspond to the three parts of the instruction's symbolic representation. The overall semantics of the symbolic instruction *dest = comp;jump* is as follows. The *comp* field instructs the ALU what to compute. The *dest* field instructs where to store the computed value (ALU output). The *jump* field specifies a jump condition, namely, which command to fetch and execute next. We now describe the format and semantics of each of the three fields.

The Computation Specification   The Hack ALU is designed to compute a fixed set of functions on the D, A, and M registers (where M stands for Memory[A]). The computed function is specified by the a-bit and the six c-bits comprising the instruction's *comp* field. This 7-bit pattern can potentially code 128 different functions, of which only the 28 listed in figure 4.3 are documented in the language specification.

   Recall that the format of the *C*-instruction is 111a cccc ccdd djjj. Suppose we want to have the ALU compute D-1, the current value of the D register minus 1. According to figure 4.3, this can be done by issuing the instruction 111**0 0011 10**00 0000 (the 7-bit operation code is in bold). To compute the value of D|M, we issue the instruction 111**1 0101 01**00 0000. To compute the constant −1, we issue the instruction 111**0 1110 10**00 0000, and so on.

The Destination Specification   The value computed by the *comp* part of the *C*-instruction can be stored in several destinations, as specified by the instruction's 3-bit

(when a=0) ***comp*** *mnemonic*	c1	c2	c3	c4	c5	c6	(when a=1) ***comp*** *mnemonic*
0	1	0	1	0	1	0	
1	1	1	1	1	1	1	
-1	1	1	1	0	1	0	
D	0	0	1	1	0	0	
A	1	1	0	0	0	0	M
!D	0	0	1	1	0	1	
!A	1	1	0	0	0	1	!M
-D	0	0	1	1	1	1	
-A	1	1	0	0	1	1	-M
D+1	0	1	1	1	1	1	
A+1	1	1	0	1	1	1	M+1
D-1	0	0	1	1	1	0	
A-1	1	1	0	0	1	0	M-1
D+A	0	0	0	0	1	0	D+M
D-A	0	1	0	0	1	1	D-M
A-D	0	0	0	1	1	1	M-D
D&A	0	0	0	0	0	0	D&M
D|A	0	1	0	1	0	1	D|M

Figure 4.3   The *compute* field of the *C*-instruction. D and A are names of registers. M refers to the memory location addressed by A, namely, to Memory[A]. The symbols + and − denote 16-bit 2's complement addition and subtraction, while !, |, and & denote the 16-bit bit-wise Boolean operators Not, Or, and And, respectively. Note the similarity between this instruction set and the ALU specification given in figure 2.6.

dest part (see figure 4.4). The first and second d-bits code whether to store the computed value in the A register and in the D register, respectively. The third d-bit codes whether to store the computed value in M (i.e., in Memory[A]). One, more than one, or none of these bits may be asserted.

Recall that the format of the *C*-instruction is 111a cccc ccdd djjj. Suppose we want the computer to increment the value of Memory[7] by 1 and to also store the result in the D register. According to figures 4.3 and 4.4, this can be accomplished by the following instructions:

```
0000 0000 0000 0111    // @7
1111 1101 1101 1000    // MD=M+1
```

d1	d2	d3	Mnemonic	Destination (where to store the computed value)
0	0	0	null	The value is not stored anywhere
0	0	1	M	Memory[A] (memory register addressed by A)
0	1	0	D	D register
0	1	1	MD	Memory[A] and D register
1	0	0	A	A register
1	0	1	AM	A register and Memory[A]
1	1	0	AD	A register and D register
1	1	1	AMD	A register, Memory[A], and D register

Figure 4.4 The *dest* field of the *C*-instruction.

The first instruction causes the computer to select the memory register whose address is 7 (the so-called M register). The second instruction computes the value of M + 1 and stores the result in both M and D.

The Jump Specification The *jump* field of the *C*-instruction tells the computer what to do next. There are two possibilities: The computer should either fetch and execute the next instruction in the program, which is the default, or it should fetch and execute an instruction located elsewhere in the program. In the latter case, we assume that the A register has been previously set to the address to which we have to jump.

Whether or not a jump should actually materialize depends on the three j-bits of the *jump* field and on the ALU output value (computed according to the *comp* field). The first j-bit specifies whether to jump in case this value is negative, the second j-bit in case the value is zero, and the third j-bit in case it is positive. This gives eight possible jump conditions, shown in figure 4.5.

The following example illustrates the jump commands in action:

Logic

```
if Memory[3]=5 then goto 100
else goto 200
```

Implementation

```
@3
D=M      // D=Memory[3]
@5
D=D-A    // D=D-5
@100
D;JEQ    // If D=0 goto 100
@200
0;JMP    // Goto 200
```

j1 (*out* < 0)	j2 (*out* = 0)	j3 (*out* > 0)	Mnemonic	Effect
0	0	0	null	No jump
0	0	1	JGT	If *out* > 0 jump
0	1	0	JEQ	If *out* = 0 jump
0	1	1	JGE	If *out* ≥ 0 jump
1	0	0	JLT	If *out* < 0 jump
1	0	1	JNE	If *out* ≠ 0 jump
1	1	0	JLE	If *out* ≤ 0 jump
1	1	1	JMP	Jump

Figure 4.5   The *jump* field of the *C*-instruction. *Out* refers to the ALU output (resulting from the instruction's *comp* part), and *jump* implies "continue execution with the instruction addressed by the A register."

The last instruction (0;JMP) effects an unconditional jump. Since the *C*-instruction syntax requires that we always effect *some* computation, we instruct the ALU to compute 0 (an arbitrary choice), which is ignored.

Conflicting Uses of the A Register   As was just illustrated, the programmer can use the A register to select either a *data memory* location for a subsequent *C*-instruction involving M, or an *instruction memory* location for a subsequent *C*-instruction involving a jump. Thus, to prevent conflicting use of the A register, in well-written programs a *C*-instruction that may cause a jump (i.e., with some non-zero j bits) should not contain a reference to M, and vice versa.

4.2.4   Symbols

Assembly commands can refer to memory locations (addresses) using either constants or *symbols*. Symbols are introduced into assembly programs in the following three ways:

■ *Predefined symbols:*   A special subset of RAM addresses can be referred to by any assembly program using the following predefined symbols:

• *Virtual registers:*   To simplify assembly programming, the symbols R0 to R15 are predefined to refer to RAM addresses 0 to 15, respectively.

• *Predefined pointers:*   The symbols SP, LCL, ARG, THIS, and THAT are predefined to refer to RAM addresses 0 to 4, respectively. Note that each of these memory locations has two labels. For example, address 2 can be referred to using either R2 or ARG. This syntactic convention will come to play in the implementation of the virtual machine, discussed in chapters 7 and 8.

· *I/O pointers:* The symbols SCREEN and KBD are predefined to refer to RAM addresses 16384 (0x4000) and 24576 (0x6000), respectively, which are the base addresses of the screen and keyboard memory maps. The use of these I/O devices is explained later.

▪ *Label symbols:* These user-defined symbols, which serve to label destinations of *goto* commands, are declared by the pseudo-command "(Xxx)". This directive defines the symbol Xxx to refer to the instruction memory location holding the next command in the program. A label can be defined only once and can be used anywhere in the assembly program, even before the line in which it is defined.

▪ *Variable symbols:* Any user-defined symbol Xxx appearing in an assembly program that is not predefined and is not defined elsewhere using the "(Xxx)" command is treated as a *variable*, and is assigned a unique memory address by the assembler, starting at RAM address 16 (0x0010).

4.2.5   Input/Output Handling

The Hack platform can be connected to two peripheral devices: a screen and a keyboard. Both devices interact with the computer platform through *memory maps*. This means that drawing pixels on the screen is achieved by writing binary values into a memory segment associated with the screen. Likewise, listening to the keyboard is done by reading a memory location associated with the keyboard. The physical I/O devices and their memory maps are synchronized via continuous refresh loops.

Screen The Hack computer includes a black-and-white screen organized as 256 rows of 512 pixels per row. The screen's contents are represented by an 8K memory map that starts at RAM address 16384 (0x4000). Each row in the physical screen, starting at the screen's top left corner, is represented in the RAM by 32 consecutive 16-bit words. Thus the pixel at row r from the top and column c from the left is mapped on the $c\%16$ bit (counting from LSB to MSB) of the word located at $RAM[16384 + r \cdot 32 + c/16]$. To write or read a pixel of the physical screen, one writes or reads the corresponding bit in the RAM-resident memory map (1 = black, 0 = white). Example:

```
// Blacken a line of 16 pixels at the screen's top left corner:
@SCREEN   // Set the A register to point to the memory
          // word that is mapped to the 16 left-most
          // pixels of the top row of the screen.
M=-1      // -1 is 1111111111111111 in binary
```

Keyboard   The Hack computer interfaces with the physical keyboard via a single-word memory map located in RAM address 24576 (0x6000). Whenever a key is pressed on the physical keyboard, its 16-bit ASCII code appears in RAM[24576]. When no key is pressed, the code 0 appears in this location. In addition to the usual ASCII codes, the Hack keyboard recognizes the keys shown in figure 4.6.

4.2.6   Syntax Conventions and File Format

Binary Code Files   A binary code file is composed of text lines. Each line is a sequence of sixteen "0" and "1" ASCII characters, coding a single machine language instruction. Taken together, all the lines in the file represent a machine language program. The contract is such that when a machine language program is loaded into the computer's instruction memory, the binary code represented by the file's nth line is stored in address n of the instruction memory (the count of both program lines and memory addresses starts at 0). By convention, machine language programs are stored in text files with a "hack" extension, for example, `Prog.hack`.

Assembly Language Files   By convention, assembly language programs are stored in text files with an "asm" extension, for example, `Prog.asm`. An assembly language

Key pressed	Code	Key pressed	Code
newline	128	end	135
backspace	129	page up	136
left arrow	130	page down	137
up arrow	131	insert	138
right arrow	132	delete	139
down arrow	133	esc	140
home	134	f1–f12	141–152

Figure 4.6   Special keyboard codes in the Hack platform.

file is composed of text lines, each representing either an *instruction* or a *symbol declaration:*

- *Instruction*:   an *A*-instruction or a *C*-instruction.
- (*Symbol*):   This pseudo-command causes the assembler to assign the label `Symbol` to the memory location in which the next command of the program will be stored. It is called "pseudo-command" since it generates no machine code.

(The remaining conventions in this section pertain to assembly programs only.)

Constants and Symbols   *Constants* must be non-negative and are always written in decimal notation. A user-defined *symbol* can be any sequence of letters, digits, underscore (_), dot (.), dollar sign ($), and colon (:) that does not begin with a digit.

Comments   Text beginning with two slashes (//) and ending at the end of the line is considered a comment and is ignored.

White Space   Space characters are ignored. Empty lines are ignored.

Case Conventions   All the assembly mnemonics must be written in uppercase. The rest (user-defined labels and variable names) is case sensitive. The convention is to use uppercase for labels and lowercase for variable names.

4.3   Perspective

The Hack machine language is almost as simple as machine languages get. Most computers have more instructions, more data types, more registers, more instruction formats, and more addressing modes. However, any feature not supported by the Hack machine language may still be implemented in software, at a performance cost. For example, the Hack platform does not supply multiplication and division as primitive machine language operations. Since these operations are obviously required by any high-level language, we will later implement them at the operating system level (chapter 12). The implementation will be as efficient as software permits.

In terms of syntax, we have chosen to give Hack a somewhat different look-and-feel than the mechanical nature of most assembly languages. In particular, we have chosen a high-level language-like syntax for the *C*-command, for example, D=M and D=D+M instead of the more traditional LOAD and ADD directives. The reader should note, however, that these are just syntactic details. For example, the + character plays no algebraic role whatsoever in the command D=D+M. Rather, the three-character string D+M, taken as a whole, is treated as a single assembly mnemonic, designed to code a single ALU operation.

One of the main characteristics that gives machine languages their particular flavor is the number of memory addresses that can appear in a single command. In this respect, Hack may be described as a "$\frac{1}{2}$ address machine": Since there is no room to pack both an instruction code and a 15-bit address in the 16-bit instruction format, operations involving memory access will normally be specified in Hack using two instructions: an *A*-instruction to specify the address on which we wish to operate, and a *C*-instruction to specify the operation. In comparison, most machine languages can directly specify at least one address in every machine instruction.

Indeed, Hack assembly code typically ends up being (mostly) an alternating sequence of *A*- and *C*-instructions, for example, @xxx followed by D=D+M, @YYY followed by 0;JMP, and so on. If you find this coding style tedious or even peculiar, you should note that friendlier *macro commands* like D=D+M[xxx] and GOTO YYY can easily be introduced into the language, causing Hack assembly code to be more readable as well as about 50 percent shorter. The trick is to have the assembler translate these macro commands into binary code effecting @xxx followed by D=D+M, @YYY followed by 0;JMP, and so on.

The *assembler*, mentioned several times in this chapter, is the program responsible for translating symbolic assembly programs into executable programs written in binary code. In addition, the assembler is responsible for managing all the system- and user-defined symbols found in the assembly program, and for replacing them with physical memory addresses, as needed. We return to this translation task in chapter 6, in which we build an assembler for the Hack language.

4.4   Project

Objective   Get a taste of low-level programming in machine language, and get acquainted with the Hack computer platform. In the process of working on this project, you will also become familiar with the assembly process, and you will appreciate visually how the translated binary code executes on the target hardware.

Resources   In this project you will use two tools supplied with the book: An *assembler*, designed to translate Hack assembly programs into binary code, and a *CPU emulator*, designed to run binary programs on a simulated Hack platform.

Contract   Write and test the two programs described in what follows. When executed on the CPU emulator, your programs should generate the results mandated by the test scripts supplied in the project directory.

- *Multiplication Program* (Mult.asm):   The inputs of this program are the current values stored in R0 and R1 (i.e., the two top RAM locations). The program computes the product R0*R1 and stores the result in R2. We assume (in this program) that R0>=0, R1>=0, and R0*R1<32768. Your program need not test these conditions, but rather assume that they hold. The supplied Mult.tst and Mult.cmp scripts will test your program on several representative data values.

- *I/O-Handling Program* (Fill.asm):   This program runs an infinite loop that listens to the keyboard input. When a key is pressed (any key), the program blackens the screen, namely, writes "black" in every pixel. When no key is pressed, the screen should be cleared. You may choose to blacken and clear the screen in any spatial order, as long as pressing a key continuously for long enough will result in a fully blackened screen and not pressing any key for long enough will result in a cleared screen. This program has a test script (Fill.tst) but no compare file—it should be checked by visibly inspecting the simulated screen.

Steps   We recommend proceeding as follows:

0.   The assembler and CPU emulator programs needed for this project are available in the tools directory of the book's software suite. Before using them, go through the assembler tutorial and the CPU emulator tutorial.

1.   Use a plain text editor to write the first program in assembly, and save it as projects/04/mult/Mult.asm.

2.   Use the supplied assembler (in either batch or interactive mode) to translate your program. If you get syntax errors, go to step 1. If there are no syntax errors, the assembler will produce a file called projects/04/mult/Mult.hack, containing binary machine instructions.

3.   Use the supplied CPU emulator to test the resulting Mult.hack code. This can be done either interactively, or batch-style using the supplied Mult.tst script. If you get run-time errors, go to step 1.

4.   Repeat stages 1–3 for the second program (Fill.asm), using the projects/04/fill directory.

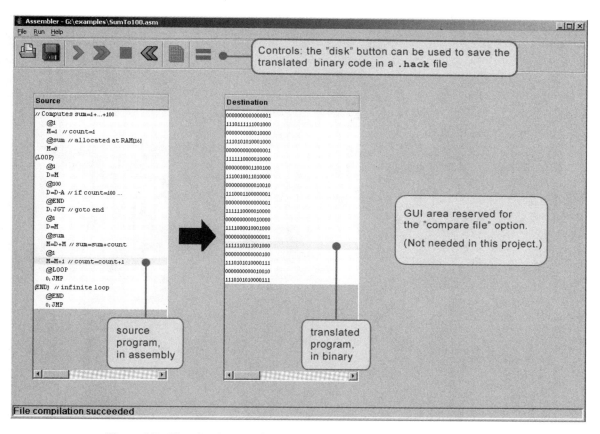

Figure 4.7   The visual assembler supplied with the book.

Debugging Tip   The Hack language is case sensitive. A common error occurs when one writes, say, @foo and @Foo in different parts of the program, thinking that both commands refer to the same variable. In fact, the assembler treats these symbols as two completely different identifiers.

The Supplied Assembler   The book's software suite includes a Hack assembler that can be used in either command mode or GUI mode. The latter mode of operation allows observing the translation process in a visual and step-wise fashion, as shown in figure 4.7.

The machine language programs produced by the assembler can be tested in two different ways. First, one can run the .hack program in the CPU emulator.

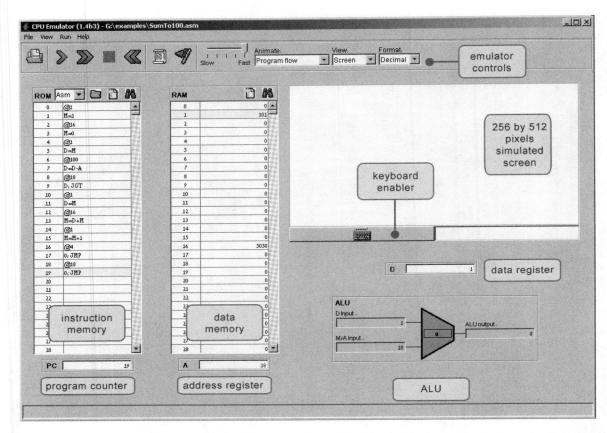

Figure 4.8   The CPU emulator supplied with the book. The loaded program can be displayed either in symbolic notation (as shown in this screen shot) or in binary code. The screen and the keyboard are not used by this particular program.

Alternatively, one can run the same program directly on the hardware, by loading it into the computer's instruction memory using the hardware simulator. Since we will finish building the hardware platform only in the next chapter, the former option makes more sense at this stage.

The Supplied CPU Emulator   This program simulates the Hack computer platform. It allows loading a Hack program into the simulated ROM and visually observing its execution on the simulated hardware, as shown in figure 4.8.

For ease of use, the CPU emulator enables loading binary `.hack` files as well as symbolic `.asm` files. In the latter case, the emulator translates the assembly program into binary code on the fly. This utility seems to render the supplied assembler unnecessary, but this is not the case. First, the supplied assembler shows the translation process visually, for instructive purposes. Second, the binary files generated by the assembler can be executed directly on the hardware platform. To do so, load the Computer chip (built in chapter 5's project) into the hardware simulator, then load the `.hack` file generated by the assembler into the computer's ROM chip.

5 Computer Architecture

Form ever follows function.
—Louis Sullivan (1856–1924), architect

Form IS function.
—Ludwig Mies van der Rohe (1886–1969), architect

This chapter is the pinnacle of the "hardware" part of our journey. We are now ready to take all the chips that we built in chapters 1–3 and integrate them into a general-purpose computer capable of running stored programs written in the machine language presented in chapter 4. The specific computer we will build, called *Hack*, has two important virtues. On the one hand, Hack is a simple machine that can be constructed in just a few hours, using previously built chips and the hardware simulator supplied with the book. On the other hand, Hack is sufficiently powerful to illustrate the key operating principles and hardware elements of any digital computer. Therefore, building it will give you an excellent understanding of how modern computers work at the low hardware and software levels.

Following an introduction of the *stored program* concept, section 5.1 gives a detailed description of the *von Neumann architecture*—a central dogma in computer science underlying the design of almost all modern computers. The Hack platform is one example of a von Neumann machine, and section 5.2 gives its exact hardware specification. Section 5.3 describes how the Hack platform can be implemented from available chips, in particular the ALU built in chapter 2 and the registers and memory systems built in chapter 3.

The computer that will emerge from this construction will be as simple as possible, but not simpler. This means that it will have the minimal configuration necessary to run interesting programs and deliver a reasonable performance. The comparison of this machine to typical computers is taken up in section 5.4, which emphasizes the critical role that *optimization* plays in the design of industrial-strength computers, but not in this chapter. As usual, the simplicity of our approach has a purpose: All the chips mentioned in the chapter, culminating in the Hack computer itself, can be built and tested on a personal computer running our hardware simulator, following the technical instructions given in section 5.5. The result will be a minimal yet surprisingly powerful computer.

5.1   Background

5.1.1   The Stored Program Concept

Compared to all the other machines around us, the most unique feature of the digital computer is its amazing versatility. Here is a machine with finite hardware that can perform a practically infinite array of tasks, from interactive games to word processing to scientific calculations. This remarkable flexibility—a boon that we have come to take for granted—is the fruit of a brilliant idea called the *stored program* concept. Formulated independently by several mathematicians in the 1930s, the stored program concept is still considered the most profound invention in, if not the very foundation of, modern computer science.

Like many scientific breakthroughs, the basic idea is rather simple. The computer is based on a fixed hardware platform, capable of executing a fixed repertoire of instructions. At the same time, these instructions can be used and combined like building blocks, yielding arbitrarily sophisticated programs. Moreover, the logic of these programs is not embedded in the hardware, as it was in mechanical computers predating 1930. Instead, the program's code is stored and manipulated in the computer memory, *just like data*, becoming what is known as "software." Since the computer's operation manifests itself to the user through the currently executing software, the same hardware platform can be made to behave completely differently each time it is loaded with a different program.

5.1.2   The von Neumann Architecture

The stored program concept is a key element of many abstract and practical computer models, most notably the *universal Turing machine* (1936) and the *von Neumann machine* (1945). The Turing machine—an abstract artifact describing a deceptively simple computer—is used mainly to analyze the logical foundations of

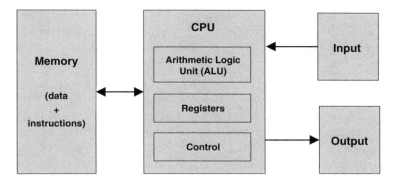

Figure 5.1   The von Neumann architecture (conceptual). At this level of detail, this model describes the architecture of almost all digital computers. The program that operates the computer resides in its memory, in accordance with the "stored program" concept.

computer systems. In contrast, the von Neumann machine is a practical architecture and the conceptual blueprint of almost all computer platforms today.

The von Neumann architecture is based on a *central processing unit* (CPU), interacting with a *memory* device, receiving data from some *input* device, and sending data to some *output* device (figure 5.1). At the heart of this architecture lies the stored program concept: The computer's memory stores not only the data that the computer manipulates, but also the very instructions that tell the computer what to do. Let us explore this architecture in some detail.

5.1.3   Memory

The memory of a von Neumann machine holds two types of information: data items and programming instructions. The two types of information are usually treated differently, and in some computers they are stored in separate memory units. In spite of their different functions though, both types of information are represented as binary numbers that are stored in the same generic random-access structure: a continuous array of cells of some fixed width, also called *words* or *locations*, each having a unique *address*. Hence, an individual word (representing either a data item or an instruction) is specified by supplying its address.

Data Memory   High-level programs manipulate abstract artifacts like variables, arrays, and objects. When translated into machine language, these data abstractions become series of binary numbers, stored in the computer's data memory. Once an individual word has been selected from the data memory by specifying its address, it can be either *read* or *written* to. In the former case, we retrieve the word's value. In the latter case, we store a new value into the selected location, erasing the old value.

Instruction Memory   When translated into machine language, each high-level command becomes a series of binary words, representing machine language instructions. These instructions are stored in the computer's *instruction memory*. In each step of the computer's operation, the CPU *fetches* (i.e., *reads*) a word from the instruction memory, decodes it, executes the specified instruction, and figures out which instruction to execute next. Thus, changing the contents of the instruction memory has the effect of completely changing the computer's operation.

The instructions that reside in the instruction memory are written in an agreed-upon formalism called *machine language*. In some computers, the specification of each operation and the codes representing its operands are represented in a single-word instruction. Other computers split this specification over several words.

5.1.4   Central Processing Unit

The CPU—the centerpiece of the computer's architecture—is in charge of executing the instructions of the currently loaded program. These instructions tell the CPU to carry out various calculations, to read and write values from and into the memory, and to conditionally jump to execute other instructions in the program. The CPU executes these tasks using three main hardware elements: an *Arithmetic-Logic Unit* (ALU), a set of *registers*, and a *control unit*.

Arithmetic Logic Unit   The ALU is built to perform all the low-level arithmetic and logical operations featured by the computer. For instance, a typical ALU can add two numbers, test whether a number is positive, manipulate the bits in a word of data, and so on.

Registers   The CPU is designed to carry out simple calculations *quickly*. In order to boost performance, it is desirable to store the results of these calculations locally, rather than ship them in and out of memory. Thus, every CPU is equipped with a small set of high-speed *registers*, each capable of holding a single word.

Control Unit   A computer instruction is represented as a binary code, typically 16, 32, or 64 bits wide. Before such an instruction can be executed, it must be decoded, and the information embedded in it must be used to signal various hardware devices (ALU, registers, memory) how to execute the instruction. The instruction decoding is done by some *control unit*, which is also responsible for figuring out which instruction to fetch and execute next.

The CPU operation can now be described as a repeated loop: fetch an instruction (word) from memory; decode it; execute it, fetch the next instruction, and so on. The instruction execution may involve one or more of the following micro tasks: have the ALU compute some value, manipulate internal registers, read a word from the memory, and write a word to the memory. In the process of executing these tasks, the CPU also figures out which instruction to fetch and execute next.

5.1.5 Registers

Memory access is a slow affair. When the CPU is instructed to retrieve the contents of address j of the memory, the following process ensues: (a) j travels from the CPU to the RAM's address input; (b) the RAM's direct-access logic selects the memory register whose address is j; (c) the contents of RAM[j] travel back to the CPU. Registers provide the same service—data retrieval and storage—without the round-trip travel and search expenses. First, the registers reside physically inside the CPU chip, so accessing them is almost instantaneous. Second, there are typically only a handful of registers, compared to millions of memory cells. Therefore, machine language instructions can specify which registers they want to manipulate using just a few bits, resulting in thinner instruction formats.

Different CPUs employ different numbers of registers, of different types, for different purposes. In some computer architectures each register can serve more than one purpose:

Data registers: These registers give the CPU short-term memory services. For example, when calculating the value of $(a - b) \cdot c$, we must first compute and remember the value of $(a - b)$. Although this result can be temporarily stored in some memory location, a better solution is to store it locally inside the CPU—in a *data register*.

Addressing registers: The CPU has to continuously access the memory in order to read data and write data. In every one of these operations, we must specify which individual memory word has to be accessed, namely, supply an address. In some cases this address appears as part of the current instruction, while in others it depends on the execution of a previous instruction. In the latter case, the address should be stored in a register whose contents can be later treated as a memory address—an *addressing register*.

Program counter register: When executing a program, the CPU must always keep track of the address of the next instruction that must be fetched from the instruction memory. This address is kept in a special register called *program counter*, or PC. The contents of the PC are then used as the address for fetching instructions from the instruction memory. Thus, in the process of executing the current instruction, the CPU updates the PC in one of two ways. If the current instruction contains no *goto* directive, the PC is incremented to point to the next instruction in the program. If the current instruction includes a *goto n* directive that should be executed, the CPU loads *n* into the PC.

5.1.6   Input and Output

Computers interact with their external environments using a diverse array of input and output (I/O) devices. These include screens, keyboards, printers, scanners, network interface cards, USB devices, and so forth, not to mention the bewildering array of proprietary components that embedded computers are called to control in automobiles, weapon systems, medical equipment, and so on. There are two reasons why we do not concern ourselves here with the anatomy of these various devices. First, every one of them represents a unique piece of machinery requiring a unique knowledge of engineering. Second, and for this very same reason, computer scientists have devised various schemes to make all these devices look exactly the same to the computer. The simplest trick in this art is called *memory-mapped I/O*.

The basic idea is to create a binary emulation of the I/O device, making it "look" to the CPU like a normal memory segment. In particular, each I/O device is allocated an exclusive area in memory, becoming its "memory map." In the case of an *input* device (keyboard, mouse, etc.), the memory map is made to continuously *reflect* the physical state of the device; in the case of an *output* device (screen, speakers, etc.), the memory map is made to continuously *drive* the physical state of the device. When external events affect some input devices (e.g., pressing a key on the keyboard or moving the mouse), certain values are written in their respective memory maps. Likewise, if we want to manipulate some output devices (e.g., draw something on the screen or play a tune), we write some values in their respective memory maps. From the hardware point of view, this scheme requires each I/O device to provide an interface similar to that of a memory unit. From a software point of view, each I/O device is required to define an interaction contract, so that programs can access it correctly. As a side comment, given the multitude of available computer platforms and I/O devices, one can appreciate the crucial role that *standards* play in designing computer architectures.

The practical implications of a memory-mapped I/O architecture are significant: The design of the CPU and the overall platform can be totally independent of the number, nature, or make of the I/O devices that interact, or *will* interact, with the computer. Whenever we want to connect a new I/O device to the computer, all we have to do is allocate to it a new memory map and "take note" of its base address (these one-time configurations are typically done by the operating system). From this point onward, any program that wants to manipulate this I/O device can do so—all it needs to do is manipulate bits in memory.

5.2   The Hack Hardware Platform Specification

5.2.1   Overview

The Hack platform is a 16-bit von Neumann machine, consisting of a CPU, two separate memory modules serving as instruction memory and data memory, and two memory-mapped I/O devices: a screen and a keyboard. Certain parts of this architecture—especially its machine language—were presented in chapter 4. A summary of this discussion is given here, for ease of reference.

The Hack computer executes programs that reside in its instruction memory. The instruction memory is a read-only device, and thus programs are loaded into it using some exogenous means. For example, the instruction memory can be implemented in a ROM chip that is preburned with the required program. Loading a new program can be done by replacing the entire ROM chip. In order to simulate this operation, hardware simulators of the Hack platform must provide a means for loading the instruction memory from a text file containing a program written in the Hack machine language. (From now on, we will refer to Hack's data memory and instruction memory as RAM and ROM, respectively.)

The Hack CPU consists of the ALU specified in chapter 2 and three registers called *data register* (D), *address register* (A), and *program counter* (PC). D and A are general-purpose 16-bit registers that can be manipulated by arithmetic and logical instructions like `A=D-1`, `D=D|A`, and so on, following the Hack machine language specified in chapter 4. While the D-register is used solely to store data values, the contents of the A-register can be interpreted in three different ways, depending on the instruction's context: as a data value, as a RAM address, or as a ROM address.

The Hack machine language is based on two 16-bit command types. The *address instruction* has the format `0vvvvvvvvvvvvvvv`, each v being 0 or 1. This instruction causes the computer to load the 15-bit constant `vvv...v` into the A-register. The *compute instruction* has the format `111accccccdddjjj`. The a- and c-bits instruct the ALU which function to compute, the d-bits instruct where to store the ALU output, and the j-bits specify an optional jump condition, all according to the Hack machine language specification.

As we will see shortly, the computer's architecture is wired in such a way that the output of the program counter (PC) chip is connected to the address input of the ROM chip. This way, the ROM chip always emits the word ROM[PC], namely, the contents of the instruction memory location whose address is "pointed at" by the PC. This value is called the *current instruction*. With that in mind, the overall computer operation during each clock cycle is as follows:

Execute: Various bit parts of the current instruction are simultaneously fed to various chips in the computer. If it's an *address instruction* (most significant bit = 0), the A-register is set to the 15-bit constant embedded in the instruction. If it's a *compute instruction* (MSB = 1), its underlying a-, c-, d- and j-bits are treated as control bits that cause the ALU and the registers to execute the instruction.

Fetch: Which instruction to fetch next is determined by the jump bits of the current instruction and by the ALU output. Taken together, these values determine whether a jump should materialize. If so, the PC is set to the value of the A-register; otherwise, the PC is incremented by 1. In the next clock cycle, the instruction that the program counter points at emerges from the ROM's output, and the cycle continues.

This particular fetch-execute cycle implies that in the Hack platform, elementary operations involving memory access usually require two instructions: an *address instruction* to set the A register to a particular address, and a subsequent *compute instruction* that operates on this address (a read/write operation on the RAM or a jump operation into the ROM).

We now turn to formally specify the Hack hardware platform. Before starting, we wish to point out that this platform can be assembled from previously built components. The CPU is based on the ALU built in chapter 2. The *registers* and the *program counter* are identical copies of the 16-bit register and 16-bit counter, respectively, built in chapter 3. Likewise, the ROM and the RAM chips are versions of the memory units built in chapter 3. Finally, the *screen* and the *keyboard* devices will interface with the hardware platform through memory maps, implemented as built-in chips that have the same interface as RAM chips.

5.2.2   Central Processing Unit (CPU)

The CPU of the Hack platform is designed to execute 16-bit instructions accord-ing to the Hack machine language specified in chapter 4. It expects to be connected to two separate memory modules: an instruction memory, from which it fetches instructions for execution, and a data memory, from which it can read, and into which it can write, data values. Figure 5.2 gives the specification details.

5.2.3   Instruction Memory

The Hack instruction memory is implemented in a direct-access Read-Only Memory device, also called ROM. The Hack ROM consists of 32K addressable 16-bit regis-ters, as shown in figure 5.3.

5.2.4   Data Memory

Hack's *data memory* chip has the interface of a typical RAM device, like that built in chapter 3 (see, e.g., figure 3.3). To read the contents of register n, we put n in the memory's `address` input and probe the memory's `out` output. This is a combina-tional operation, independent of the clock. To write a value v into register n, we put v in the `in` input, n in the `address` input, and assert the memory's `load` bit. This is a sequential operation, and so register n will commit to the new value v in the next clock cycle.

   In addition to serving as the computer's general-purpose data store, the data memory also interfaces between the CPU and the computer's input/output devices, using *memory maps*.

Memory Maps   In order to facilitate interaction with a user, the Hack platform can be connected to two peripheral devices: *screen* and *keyboard*. Both devices interact with the computer platform through *memory-mapped* buffers. Specifically, screen images can be drawn and probed by writing and reading, respectively, words in a designated memory segment called *screen memory map*. Similarly, one can check which key is presently pressed on the keyboard by probing a designated memory word called *keyboard memory map*. The memory maps interact with their respective I/O devices via peripheral logic that resides outside the computer. The contract is as follows: Whenever a bit is changed in the screen's memory map, a respective pixel is drawn on the physical screen. Whenever a key is pressed on the physical keyboard, the respective code of this key appears in the keyboard's memory map.

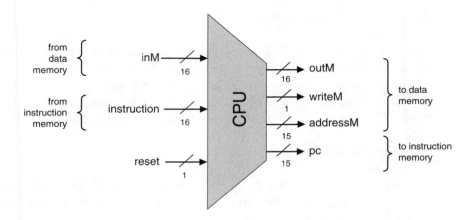

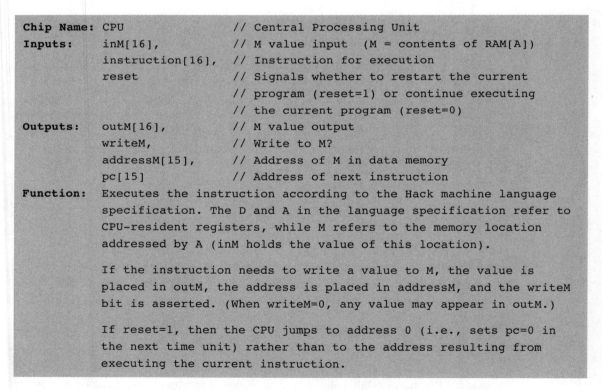

Figure 5.2   The Central Processing Unit. Assembled from the ALU and the registers built in chapters 2 and 3, respectively.

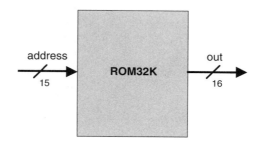

```
Chip Name:  ROM32K             // 16-bit read-only 32K memory
Input:      address[15]        // Address in the ROM
Output:     out[16]            // Value of ROM[address]
Function:   out=ROM[address]   // 16-bit assignment
Comment:    The ROM is preloaded with a machine language program.
            Hardware implementations can treat the ROM as a
            built-in chip. Software simulators must supply a
            mechanism for loading a program into the ROM.
```

Figure 5.3   Instruction memory.

We specify first the built-in chips that interface between the hardware interface and the I/O devices, then the complete memory module that embeds these chips.

Screen   The Hack computer can interact with a black-and-white screen organized as 256 rows of 512 pixels per row. The computer interfaces with the physical screen via a memory map, implemented by a chip called Screen. This chip behaves like regular memory, meaning that it can be read and written to. In addition, it features the side effect that any bit written to it is reflected as a pixel on the physical screen (1 = black, 0 = white). The exact mapping between the memory map and the physical screen coordinates is given in figure 5.4.

Keyboard   The Hack computer can interact with a standard keyboard, like that of a personal computer. The computer interfaces with the physical keyboard via a chip called Keyboard (figure 5.5). Whenever a key is pressed on the physical keyboard, its 16-bit ASCII code appears as the output of the Keyboard chip. When no key is pressed, the chip outputs 0. In addition to the usual ASCII codes, the Keyboard chip recognizes, and responds to, the keys listed in figure 5.6.

```
Chip Name: Screen          // Memory map of the physical screen
Inputs:    in[16],         // What to write
           load,           // Write-enable bit
           address[13]     // Where to write
Output:    out[16]         // Screen value at the given address
Function:  Functions exactly like a 16-bit 8K RAM:
           1. out(t)=Screen[address(t)](t)
           2. If load(t-1) then Screen[address(t-1)](t)=in(t-1)
           (t is the current time unit, or cycle)
Comment:   Has the side effect of continuously refreshing a 256
           by 512 black-and-white screen (simulators must
           simulate this device). Each row in the physical
           screen is represented by 32 consecutive 16-bit words,
           starting at the top left corner of the screen. Thus
           the pixel at row r from the top and column c from the
           left (0<=r<=255, 0<=c<=511) reflects the c%16 bit
           (counting from LSB to MSB) of the word found at
           Screen[r*32+c/16].
```

Figure 5.4 Screen interface.

```
Chip Name: Keyboard        // Memory map of the physical keyboard.
                           // Outputs the code of the currently
                           // pressed key.
Output:    out[16]         // The ASCII code of the pressed key, or
                           // one of the special codes listed in
                           // figure 5.6, or 0 if no key is pressed.
Function:  Outputs the code of the key presently pressed on the
           physical keyboard.
Comment:   This chip is continuously being refreshed from a
           physical keyboard unit (simulators must simulate this
           service).
```

Figure 5.5 Keyboard interface.

Key pressed	Keyboard output	Key pressed	Keyboard output
newline	128	end	135
backspace	129	page up	136
left arrow	130	page down	137
up arrow	131	insert	138
right arrow	132	delete	139
down arrow	133	esc	140
home	134	f1–f12	141–152

Figure 5.6   Special keyboard keys in the Hack platform.

Now that we've described the internal parts of the data memory, we are ready to specify the entire data memory address space.

Overall Memory   The overall address space of the Hack platform (i.e., its entire data memory) is provided by a chip called Memory. The memory chip includes the RAM (for regular data storage) and the screen and keyboard memory maps. These modules reside in a single address space that is partitioned into four sections, as shown in figure 5.7.

5.2.5   Computer

The topmost chip in the Hack hardware hierarchy is a complete computer system designed to execute programs written in the Hack machine language. This abstraction is described in figure 5.8. The Computer chip contains all the hardware devices necessary to operate the computer including a CPU, a data memory, an instruction memory (ROM), a screen, and a keyboard, all implemented as internal parts. In order to execute a program, the program's code must be preloaded into the ROM. Control of the screen and the keyboard is achieved via their memory maps, as described in the Screen and Keyboard chip specifications.

5.3   Implementation

This section gives general guidelines on how the Hack computer platform can be built to deliver the various services described in its specification (section 5.2). As usual, we don't give exact building instructions, expecting readers to come up with

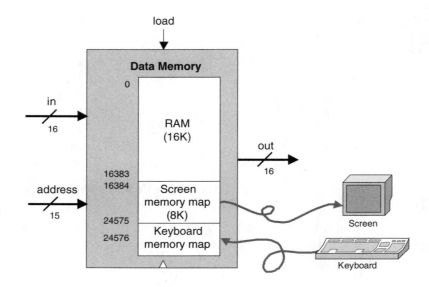

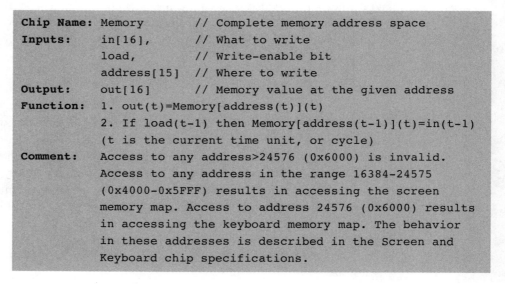

Figure 5.7 Data memory.

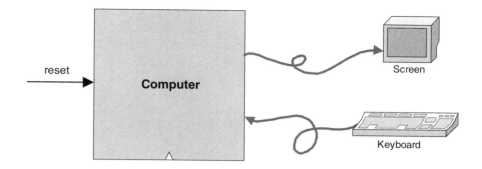

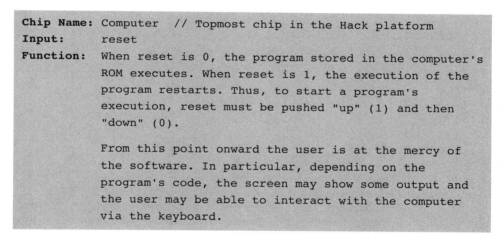

```
Chip Name: Computer   // Topmost chip in the Hack platform
Input:     reset
Function:  When reset is 0, the program stored in the computer's
           ROM executes. When reset is 1, the execution of the
           program restarts. Thus, to start a program's
           execution, reset must be pushed "up" (1) and then
           "down" (0).

           From this point onward the user is at the mercy of
           the software. In particular, depending on the
           program's code, the screen may show some output and
           the user may be able to interact with the computer
           via the keyboard.
```

Figure 5.8   Computer. Topmost chip of the Hack hardware platform.

their own designs. All the chips can be built in HDL and simulated on a personal computer using the hardware simulator that comes with the book. As usual, technical details are given in the final Project section of this chapter.

Since most of the action in the Hack platform occurs in its Central Processing Unit, the main implementation challenge is building the CPU. The construction of the rest of the computer platform is straightforward.

5.3.1   The Central Processing Unit

The CPU implementation objective is to create a logic gate architecture capable of executing a given Hack instruction and fetching the next instruction to be executed. Naturally, the CPU will include an ALU capable of executing Hack instructions, a

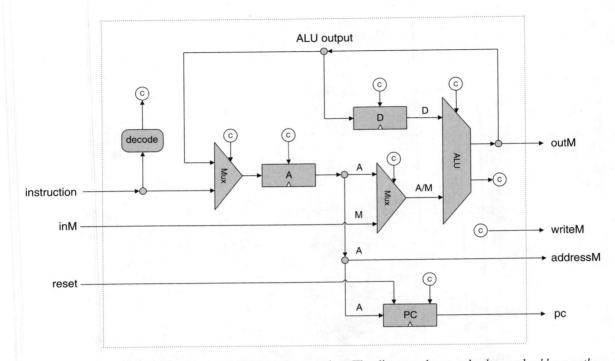

Figure 5.9 Proposed CPU implementation. The diagram shows only *data* and *address paths*, namely, wires that carry data and addresses from one place to another. The diagram does not show the CPU's *control logic*, except for inputs and outputs of control bits, labeled with a circled "c". Each one of the incoming circled "c" labels stands for one or more control bits. These bits are extracted from the current instruction and routed to the various chips whose behavior they seek to control. Since we don't specify the exact number and wiring of these bits, the diagram is incomplete.

set of registers, and some control logic designed to fetch and decode instructions. Since almost all these hardware elements were already built in previous chapters, the key question here is how to connect them in order to effect the desired CPU operation. One possible solution is illustrated in figure 5.9.

The key element missing in figure 5.9 is the CPU's *control logic*, designed to perform the following tasks:

▪ *Instruction decoding:* Parse the instruction into its underlying fields, i.e., subsets of bits. We call these bits "control bits," hinting at their intended use.

▪ *Instruction execution:* Signal the various chip parts of the computer what they should do in order to execute the instruction; this is done by routing the control bits to their intended destinations.

■ *Next instruction fetching:* Figure out which instruction to execute next. This decision depends on the jump bits of the instruction as well as on the two control bits emitted by the ALU.

(In what follows, the term *proposed CPU implementation* refers to figure 5.9.)

Instruction Decoding The 16-bit word located in the CPU's instruction input can represent either an *A*-instruction or a *C*-instruction. In order to figure out what this 16-bit word means, it can be broken into the fields "i xx a ccccc ddd jjj". The i-bit codes the instruction type, which is 0 for an *A*-instruction and 1 for a *C*-instruction. In case of a *C*-instruction, the a-bit and the c-bits code the *comp* part, the d-bits code the *dest* part, and the j-bits code the *jump* part of the instruction. In case of an *A*-instruction, the 15 bits other than the i-bit should be interpreted as a 15-bit constant.

Instruction Execution The various fields of the instruction (i-, a-, c-, d-, and j-bits) are routed simultaneously to various parts of the architecture, where they cause different chips to do what they are supposed to do in order to execute either the *A*-instruction or the *C*-instruction, as mandated by the machine language specification. In particular, the a-bit determines whether the ALU will operate on the A register input or on the Memory input, the c-bits determine which function the ALU will compute, and the d-bits enable various registers to accept the ALU result.

Next Instruction Fetching As a side effect of executing the current instruction, the CPU also determines the address of the next instruction and emits it via its pc output. The "driver" of this task is the *program counter*—an internal part of the CPU whose output is fed directly to the CPU's pc output. This is precisely the PC chip built in chapter 3 (see figure 3.5).

Most of the time, the programmer wants the computer to fetch and execute the next instruction in the program. Thus if t is the current time-unit, the default program counter operation should be $PC(t) = PC(t - 1) + 1$. When we want to effect a *goto n* operation, the machine language specification requires to first set the A register to n (via an *A*-instruction) and then issue a jump directive (coded by the j-bits of a subsequent *C*-instruction). Hence, our challenge is to come up with a hardware implementation of the following logic:

If jump(t) then $PC(t) = A(t - 1)$
else $PC(t) = PC(t - 1) + 1$

Conveniently, and actually by careful design, this jump control logic can be easily effected by the proposed CPU implementation. Recall that the PC chip interface (figure 3.5) has a `load` control bit that enables it to accept a new input value. Thus, to effect the desired jump control logic, we start by connecting the output of the A register to the input of the PC. The only remaining question is when to enable the PC to accept this value (rather than continuing its steadfast counting), namely, when does a jump need to occur. This is a function of two signals: (a) the `j`-bits of the current instruction, specifying on which condition we are supposed to jump, and (b) the ALU output status bits, indicating whether the condition is satisfied. If we have a jump, the PC should be loaded with A's output. Otherwise, the PC should increment by 1.

Additionally, if we want the computer to restart the program's execution, all we have to do is reset the program counter to 0. That's why the proposed CPU implementation feeds the CPU's reset input directly into the reset pin of the PC chip.

5.3.2 Memory

According to its specification, the Memory chip of the Hack platform is essentially a package of three lower-level chips: RAM16K, Screen, and Keyboard. At the same-time, users of the Memory chip must see a single logical address space, spanning from location 0 to 24576 (`0x0000` to `0x6000`—see figure 5.7). The implementation of the Memory chip should create this continuum effect. This can be done by the same technique used to combine small RAM units into larger ones, as we have done in chapter 3 (see figure 3.6 and the discussion of *n-register memory* that accompanies it).

5.3.3 Computer

Once the CPU and the Memory chips have been implemented and tested, the construction of the overall computer is straightforward. Figure 5.10 depicts a possible implementation.

5.4 Perspective

Following the general spirit of the book, the architecture of the Hack computer is rather minimal. Typical computer platforms have more registers, more data types, more powerful ALUs, and richer instruction sets. However, these differences are

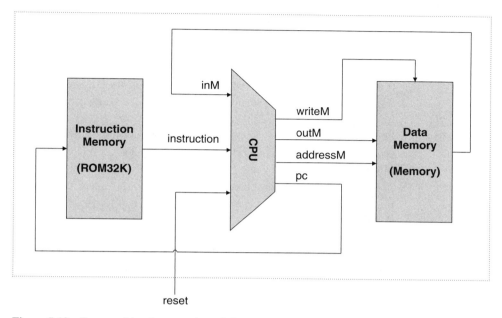

Figure 5.10   Proposed implementation of the topmost Computer chip.

mainly quantitative. From a qualitative standpoint, Hack is quite similar to most digital computers, as they all follow the same conceptual paradigm: the von Neumann architecture.

In terms of function, computer systems can be classified into two categories: *general-purpose computers*, designed to easily switch from executing one program to another, and *dedicated computers*, usually embedded in other systems like cell phones, game consoles, digital cameras, weapon systems, factory equipment, and so on. For any particular application, a single program is burned into the dedicated computer's ROM, and is the only one that can be executed (in game consoles, for example, the game software resides in an external cartridge that is simply a replaceable ROM module encased in some fancy package). Aside from this difference, general-purpose and dedicated computers share the same architectural ideas: stored programs, fetch-decode-execute logic, CPU, registers, program counter, and so on.

Unlike Hack, most general-purpose computers use a single address space for storing both data and instructions. In such architectures, the instruction address as well as the optional data address specified by the instruction must be fed into the same destination: the single address input of the shared address space. Clearly, this cannot be done at the same time. The standard solution is to base the computer implementation on a two-cycle logic. During the *fetch cycle*, the instruction address is fed to the address input of the memory, causing it to immediately emit the current instruction, which is then stored in an *instruction register*. In the subsequent *execute cycle*, the instruction is decoded, and the optional data address inferred from it is fed to the memory's address input, allowing the instruction to manipulate the selected memory location. In contrast, the Hack architecture is unique in that it partitions the address space into two separate parts, allowing a single-cycle fetch-execute logic. The price of this simpler hardware design is that programs cannot be changed dynamically.

In terms of I/O, the Hack keyboard and screen are rather spartan. General-purpose computers are typically connected to multiple I/O devices like printers, disks, network connections, and so on. Also, typical screens are obviously much more powerful than the Hack screen, featuring more pixels, many brightness levels in each pixel, and colors. Still, the basic principle that each pixel is controlled by a memory-resident binary value is maintained: instead of a single bit controlling the pixel's black or white color, several bits are devoted to control the level of brightness of each of the three primary colors that, together, produce the pixel's ultimate color. Likewise, the memory mapping of the Hack screen is simplistic. Instead of mapping pixels directly into bits of memory, most modern computers allow the CPU to send high-level graphic instructions to a *graphics card* that controls the screen. This way, the CPU is relieved from the tedium of drawing figures like circles and polygons directly—the graphics card takes care of this task using its own embedded chip-set.

Finally, it should be stressed that most of the effort and creativity in designing computer hardware is invested in achieving better performance. Thus, hardware architecture courses and textbooks typically evolve around such issues as implementing memory hierarchies (cache), better access to I/O devices, pipelining, parallelism, instruction prefetching, and other optimization techniques that were sidestepped in this chapter.

Historically, attempts to enhance the processor's performance have led to two main schools of hardware design. Advocates of the *Complex Instruction Set Computing* (CISC) approach argue for achieving better performance by providing rich and elaborate instruction sets. Conversely, the *Reduced Instruction Set Computing* (RISC) camp uses simpler instruction sets in order to promote as fast a hardware implementation as possible. The Hack computer does not enter this debate, featuring neither a strong instruction set nor special hardware acceleration techniques.

5.5   Project

Objective   Build the Hack computer platform, culminating in the topmost Computer chip.

Resources   The only tools that you need for completing this project are the hardware simulator supplied with the book and the test scripts described here. The computer platform should be implemented in the HDL language specified in appendix A.

Contract   The computer platform built in this project should be capable of executing programs written in the Hack machine language, specified in chapter 4. Demonstrate this capability by having your Computer chip run the three programs given here.

Component Testing   We supply test scripts and compare files for unit-testing the Memory and CPU chips in isolation. It's important to complete the testing of these chips before building and testing the overall Computer chip.

Test Programs   A natural way to test the overall Computer chip implementation is to have it execute some sample programs written in the Hack machine language. In order to run such a test, one can write a test script that loads the Computer chip into the hardware simulator, loads a program from an external text file into its ROM chip, and then runs the clock enough cycles to execute the program. We supply all the files necessary to run three such tests, as follows:

1. `Add.hack`:   Adds the two constants 2 and 3 and writes the result in RAM[0].

2. `Max.hack`:   Computes the maximum of RAM[0] and RAM[1] and writes the result in RAM[2].

3. `Rect.hack`:   Draws a rectangle of width 16 pixels and length RAM[0] at the top left of the screen.

Before testing your Computer chip on any one of the above programs, read the test script associated with the program and be sure to understand the instructions given to the simulator. Appendix B may be a useful reference here.

Steps   Build the computer in the following order:

■ *Memory:*   Composed from three chips: RAM16K, Screen, and Keyboard. The Screen and the Keyboard are available as built-in chips and there is no need to build them. Although the RAM16K chip was built in the project in chapter 3, we recommend using its built-in version, as it provides a debugging-friendly GUI.

- *CPU:*   Can be composed according to the proposed implementation given in figure 5.9, using the ALU and register chips built in chapters 2 and 3, respectively. We recommend using the built-in versions of these chips, in particular ARegister and DRegister. These chips have exactly the same functionality of the Register chip specified in chapter 3, plus GUI side effects.

In the course of implementing the CPU, it is allowed (but not necessarily recommended) to specify and build some internal chips of your own. This is up to you. If you choose to create new chips not mentioned in the book, be sure to document and test them carefully before you plug them into the architecture.

- *Instruction Memory:*   Use the built-in ROM32K chip.

- *Computer:*   The topmost Computer chip can be composed from the chips mentioned earlier, using figure 5.10 as a blueprint.

The Hardware Simulator   As in the projects in chapters 1–3, all the chips in this project (including the topmost Computer chip) can be implemented and tested using the hardware simulator supplied with the book. Figure 5.11 is a screen shot of testing the Rect.hack program on a Computer chip implementation.

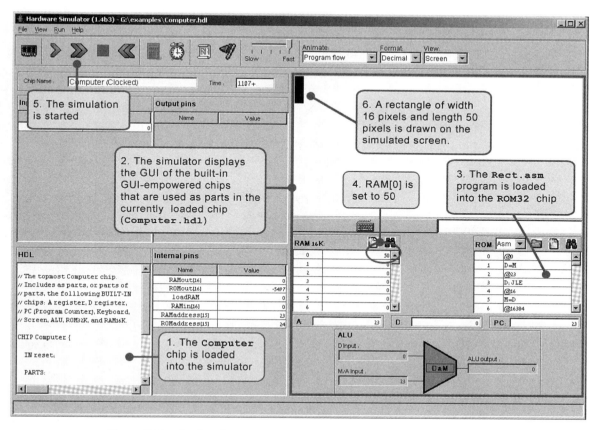

Figure 5.11   Testing the Computer chip on the hardware simulator. The Rect program draws a rectangle of width 16 pixels and length RAM[0] at the top left of the screen. Note that the program is correct. Thus, if it does not work properly, it means that the computer platform on which it runs (Computer.hdl and/or some of its lower-level parts) is buggy.

6   Assembler

What's in a name? That which we call a rose by any other name would smell as sweet.
—Shakespeare, from *Romeo and Juliet*

The first half of the book (chapters 1–5) described and built a computer's *hardware platform*. The second half of the book (chapters 6–12) focuses on the computer's *software hierarchy*, culminating in the development of a compiler and a basic operating system for a simple, object-based programming language. The first and most basic module in this software hierarchy is the *assembler*. In particular, chapter 4 presented machine languages in both their *assembly* and *binary* representations. This chapter describes how assemblers can systematically translate programs written in the former into programs written in the latter. As the chapter unfolds, we explain how to develop a *Hack assembler*—a program that generates binary code that can run as is on the hardware platform built in chapter 5.

Since the relationship between symbolic assembly commands and their corresponding binary codes is straightforward, writing an assembler (using some high-level language) is not a difficult task. One complication arises from allowing assembly programs to use symbolic references to memory addresses. The assembler is expected to manage these user-defined symbols and resolve them to physical memory addresses. This task is normally done using a *symbol table*—a classical data structure that comes to play in many software translation projects.

As usual, the Hack assembler is not an end in itself. Rather, it provides a simple and concise demonstration of the key software engineering principles used in the construction of any assembler. Further, writing the assembler is the first in the series of seven software development projects that accompany the rest of the book. Unlike the hardware projects, which were implemented in HDL, the software projects that construct the translator programs (*assembler*, *virtual machine*, and *compiler*) may be implemented in any programming language. In each project, we provide a language-neutral API and a detailed step-by-step test plan, along with all the necessary test programs and test scripts. Each one of these projects, beginning with the assembler, is a stand-alone module that can be developed and tested in isolation from all the other projects.

6.1 Background

Machine languages are typically specified in two flavors: *symbolic* and *binary*. The binary codes—for example, 11000010100000011000000000000111—represent actual machine instructions, as understood by the underlying hardware. For example, the instruction's leftmost 8 bits can represent an operation code, say LOAD, the next 8 bits a register, say R3, and the remaining 16 bits an address, say 7. Depending on the hardware's logic design and the agreed-upon machine language, the overall 32-bit pattern can thus cause the hardware to effect the operation "load the contents of Memory[7] into register R3." Modern computer platforms support dozens if not hundreds of such elementary operations. Thus, machine languages are rather complex, involving a multitude of operation codes, memory addressing modes, and instruction formats.

One way to cope with this complexity is to document machine instructions using an agreed-upon syntax, say LOAD R3,7 rather than 110000101000000110 000000000000111. And since the translation from symbolic notation to binary code is straightforward, it makes sense to allow low-level programs to be written in symbolic notation and to have a computer program translate them into binary code. The symbolic language is called *assembly*, and the translator program *assembler*. The assembler parses each assembly command into its underlying fields, translates each field into its equivalent binary code, and assembles the generated codes into a binary instruction that can be actually executed by the hardware.

Symbols Binary instructions are represented in binary code. By definition, they refer to memory addresses using actual numbers. For example, consider a program that uses a variable to represent the *weight* of various things, and suppose that this variable has been mapped on location 7 in the computer's memory. At the binary code level, instructions that manipulate the *weight* variable must refer to it using the explicit address 7. Yet once we step up to the assembly level, we can allow writing commands like LOAD R3,weight instead of LOAD R3,7. In both cases, the command will effect the same operation: "set R3 to the contents of Memory[7]." In a similar fashion, rather than using commands like goto 250, assembly languages allow commands like goto LOOP, assuming that somewhere in the program the symbol LOOP is made to refer to address 250. In general then, symbols are introduced into assembly programs from two sources:

- *Variables:* The programmer can use symbolic variable names, and the translator will "automatically" assign them to memory addresses. Note that the actual values of these addresses are insignificant, so long as each symbol is resolved to the same address throughout the program's translation.

- *Labels:* The programmer can mark various locations in the program with symbols. For example, one can declare the label LOOP to refer to the beginning of a certain code segment. Other commands in the program can then goto LOOP, either conditionally or unconditionally.

The introduction of symbols into assembly languages suggests that assemblers must be more sophisticated than dumb text processing programs. Granted, translating agreed-upon symbols into agreed-upon binary codes is not a complicated task. At the same time, the mapping of user-defined variable names and symbolic labels on actual memory addresses is not trivial. In fact, this symbol resolution task is the first nontrivial translation challenge in our ascent up the software hierarchy from the hardware level. The following example illustrates the challenge and the common way to address it.

Symbol Resolution   Consider figure 6.1, showing a program written in some self-explanatory low-level language. The program contains four user-defined symbols: two variable names (i and sum) and two labels (LOOP and END). How can we systematically convert this program into a symbol-less code?

We start by making two arbitrary game rules: The translated code will be stored in the computer's memory starting at address 0, and variables will be allocated to memory locations starting at address 1024 (these rules depend on the specific target hardware platform). Next, we build a *symbol table*, as follows. For each new symbol *xxx* encountered in the source code, we add a line (xxx, n) to the symbol table, where *n* is the memory address associated with the symbol according to the game rules. After completing the construction of the symbol table, we use it to translate the program into its symbol-less version.

Note that according to the assumed game rules, variables i and sum are allocated to addresses 1024 and 1025, respectively. Of course any other two addresses will be just as good, so long as *all* references to i and sum in the program resolve to the same physical addresses, as indeed is the case. The remaining code is self-explanatory, except perhaps for instruction 6. This instruction terminates the program's execution by putting the computer in an infinite loop.

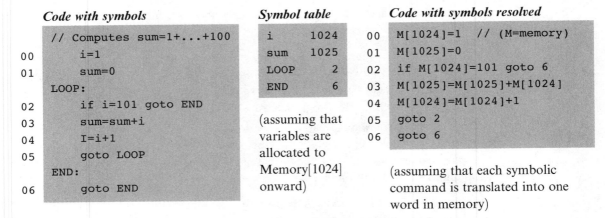

Code with symbols

```
// Computes sum=1+...+100
00      i=1
01      sum=0
LOOP:
02      if i=101 goto END
03      sum=sum+i
04      I=i+1
05      goto LOOP
END:
06      goto END
```

Symbol table

i	1024
sum	1025
LOOP	2
END	6

(assuming that
variables are
allocated to
Memory[1024]
onward)

Code with symbols resolved

```
00  M[1024]=1   // (M=memory)
01  M[1025]=0
02  if M[1024]=101 goto 6
03  M[1025]=M[1025]+M[1024]
04  M[1024]=M[1024]+1
05  goto 2
06  goto 6
```

(assuming that each symbolic
command is translated into one
word in memory)

Figure 6.1 Symbol resolution using a symbol table. The line numbers are not part of the program—they simply count all the lines in the program that represent real instructions, namely, neither comments nor label declarations. Note that once we have the symbol table in place, the symbol resolution task is straightforward. Note also that the code shown above assumes a hypothetical hardware and language that are unrelated to the Hack computer.

Three comments are in order here. First, note that the variable allocation assumption implies that the largest program that we can run is 1,024 instructions long. Since realistic programs (like the operating system) are obviously much larger, the base address for storing variables will normally be much farther. Second, the assumption that each source command is mapped on one word may be naïve. Typically, some assembly commands (e.g., if i=101 goto END) may translate into several machine instructions and thus will end up occupying several memory locations. The translator can deal with this variance by keeping track of how many words each source command generates, then updating its "instruction memory counter" accordingly.

Finally, the assumption that each variable is represented by a single memory location is also naïve. Programming languages feature variables of different types, and these occupy different memory spaces on the target computer. For example, the C language data types short and double represent 16-bit and 64-bit numbers, respectively. When a C program is run on a 16-bit machine, these variables will occupy a single memory address and a block of four consecutive addresses, respectively. Thus, when allocating memory space for variables, the translator must take into account both their data types and the word width of the target hardware.

The Assembler   Before an assembly program can be executed on a computer, it must be translated into the computer's binary machine language. The translation task is done by a program called *assembler*. The assembler takes as input a stream of assembly commands and generates as output a stream of equivalent binary instructions. The resulting code can be loaded as is into the computer's memory and executed by the hardware.

We see that the assembler is essentially a text-processing program, designed to provide translation services. The programmer who is commissioned to write the assembler must be given the full documentation of the assembly syntax, on the one hand, and the respective binary codes, on the other. Following this contract—typically called *machine language specification*—it is not difficult to write a program that, for each symbolic command, carries out the following tasks (not necessarily in that order):

- Parse the symbolic command into its underlying fields.

- For each field, generate the corresponding bits in the machine language.

- Replace all symbolic references (if any) with numeric addresses of memory locations.

- Assemble the binary codes into a complete machine instruction.

Three of the above tasks (parsing, code generation, and final assembly) are rather easy to implement. The fourth task—symbols handling—is more challenging, and considered one of the main functions of the assembler. This function was described in the previous section. The next two sections specify the Hack assembly language and propose an assembler implementation for it, respectively.

6.2   Hack Assembly-to-Binary Translation Specification

The Hack assembly language and its equivalent binary representation were specified in chapter 4. A compact and formal version of this language specification is repeated here, for ease of reference. This specification can be viewed as the contract that Hack assemblers must implement, one way or another.

6.2.1   Syntax Conventions and File Formats

File Names   By convention, Hack programs in binary machine code and in assembly code are stored in text files with "hack" and "asm" extensions, respectively. Thus, a `Prog.asm` file is translated by the assembler into a `Prog.hack` file.

Binary Code (.hack) Files   A binary code file is composed of text lines. Each line is a sequence of 16 "0" and "1" ASCII characters, coding a single 16-bit machine language instruction. Taken together, all the lines in the file represent a machine language program. When a machine language program is loaded into the computer's instruction memory, the binary code represented by the file's *n*th line is stored in address *n* of the instruction memory (the count of both program lines and memory addresses starts at 0).

Assembly Language (.asm) Files   An assembly language file is composed of text lines, each representing either an *instruction* or a *symbol declaration*:

- *Instruction*:   an *A*-instruction or a *C*-instruction, described in section 6.2.2.
- *(Symbol)*:   This pseudo-command binds the `symbol` to the memory location into which the next command in the program will be stored. It is called "pseudo-command" since it generates no machine code.

(The remaining conventions in this section pertain to assembly programs only.)

Constants and Symbols   *Constants* must be non-negative and are written in decimal notation. A user-defined *symbol* can be any sequence of letters, digits, underscore (_), dot (.), dollar sign ($), and colon (:) that does not begin with a digit.

Comments   Text beginning with two slashes (//) and ending at the end of the line is considered a comment and is ignored.

White Space   Space characters are ignored. Empty lines are ignored.

Case Conventions   All the assembly mnemonics must be written in uppercase. The rest (user-defined labels and variable names) is case sensitive. The convention is to use uppercase for labels and lowercase for variable names.

6.2.2   Instructions

The Hack machine language consists of two instruction types called *addressing instruction* (*A*-instruction) and *compute instruction* (*C*-instruction). The instruction format is as follows.

A-instruction: *@value*   // Where *value* is either a non-negative decimal number
                                     // or a symbol referring to such number.

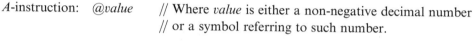

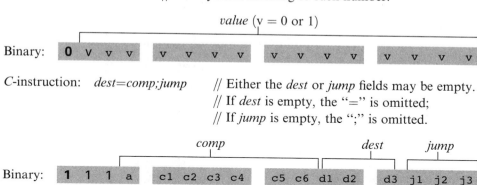

C-instruction: *dest=comp;jump*   // Either the *dest* or *jump* fields may be empty.
                                       // If *dest* is empty, the "=" is omitted;
                                       // If *jump* is empty, the ";" is omitted.

The translation of each of the three fields *comp, dest, jump* to their binary forms is specified in the following three tables.

comp (when a=0)	c1	c2	c3	c4	c5	c6	*comp* (when a=1)
0	1	0	1	0	1	0	
1	1	1	1	1	1	1	
-1	1	1	1	0	1	0	
D	0	0	1	1	0	0	
A	1	1	0	0	0	0	M
!D	0	0	1	1	0	1	
!A	1	1	0	0	0	1	!M
-D	0	0	1	1	1	1	
-A	1	1	0	0	1	1	-M
D+1	0	1	1	1	1	1	
A+1	1	1	0	1	1	1	M+1
D-1	0	0	1	1	1	0	
A-1	1	1	0	0	1	0	M-1
D+A	0	0	0	0	1	0	D+M
D-A	0	1	0	0	1	1	D-M
A-D	0	0	0	1	1	1	M-D
D&A	0	0	0	0	0	0	D&M
D|A	0	1	0	1	0	1	D|M

dest	d1	d2	d3
null	0	0	0
M	0	0	1
D	0	1	0
MD	0	1	1
A	1	0	0
AM	1	0	1
AD	1	1	0
AMD	1	1	1

jump	j1	j2	j3
null	0	0	0
JGT	0	0	1
JEQ	0	1	0
JGE	0	1	1
JLT	1	0	0
JNE	1	0	1
JLE	1	1	0
JMP	1	1	1

6.2.3 Symbols

Hack assembly commands can refer to memory locations (addresses) using either constants or symbols. Symbols in assembly programs arise from three sources.

Predefined Symbols   Any Hack assembly program is allowed to use the following predefined symbols.

Label	RAM address	(hexa)
SP	0	0x0000
LCL	1	0x0001
ARG	2	0x0002
THIS	3	0x0003
THAT	4	0x0004
R0–R15	0-15	0x0000-f
SCREEN	16384	0x4000
KBD	24576	0x6000

Note that each one of the top five RAM locations can be referred to using two predefined symbols. For example, either R2 or ARG can be used to refer to RAM[2]. These predefined symbols mean nothing now, but they will come into play when we implement the virtual machine in the next chapter.

Label Symbols   The pseudo-command (Xxx) defines the symbol Xxx to refer to the instruction memory location holding the next command in the program. A label can be defined only once and can be used anywhere in the assembly program, even before the line in which it is defined.

Variable Symbols Any symbol xxx appearing in an assembly program that is not predefined and is not defined elsewhere using the (xxx) command is treated as a variable. Variables are mapped to consecutive memory locations as they are first encountered, starting at RAM address 16 (0x0010).

6.2.4 Example

Chapter 4 presented a program that sums up the integers 1 to 100. Figure 6.2 repeats this example, showing both its assembly and binary versions.

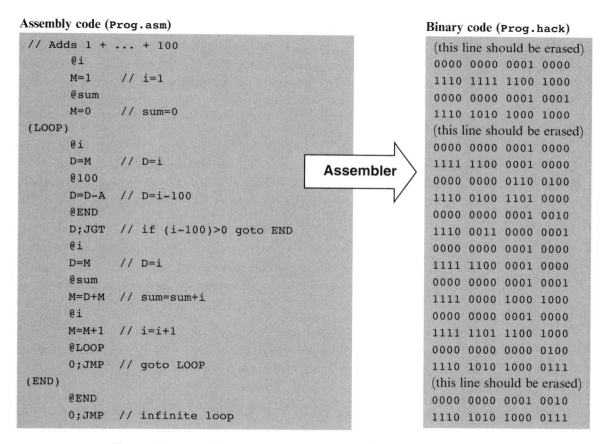

Assembly code (Prog.asm)

```
// Adds 1 + ... + 100
    @i
    M=1     // i=1
    @sum
    M=0     // sum=0
(LOOP)
    @i
    D=M     // D=i
    @100
    D=D-A   // D=i-100
    @END
    D;JGT   // if (i-100)>0 goto END
    @i
    D=M     // D=i
    @sum
    M=D+M   // sum=sum+i
    @i
    M=M+1   // i=i+1
    @LOOP
    0;JMP   // goto LOOP
(END)
    @END
    0;JMP   // infinite loop
```

Binary code (Prog.hack)

```
(this line should be erased)
0000 0000 0001 0000
1110 1111 1100 1000
0000 0000 0001 0001
1110 1010 1000 1000
(this line should be erased)
0000 0000 0001 0000
1111 1100 0001 0000
0000 0000 0110 0100
1110 0100 1101 0000
0000 0000 0001 0010
1110 0011 0000 0001
0000 0000 0001 0000
1111 1100 0001 0000
0000 0000 0001 0001
1111 0000 1000 1000
0000 0000 0001 0000
1111 1101 1100 1000
0000 0000 0000 0100
1110 1010 1000 0111
(this line should be erased)
0000 0000 0001 0010
1110 1010 1000 0111
```

Assembler

Figure 6.2 Assembly and binary representations of the same program.

6.3 Implementation

The Hack assembler reads as input a text file named `Prog.asm`, containing a Hack assembly program, and produces as output a text file named `Prog.hack`, containing the translated Hack machine code. The name of the input file is supplied to the assembler as a command line argument:

```
prompt> Assembler Prog.asm
```

The translation of each individual assembly command to its equivalent binary instruction is direct and one-to-one. Each command is translated separately. In particular, each mnemonic component (field) of assembly *C*-commands is translated into its corresponding bit code according to the tables in section 6.2.2, and each symbol in assembly *A*-commands is resolved to its numeric address as specified in section 6.2.3.

We propose an assembler implementation based on four modules: a *Parser* module that parses the input, a *Code* module that provides the binary codes of all the assembly mnemonics, a *SymbolTable* module that handles symbols, and a main program that drives the entire translation process.

A Note about API Notation   The assembler development is the first in a series of five software construction projects that build our hierarchy of translators (*assembler*, *virtual machine*, and *compiler*). Since readers can develop these projects in the programming language of their choice, we base our proposed implementation guidelines on language independent API.

A typical project API describes several *modules*, each containing one or more *routines*. In object-oriented languages like Java, C++, and C#, a module usually corresponds to a *class*, and a routine usually corresponds to a *method*. In procedural languages, routines correspond to *functions*, *subroutines*, or *procedures*, and modules correspond to collections of routines that handle related data. In some languages (e.g., Modula-2) a module may be expressed explicitly, in others implicitly (e.g., a *file* in the C language), and in others (e.g., Pascal) it will have no corresponding language construct, and will just be a conceptual grouping of routines.

6.3.1 The *Parser* Module

The main function of the parser is to break each assembly command into its underlying components (fields and symbols). The API is as follows.

Parser: Encapsulates access to the input code. Reads an assembly language command, parses it, and provides convenient access to the command's components (fields and symbols). In addition, removes all white space and comments.

Routine	Arguments	Returns	Function
Constructor/ initializer	Input file/ stream	—	Opens the input file/stream and gets ready to parse it.
hasMoreCommands	—	Boolean	Are there more commands in the input?
advance	—	—	Reads the next command from the input and makes it the current command. Should be called only if hasMoreCommands() is true. Initially there is no current command.
commandType	—	A_COMMAND, C_COMMAND, L_COMMAND	Returns the type of the current command: ■ A_COMMAND for @Xxx where Xxx is either a symbol or a decimal number ■ C_COMMAND for dest=comp;jump ■ L_COMMAND (actually, pseudo-command) for (Xxx) where Xxx is a symbol.
symbol	—	string	Returns the symbol or decimal Xxx of the current command @Xxx or (Xxx). Should be called only when commandType() is A_COMMAND or L_COMMAND.
dest	—	string	Returns the dest mnemonic in the current *C*-command (8 possibilities). Should be called only when commandType() is C_COMMAND.

Routine	Arguments	Returns	Function
comp	—	string	Returns the comp mnemonic in the current *C*-command (28 possibilities). Should be called only when commandType() is C_COMMAND.
jump	—	string	Returns the jump mnemonic in the current *C*-command (8 possibilities). Should be called only when commandType() is C_COMMAND.

6.3.2   The *Code* Module

Code: Translates Hack assembly language mnemonics into binary codes.

Routine	Arguments	Returns	Function
dest	mnemonic (string)	3 bits	Returns the binary code of the dest mnemonic.
comp	mnemonic (string)	7 bits	Returns the binary code of the comp mnemonic.
jump	mnemonic (string)	3 bits	Returns the binary code of the jump mnemonic.

6.3.3   Assembler for Programs with No Symbols

We suggest building the assembler in two stages. In the first stage, write an assembler that translates assembly programs without symbols. This can be done using the Parser and Code modules just described. In the second stage, extend the assembler with symbol handling capabilities, as we explain in the next section.

The contract for the first symbol-less stage is that the input Prog.asm program contains no symbols. This means that (a) in all address commands of type @Xxx the Xxx constants are decimal numbers and not symbols, and (b) the input file contains no label commands, namely, no commands of type (Xxx).

The overall symbol-less assembler program can now be implemented as follows. First, the program opens an output file named `Prog.hack`. Next, the program marches through the lines (assembly instructions) in the supplied `Prog.asm` file. For each *C*-instruction, the program concatenates the translated binary codes of the instruction fields into a single 16-bit word. Next, the program writes this word into the `Prog.hack` file. For each *A*-instruction of type `@Xxx`, the program translates the decimal constant returned by the parser into its binary representation and writes the resulting 16-bit word into the `Prog.hack` file.

6.3.4   The *SymbolTable* Module

Since Hack instructions can contain symbols, the symbols must be resolved into actual addresses as part of the translation process. The assembler deals with this task using a *symbol table*, designed to create and maintain the correspondence between symbols and their meaning (in Hack's case, RAM and ROM addresses). A natural data structure for representing such a relationship is the classical *hash table*. In most programming languages, such a data structure is available as part of a standard library, and thus there is no need to develop it from scratch. We propose the following API.

SymbolTable: Keeps a correspondence between symbolic labels and numeric addresses.

Routine	Arguments	Returns	Function
Constructor	—	—	Creates a new empty symbol table.
addEntry	symbol (string), address (int)	—	Adds the pair (`symbol`, `address`) to the table.
contains	symbol (string)	Boolean	Does the symbol table contain the given `symbol`?
GetAddress	symbol (string)	int	Returns the address associated with the `symbol`.

6.3.5   Assembler for Programs with Symbols

Assembly programs are allowed to use symbolic labels (destinations of *goto* commands) before the symbols are defined. This convention makes the life of assembly programmers easier and that of assembler developers harder. A common solution to this complication is to write a two-pass assembler that reads the code twice, from start to end. In the first pass, the assembler builds the symbol table and generates no code. In the second pass, all the label symbols encountered in the program have already been bound to memory locations and recorded in the symbol table. Thus, the assembler can replace each symbol with its corresponding meaning (numeric address) and generate the final binary code.

Recall that there are three types of symbols in the Hack language: *predefined symbols*, *labels*, and *variables*. The symbol table should contain and handle all these symbols, as follows.

Initialization   Initialize the symbol table with all the predefined symbols and their pre-allocated RAM addresses, according to section 6.2.3.

First Pass   Go through the entire assembly program, line by line, and build the symbol table without generating any code. As you march through the program lines, keep a running number recording the ROM address into which the current command will be eventually loaded. This number starts at 0 and is incremented by 1 whenever a C-instruction or an A-instruction is encountered, but does not change when a label pseudocommand or a comment is encountered. Each time a pseudocommand (Xxx) is encountered, add a new entry to the symbol table, associating Xxx with the ROM address that will eventually store the next command in the program. This pass results in entering all the program's *labels* along with their ROM addresses into the symbol table. The program's variables are handled in the second pass.

Second Pass   Now go again through the entire program, and parse each line. Each time a symbolic A-instruction is encountered, namely, @Xxx where Xxx is a symbol and not a number, look up Xxx in the symbol table. If the symbol is found in the table, replace it with its numeric meaning and complete the command's translation. If the symbol is not found in the table, then it must represent a new variable. To handle it, add the pair (Xxx, *n*) to the symbol table, where *n* is the next available RAM address, and complete the command's translation. The allocated RAM addresses are consecutive numbers, starting at address 16 (just after the addresses allocated to the predefined symbols).

This completes the assembler's implementation.

6.4   Perspective

Like most assemblers, the Hack assembler is a relatively simple program, dealing mainly with text processing. Naturally, assemblers for richer machine languages are more complex. Also, some assemblers feature more sophisticated symbol handling capabilities not found in Hack. For example, the assembler may allow programmers to explicitly associate symbols with particular data addresses, to perform "constant arithmetic" on symbols (e.g., to use `table+5` to refer to the fifth memory location after the address referred to by `table`), and so on. Additionally, many assemblers are capable of handling *macro commands*. A macro command is simply a sequence of machine instructions that has a name. For example, our assembler can be extended to translate an agreed-upon macro-command, say `D=M[`*xxx*`]`, into the two instructions `@`*xxx* followed immediately by `D=M` (*xxx* being an address). Clearly, such macro commands can considerably simplify the programming of commonly occurring operations, at a low translation cost.

We note in closing that stand-alone assemblers are rarely used in practice. First, assembly programs are rarely written by humans, but rather by compilers. And a compiler—being an automaton—does not have to bother to generate symbolic commands, since it may be more convenient to directly produce binary machine code. On the other hand, many high-level language compilers allow programmers to embed segments of assembly language code within high-level programs. This capability, which is rather common in C language compilers, gives the programmer direct control of the underlying hardware, for optimization.

6.5   Project

Objective   Develop an assembler that translates programs written in Hack assembly language into the binary code understood by the Hack hardware platform. The assembler must implement the translation specification described in section 6.2.

Resources   The only tool needed for completing this project is the programming language in which you will implement your assembler. You may also find the following two tools useful: the assembler and CPU emulator supplied with the book. These tools allow you to experiment with a working assembler before you set out to build one yourself. In addition, the supplied assembler provides a visual line-by-line translation GUI and allows online code comparisons with the outputs that *your* assembler will generate. For more information about these capabilities, refer to the assembler tutorial (part of the book's software suite).

Contract   When loaded into your assembler, a `Prog.asm` file containing a valid Hack assembly language program should be translated into the correct Hack binary code and stored in a `Prog.hack` file. The output produced by your assembler must be identical to the output produced by the assembler supplied with the book.

Building Plan   We suggest building the assembler in two stages. First write a symbol-less assembler, namely, an assembler that can only translate programs that contain no symbols. Then extend your assembler with symbol handling capabilities. The test programs that we supply here come in two such versions (without and with symbols), to help you test your assembler incrementally.

Test Programs   Each test program except the first one comes in two versions: `ProgL.asm` is symbol-less, and `Prog.asm` is with symbols.

Add: Adds the constants 2 and 3 and puts the result in R0.

Max: Computes $\max(R0, R1)$ and puts the result in R2.

Rect: Draws a rectangle at the top left corner of the screen. The rectangle is 16 pixels wide and R0 pixels high.

Pong: A single-player Ping-Pong game. A ball bounces constantly off the screen's "walls." The player attempts to hit the ball with a bat by pressing the left and right arrow keys. For every successful hit, the player gains one point and the bat shrinks a little to make the game harder. If the player misses the ball, the game is over. To quit the game, press ESC.

The *Pong* program was written in the *Jack* programming language (chapter 9) and translated into the supplied assembly program by the *Jack compiler* (chapters 10–11). Although the original Jack program is only about 300 lines of code, the executable Pong application is about 20,000 lines of binary code, most of which being the Jack operating system (chapter 12). Running this interactive program in the CPU emulator is a slow affair, so don't expect a high-powered Pong game. This slowness is actually a virtue, since it enables your eye to track the graphical behavior of the program. In future projects in the book, this game will run much faster.

Steps Write and test your assembler program in the two stages described previously. You may use the assembler supplied with the book to compare the output of your assembler to the correct output. This testing procedure is described next. For more information about the supplied assembler, refer to the assembler tutorial.

The Supplied Assembler The practice of using the supplied assembler (which produces correct binary code) to test another assembler (which is not necessarily correct) is illustrated in figure 6.3. Let `Prog.asm` be some program written in Hack assembly. Suppose that we translate this program using the supplied assembler, producing

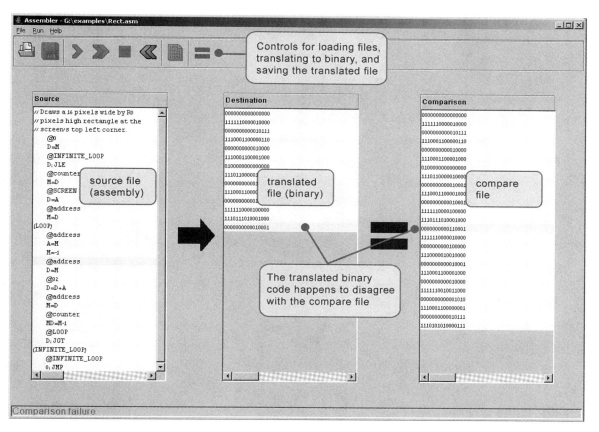

Figure 6.3 Using the supplied assembler to test the code generated by another assembler.

a binary file called `Prog.hack`. Next, we use another assembler (e.g., the one that you wrote) to translate the same program into another file, say `Prog1.hack`. Now, if the latter assembler is working correctly, it follows that `Prog.hack` = `Prog1.hack`. Thus, one way to test a newly written assembler is to load `Prog.asm` into the supplied assembler program, load `Prog1.hack` as a compare file, then translate and compare the two binary files (see figure 6.3). If the comparison fails, the assembler that produced `Prog1.hack` must be buggy; otherwise, it may be error-free.

7   Virtual Machine I: Stack Arithmetic

Programmers are creators of universes for which they alone are responsible. Universes of virtually unlimited complexity can be created in the form of computer programs.
—Joseph Weizenbaum, *Computer Power and Human Reason* (1974)

This chapter describes the first steps toward building a *compiler* for a typical object-based high-level language. We will approach this substantial task in two stages, each spanning two chapters. High-level programs will first be translated into an intermediate code (chapters 10–11), and the intermediate code will then be translated into machine language (chapters 7–8). This two-tier translation model is a rather old idea that goes back to the 1970s. In the late 1990s, it made a significant comeback following its adoption by modern languages like Java and C#.

The basic idea is as follows: Instead of running on a real platform, the intermediate code is designed to run on a *Virtual Machine*. The VM is an abstract computer that does not exist for real, but can rather be realized on other computer platforms. There are many reasons why this idea makes sense, one of which being code transportability. Since the VM may be implemented with relative ease on multiple target platforms, VM-based software can run on many processors and operating systems without having to modify the original source code. The VM implementations can be realized in several ways, by software interpreters, by special-purpose hardware, or by translating the VM programs into the machine language of the target platform.

This chapter presents a typical VM architecture, modeled after the *Java Virtual Machine* (JVM) paradigm. As usual, we focus on two perspectives. First, we motivate and specify the VM abstraction. Next, we implement it over the Hack platform. Our implementation entails writing a program called *VM translator*, designed to translate VM code into Hack assembly code. The software suite that comes with the book illustrates yet another implementation vehicle, called *VM emulator*. This program implements the VM by emulating it on a standard personal computer using Java.

A virtual machine model typically has a *language*, in which one can write *VM programs*. The VM language that we present here consists of four types of commands: arithmetic, memory access, program flow, and subroutine calling commands. We split the discussion and implementation of this language into two parts, each covered in a separate chapter and project. In this chapter we build a basic VM translator, capable of translating the VM's arithmetic and memory access commands into machine language. In the next chapter we extend the basic translator with program flow and subroutine calling functionality. The result is a full-scale virtual machine that will serve as the backend of the compiler that we will build in chapters 10–11.

The virtual machine that emerges from this effort illustrates many important ideas in computer science. First, the notion of having one computer emulating another is a fundamental idea in the field, tracing back to Alan Turing in the 1930s. Over the years it had many practical implications, for example, using an emulator of an old generation computer running on a new platform in order to achieve upward code compatibility. More recently, the virtual machine model became the centerpiece of two competing mainstreams—the Java architecture and the .NET infrastructure. These software environments are rather complex, and one way to gain an inside view of their underlying structure is to build a simple version of their VM cores, as we do here.

Another important topic embedded in this chapter is *stack processing*. The *stack* is a fundamental and elegant data structure that comes to play in many computer systems and algorithms. Since the VM presented in this chapter is stack-based, it provides a working example of this remarkably versatile data structure.

7.1   Background

7.1.1   The Virtual Machine Paradigm

Before a high-level program can run on a target computer, it must be translated into the computer's machine language. This translation—known as *compilation*—is a rather complex process. Normally, a separate compiler is written specifically for any given pair of high-level language and target machine language. This leads to a proliferation of many different compilers, each depending on every detail of both its source and destination languages. One way to decouple this dependency is to break the overall compilation process into two nearly separate stages. In the first stage, the high-level program is parsed and its commands are translated into intermediate processing steps—steps that are neither "high" nor "low." In the second stage, the intermediate steps are translated further into the machine language of the target hardware.

This decomposition is very appealing from a software engineering perspective: The first stage depends only on the specifics of the source high-level language, and the second stage only on the specifics of the target machine language. Of course, the interface between the two compilation stages—the exact definition of the intermediate processing steps—must be carefully designed. In fact, this interface is sufficiently important to merit its own definition as a stand-alone language of an abstract machine. Specifically, one can formulate a *virtual machine* whose instructions are the intermediate processing steps into which high-level commands are decomposed. The compiler that was formerly a single monolithic program is now split into two separate programs. The first program, still termed *compiler,* translates the high-level code into intermediate VM instructions, while the second program translates this VM code into the machine language of the target platform.

This two-stage compilation model has been used—one way or another—in many compiler construction projects. Some developers went as far as defining a formal and stand-alone virtual machine language, most notably the *p-code* generated by several Pascal compilers in the 1970s. Java compilers are also two-tiered, generating commands in a *bytecode* language that runs on the JVM virtual machine (also called the *Java Runtime Environment*). More recently, the approach has been adopted by the .NET infrastructure. In particular, .NET requires compilers to generate code written in an *intermediate language* (IL) that runs on a virtual machine called CLR (*Common Language Runtime*). Different alphabet soup, same ideas.

Indeed, the notion of an explicit and formal virtual machine language has several practical advantages. First, compilers for different target platforms can be obtained with relative ease by replacing only the virtual machine implementation (sometimes called the compiler's *backend*). This, in turn, allows the VM code to become transportable across different hardware platforms, permitting a range of implementation trade-offs among code efficiency, hardware cost, and programming effort. Second, compilers for many languages can share the same VM backend, allowing code sharing and language interoperability. For example, one high-level language may be good at scientific calculations, while another may excel in handling the user interface. If both languages compile into a common VM layer, it is rather natural to have routines in one language call routines in the other, using an agreed-upon invocation syntax.

Another benefit of the virtual machine approach is modularity. Every improvement in the efficiency of the VM implementation is immediately inherited by all the compilers above it. Likewise, every new digital device or appliance that is equipped with a VM implementation can immediately benefit from a huge base of available software, as seen in figure 7.1.

7.1.2   The Stack Machine Model

Like most programming languages, the VM language consists of arithmetic, memory access, program flow, and subroutine calling operations. There are several possible software paradigms on which to base such a language implementation. One of the key questions regarding this choice is *where will the operands and the results of the VM operations reside*? Perhaps the cleanest solution is to put them on a data structure called *stack*.

In a *stack machine* model, arithmetic commands pop their operands from the top of the stack and push their results back onto the top of the stack. Other commands transfer data items from the stack's top to designated memory locations, and vice versa. As it turns out, these simple stack operations can be used to implement the evaluation of any arithmetic or logical expression. Further, any program, written in any programming language, can be translated into an equivalent stack machine program. One such stack machine model is used in the *Java Virtual Machine* as well as in the VM described and built in what follows.

Elementary Stack Operations   A stack is an abstract data type that supports several operations of which the two most important ones are *push* and *pop*. The *push* operation adds an element to the top of the stack; the element that was previously on top is "pushed" below the newly added element. The *pop* operation retrieves and removes the top element from the stack; the element just below it "moves up" to the top position. Thus the stack implements a *last-in-first-out* (LIFO) storage model, illustrated in figure 7.2.

We see that stack access differs from conventional memory access in several respects. First, the stack is accessible only from the top, one item at a time. Second, reading the stack is a lossy operation: The only way to retrieve the top value is to *remove* it from the stack. In contrast, the act of reading a value from a regular memory location has no impact on the memory's state. Finally, writing an item onto the stack adds it to the stack's top, without changing the rest of the stack. In contrast, writing an item into a regular memory location is a lossy operation, since it overrides the location's previous value.

The stack data structure can be implemented in several different ways. The simplest approach is to keep an array, say *stack*, and a *stack pointer* variable, say *sp*, that points to the available location just above the topmost element. The *push x*

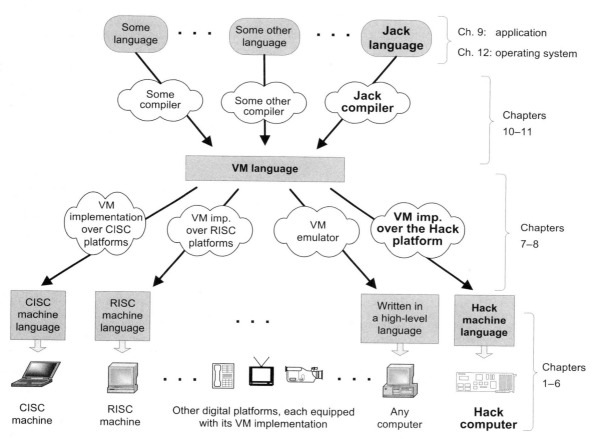

Figure 7.1 The virtual machine paradigm. Once a high-level program has been translated by a compiler into VM code, the resulting VM code can execute on any hardware platform equipped with a suitable *VM implementation*. The VM implementation either translates the VM code further into the machine language of the target hardware platform, or it runs the VM code on some emulation software (which is easier to implement, but results in slower performance). In this chapter and in the next one we build a *VM implementation on the Hack platform*, designed to translate VM code into Hack machine code. We will also make use of a Java-based *VM emulator*, supplied in the book's web site.

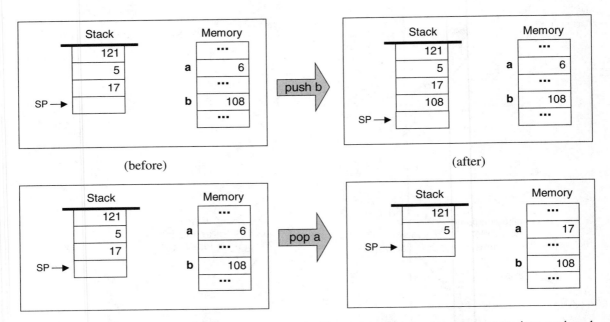

Figure 7.2 Stack processing example, illustrating the two elementary operations *push* and *pop*. Following convention, the stack is drawn upside down, as if it grows downward. The location just after the top position is always referred to by a special pointer called sp, or *stack pointer*. The labels *a* and *b* refer to two arbitrary memory addresses.

command is then implemented by storing *x* at the array entry pointed by *sp* and then incrementing *sp* (i.e., `stack[sp]=x; sp=sp+1`, or, `stack[sp++]`). The *pop* operation is implemented by first decrementing *sp* and then returning the value stored in the top position (i.e., `sp=sp-1; return stack[sp]`, or, `return stack[--sp]`).

As usual in computer science, simplicity and elegance imply power of expression. The simple stack model is a versatile data structure that comes to play in many computer systems and algorithms. In the virtual machine architecture that we build here, it serves two key purposes. First, it is used for handling all the arithmetic and logical operations of the VM. Second, it facilitates subroutine calls and the associated memory allocation—the subjects of the next chapter.

Stack Arithmetic   Stack-based arithmetic is a simple matter: the operands are popped from the stack, the required operation is performed on them, and the result is pushed back onto the stack. For example, here is how addition is handled:

The stack version of other operations (subtract, multiply, etc.) are precisely the same. For example, consider the expression d=(2−x)*(y+5), taken from some high-level program. The stack-based evaluation of this expression is shown in figure 7.3.

Stack-based evaluation of Boolean expressions has precisely the same flavor. For example, consider the high-level command if (x<7) or (y=8) then.... The stack-based evaluation of this expression is shown in figure 7.4.

The previous examples illustrate a general observation: any arithmetic and Boolean expression—no matter how complex—can be systematically converted into, and evaluated by, a sequence of simple operations on a stack. Thus, one can write a *compiler* that translates high-level arithmetic and Boolean expressions into sequences of stack commands, as we will do in chapters 10–11. We now turn to specify these commands (section 7.2), and describe their implementation on the Hack platform (section 7.3).

7.2   VM Specification, Part I

7.2.1   General

The virtual machine is *stack-based*: all operations are done on a stack. It is also *function-based*: a complete VM program is organized in program units called *functions*, written in the VM language. Each function has its own stand-alone code and is separately handled. The VM language has a single 16-bit data type that can be used as an integer, a Boolean, or a pointer. The language consists of four types of commands:

- *Arithmetic commands* perform arithmetic and logical operations on the stack.

- *Memory access commands* transfer data between the stack and virtual memory segments.

- *Program flow commands* facilitate conditional and unconditional branching operations.

- *Function calling commands* call functions and return from them.

```
// d=(2-x)*(y+5)
push 2
push x
sub
push y
push 5
add
mult
pop d
```

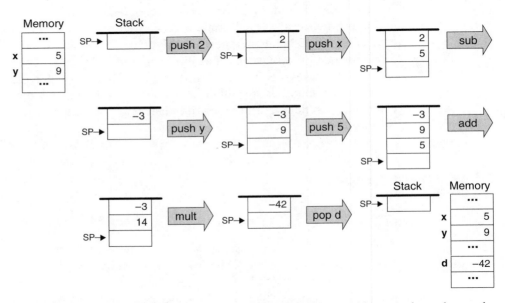

Figure 7.3 Stack-based evaluation of arithmetic expressions. This example evaluates the expression $d = (2 - x) * (y + 5)$, assuming the initial memory state $x = 5$, $y = 9$.

```
// if (x<7) or (y=8)
push x
push 7
lt
push y
push 8
eq
or
```

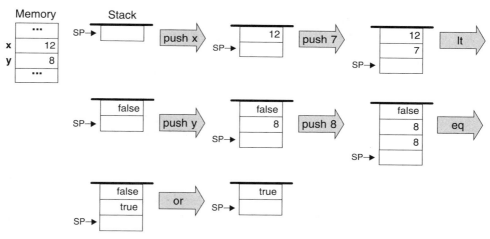

Figure 7.4 Stack-based evaluation of logical expressions. This example evaluates the Boolean expression $(x < 7)$ or $(y = 8)$, assuming the initial memory state $x = 12$, $y = 8$.

Building a virtual machine is a complex undertaking, and so we divide it into two stages. In this chapter we specify the *arithmetic* and *memory access* commands and build a basic VM translator that implements them only. The next chapter specifies the *program flow* and *function calling* commands commands and extends the basic translator into a full-scale virtual machine implementation.

Program and Command Structure   A VM *program* is a collection of one or more *files* with a .vm extension, each consisting of one or more *functions*. From a compilation standpoint, these constructs correspond, respectively, to the notions of *program*, *class*, and *method* in an object-oriented language.

Within a .vm file, each VM command appears in a separate line, and in one of the following formats: *command* (e.g., add), *command arg* (e.g., goto loop), or *command arg1 arg2* (e.g., push local 3). The arguments are separated from each other and from the *command* part by one or more spaces. "//" comments can appear at the end of any line and are ignored. Blank lines are permitted and ignored.

7.2.2 Arithmetic and Logical Commands

The VM language features nine stack-oriented arithmetic and logical commands. Seven of these commands are binary: They pop two items off the stack, compute a binary function on them, and push the result back onto the stack. The remaining two commands are unary: they pop a single item off the stack, compute a unary function on it, and push the result back onto the stack. We see that each command has the net impact of replacing its operand(s) with the command's result, without affecting the rest of the stack. Figure 7.5 gives the details.

Three of the commands listed in figure 7.5 (eq, gt, lt) return Boolean values. The VM represents *true* and *false* as −1 (0xFFFF, or 1111111111111111 in binary) and 0 (0x0000, or 0000000000000000 in binary), respectively.

7.2.3 Memory Access Commands

So far in the chapter, memory access commands were illustrated using the pseudo-commands *pop* and *push x*, where the symbol *x* referred to an individual location

Command	Return value (after popping the operand/s)	Comment	
add	$x + y$	Integer addition	(2's complement)
sub	$x - y$	Integer subtraction	(2's complement)
neg	$-y$	Arithmetic negation	(2's complement)
eq	true if $x = y$, else false	Equality	
gt	true if $x > y$, else false	Greater than	
lt	true if $x < y$, else false	Less than	
and	x And y	Bit-wise	
or	x Or y	Bit-wise	
not	Not y	Bit-wise	

Figure 7.5 Arithmetic and logical stack commands.

in some global memory. Yet formally, our VM manipulates eight separate *virtual memory segments*, listed in figure 7.6.

Memory Access Commands   All the memory segments are accessed by the same two commands:

- `push` *segment index*   Push the value of *segment*[*index*] onto the stack.

- `pop` *segment index*   Pop the top stack value and store it in *segment*[*index*].

Segment	Purpose	Comments
`argument`	Stores the function's arguments.	Allocated dynamically by the VM implementation when the function is entered.
`local`	Stores the function's local variables.	Allocated dynamically by the VM implementation and initialized to 0's when the function is entered.
`static`	Stores static variables shared by all functions in the same `.vm` file.	Allocated by the VM imp. for each `.vm` file; shared by all functions in the `.vm` file.
`constant`	Pseudo-segment that holds all the constants in the range $0 \ldots 32767$.	Emulated by the VM implementation; Seen by all the functions in the program.
`this` `that`	General-purpose segments. Can be made to correspond to different areas in the heap. Serve various programming needs.	Any VM function can use these segments to manipulate selected areas on the heap.
`pointer`	A two-entry segment that holds the base addresses of the `this` and `that` segments.	Any VM function can set `pointer` 0 (or 1) to some address; this has the effect of aligning the `this` (or `that`) segment to the heap area beginning in that address.
`temp`	Fixed eight-entry segment that holds temporary variables for general use.	May be used by any VM function for any purpose. Shared by all functions in the program.

Figure 7.6   The memory segments seen by every VM function. For now, there is no need to understand the intended use, purpose, or allocation of these segments—all these details will become clear in later chapters.

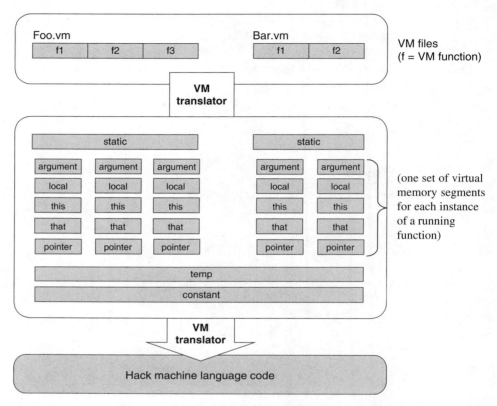

Figure 7.7 The virtual memory segments are maintained by the VM implementation. We reiterate that the intended use, purpose, and allocation of these segments will become clear in later chapters.

Where *segment* is one of the eight segment names and *index* is a non-negative integer. For example, push `argument 2` followed by pop `local 1` will store the value of the function's third argument in the function's second local variable (each segment's index starts at 0).

The relationship among VM files, VM functions, and their respective virtual memory segments is depicted in figure 7.7.

In addition to the eight memory segments, which are managed explicitly by VM push and pop commands, the VM implementation manages two implicit data structures called *stack* and *heap*. These data structures are never mentioned directly, but their states change in the background, as a side effect of VM commands.

The Stack   Consider the commands sequence `push argument 2` and `pop local 1`, mentioned before. The working memory of such VM operations is the *stack*. The data value did not simply jump from one segment to another—it went through the stack. Note however that in spite of its central role in the VM architecture, the stack proper is never mentioned explicitly in the VM language.

The Heap   Another memory element that exists in the VM's background is the *heap*. The heap is the name of the RAM area dedicated for storing objects and arrays data. These objects and arrays can be manipulated by VM commands, as we will see shortly.

7.2.4   Program Flow and Function Calling Commands

The VM features six additional commands that are discussed at length in the next chapter. For completeness, these commands are listed here.

Program Flow Commands

`label` *symbol*	// Label declaration
`goto` *symbol*	// Unconditional branching
`if-goto` *symbol*	// Conditional branching

Function Calling Commands

`function` *functionName nLocals*	// Function declaration, specifying the // number of the function's local variables
`call` *functionName nArgs*	// Function invocation, specifying the // number of the function's arguments
`return`	// Transfer control back to the calling function

(In this list of commands, *functionName* is a symbol and *nLocals* and *nArgs* are non-negative integers.)

7.2.5   Program Elements in the Jack-VM-Hack Platform

We end the first part of the VM specification with a top-down view of all the program elements that emerge from the full compilation of a typical high-level program. At the top of figure 7.8 we see a Jack program, consisting of two classes (Jack, a

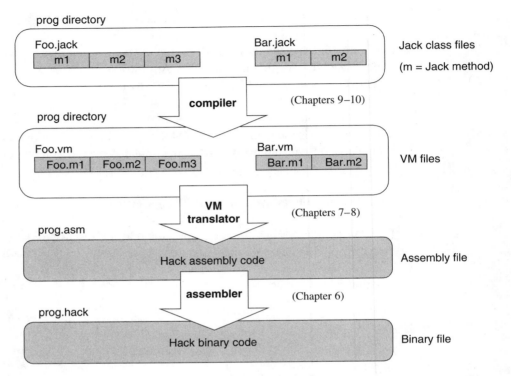

Figure 7.8   Program elements in the Jack-VM-Hack platform.

simple Java-like language, is described in chapter 9). Each Jack class consists of one or more methods. When the Jack compiler is applied to a directory that includes *n* class files, it produces *n* VM files (in the same directory). Each Jack *method* xxx within a class yyy is translated into one *VM function* called yyy.xxx within the corresponding VM file.

Next, the figure shows how the *VM translator* can be applied to the directory in which the VM files reside, generating a single assembly program. This assembly program does two main things. First, it emulates the virtual memory segments of each VM function and file, as well as the implicit stack. Second, it effects the VM commands on the target platform. This is done by manipulating the emulated VM data structures using machine language instructions—those translated from the VM commands. If all works well, that is, if the compiler and the VM translator and the assembler are implemented correctly, the target platform will end up effecting the behavior mandated by the original Jack program.

7.2.6   VM Programming Examples

Before You Read This Section   This section illustrates how the VM abstraction can be used to realize three typical programming tasks that occur frequently in high-level programs: arithmetic expression handling, array handling, and object handling. These tasks are normally expressed in some high-level language, and then translated by a compiler into equivalent VM code segments. We show three such code segments, as a sneak preview of the compilation process that will be discussed later in the book. The reader is advised that none of these examples are relevant to the VM implementation. Therefore, section 7.2.6 can be skipped in its entirety without losing the thread of neither this chapter nor its accompanying project.

In case you decide to hang on, here goes. VM programs are rarely written by human programmers, but rather by compilers. Therefore, we begin each one of the three examples with a high-level code fragment, and then show its equivalent representation in VM code. We use a C-style syntax for all the high-level examples.

A Typical Arithmetic Task   Consider the multiplication algorithm shown at the top of figure 7.9. How should we (or more likely, the compiler) express this algorithm in the VM language? First, high-level structures like `for` and `while` must be rewritten using the VM's simple "goto logic." In a similar fashion, high-level arithmetic and Boolean operations must be expressed using stack-oriented commands. The resulting code is shown in figure 7.9. (The exact semantics of the VM commands `function`, `label`, `goto`, `if-goto`, and `return` are described in chapter 8, but their intuitive meaning is self-explanatory.)

Let us focus on the virtual segments depicted at the bottom of figure 7.9. We see that when a VM function starts running, it assumes that (i) the stack is empty, (ii) the argument values on which it is supposed to operate are located in the `argument` segment, and (iii) the local variables that it is supposed to use are initialized to 0 and located in the `local` segment.

Let us now focus on the VM representation of the algorithm. Recall that VM commands cannot use symbolic argument and variable names—they are limited to making ⟨*segment index*⟩ references only. However, the translation from the former to the latter is straightforward. All we have to do is map x, y, sum and j on `argument 0`, `argument 1`, `local 0` and `local 1`, respectively, and replace all their symbolic occurrences in the pseudo code with corresponding ⟨*segment index*⟩ references.

To sum up, when a VM function starts running, it assumes that it is surrounded by a private world, all of its own, consisting of initialized `argument` and `local` segments and an empty stack, waiting to be manipulated by its commands. The agent responsible for staging this virtual worldview for every VM function just before it starts running is the VM implementation, as we will see in the next chapter.

High-level code (C style)

```
int mult(int x, int y) {
  int sum;
  sum = 0;
  for(int j = y; j != 0; j--)
      sum += x;  // Repetitive addition
  return sum;
}
```

First approximation

```
function mult
  args x, y
  vars sum, j
  sum = 0
  j = y
loop:
  if j = 0 goto end
  sum = sum + x
  j = j - 1
  goto loop
end:
  return sum
```

Pseudo VM code

```
function mult(x,y)
  push 0
  pop sum
  push y
  pop j
label loop
  push 0
  push j
  eq
  if-goto end
  push sum
  push x
  add
  pop sum
  push j
  push 1
  sub
  pop j
  goto loop
label end
  push sum
  return
```

Final VM code

```
function mult 2       // 2 local variables
  push constant 0
  pop local 0         // sum=0
  push argument 1
  pop local 1         // j=y
label loop
  push constant 0
  push local 1
  Eq
  if-goto end         // if j=0 goto end
  push local 0
  push argument 0
  Add
  pop local 0         // sum=sum+x
  push local 1
  push constant 1
  Sub
  pop local 1         // j=j-1
  goto loop
label end
  push local 0
  return              // return sum
```

Figure 7.9   VM programming example.

Just after mult(7,3) is entered: Just after mult(7,3) returns:

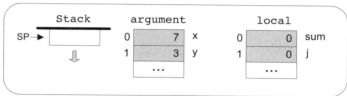
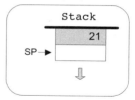

(The symbols x, y, sum, and j are not part of the VM program and are shown here only for ease of reference.)

Figure 7.9 (continued)

Array Handling   An array is an indexed collection of objects. Suppose that a high-level program has created an array of ten integers called bar and filled it with some ten numbers. Let us assume that the array's base has been mapped (behind the scene) on RAM address 4315. Suppose now that the high-level program wants to execute the command bar[2]=19. How can we implement this operation at the VM level?

In the C language, such an operation can be also specified as *(bar+2)=19, meaning "*set the RAM location whose address is* (bar+2) *to* 19." As shown in figure 7.10, this operation lends itself perfectly well to the VM language.

It remains to be seen, of course, how a high-level command like bar[2]=19 is translated in the first place into the VM code shown in figure 7.10. This transformation is described in section 11.1.1, when we discuss the code generation features of the compiler.

Object Handling   High-level programmers view objects as entities that encapsulate data (organized as *fields*, or *properties*) and relevant code (organized as *methods*). Yet physically speaking, the data of each object instance is serialized on the RAM as a list of numbers representing the object's field values. Thus the low-level handling of objects is quite similar to that of arrays.

For example, consider an animation program designed to juggle some balls on the screen. Suppose that each Ball object is characterized by the integer fields x, y, radius, and color. Let us assume that the program has created one such Ball object and called it b. What will be the internal representation of this object in the computer?

Like all other object instances, it will be stored in the RAM. In particular, whenever a program creates a new object, the compiler computes the object's size in terms of words and the operating system finds and allocates enough RAM space to store

High-level program view

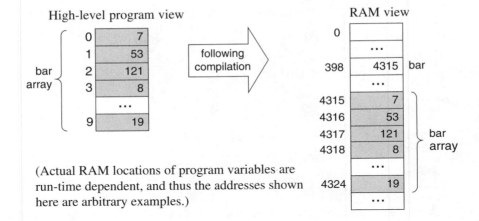

(Actual RAM locations of program variables are
run-time dependent, and thus the addresses shown
here are arbitrary examples.)

VM code

```
// Assume that the bar array is the first local variable declared in the
// high-level program. The following VM code implements the operation
// bar[2]=19,  i.e., *(bar+2)=19.
push local 0        // Get bar's base address
push constant 2
add
pop  pointer 1      // Set that's base to (bar+2)
push constant 19
pop  that 0         // *(bar+2)=19
...
```

Figure 7.10   VM-based array manipulation using the pointer and that segments.

it (the exact details of this operation are discussed in chapter 11). For now, let us assume that our b object has been allocated RAM addresses 3012 to 3015, as shown in figure 7.11.

Suppose now that a certain method in the high-level program, say `resize`, takes a `Ball` object and an integer r as arguments, and, among other things, sets the ball's `radius` to r. The VM representation of this logic is shown in figure 7.11.

When we set `pointer 0` to the value of `argument 0`, we are effectively setting the base of the virtual `this` segment to the object's base address. From this point on, VM commands can access any field in the object using the virtual memory segment `this` and an index relative to the object's base-address in memory.

But how did the compiler translate `b.radius=17` into the VM code shown in figure 7.11? And how did the compiler know that the *radius* field of the object corresponds to the *third* field in its actual representation? We return to these questions in section 11.1.1, when we discuss the code generation features of the compiler.

7.3   Implementation

The virtual machine that was described up to this point is an abstract artifact. If we want to use it for real, we must implement it on a real platform. Building such a VM implementation consists of two conceptual tasks. First, we have to emulate the VM world on the target platform. In particular, each data structure mentioned in the VM specification, namely, the stack and the virtual memory segments, must be represented in some way by the target platform. Second, each VM command must be translated into a series of instructions that effect the command's semantics on the target platform.

This section describes how to implement the VM specification (section 7.2) on the Hack platform. We start by defining a "standard mapping" from VM elements and operations to the Hack hardware and machine language. Next, we suggest guidelines for designing the software that achieves this mapping. In what follows, we will refer to this software using the terms *VM implementation* or *VM translator* interchangeably.

7.3.1   Standard VM Mapping on the Hack Platform, Part I

If you reread the virtual machine specification given so far, you will realize that it contains no assumption whatsoever about the architecture on which the VM can

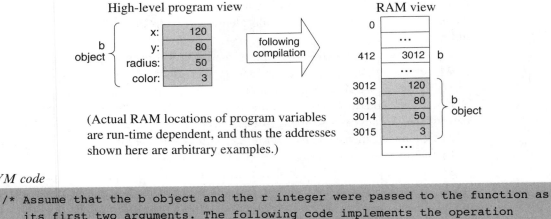

High-level program view

RAM view

(Actual RAM locations of program variables
are run-time dependent, and thus the addresses
shown here are arbitrary examples.)

VM code

```
/* Assume that the b object and the r integer were passed to the function as
   its first two arguments. The following code implements the operation
   b.radius=r. */
push argument 0  // Get b's base address
pop pointer 0    // Point the this segment to b
push argument 1  // Get r's value
pop this 2       // Set b's third field to r
...
```

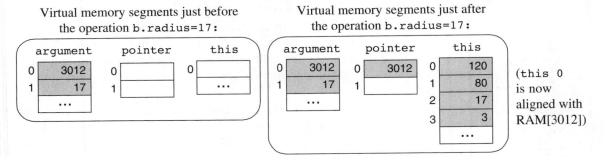

Virtual memory segments just before
the operation b.radius=17:

Virtual memory segments just after
the operation b.radius=17:

Figure 7.11   VM-based object manipulation using the pointer and this segments.

be implemented. When it comes to virtual machines, this platform independence is the whole point: You don't want to commit to any particular hardware platform, since you want your machine to potentially run on *all* of them, including those that were not built yet.

It follows that the VM designer can principally let programmers implement the VM on target platforms in any way they see fit. However, it is usually recommended that some guidelines be provided as to how the VM should map on the target platform, rather than leaving these decisions completely to the implementer's discretion. These guidelines, called *standard mapping*, are provided for two reasons. First, they entail a public contract that regulates how VM-based programs can interact with programs produced by compilers that don't use this VM (e.g., compilers that produce binary code directly). Second, we wish to allow the developers of the VM implementation to run standardized tests, namely, tests that conform to the standard mapping. This way, the tests and the software can be written by different people, which is always recommended. With that in mind, the remainder of this section specifies the standard mapping of the VM on a familiar hardware platform: the Hack computer.

VM to Hack Translation   Recall that a VM program is a collection of one or more .vm files, each containing one or more VM functions, each being a sequence of VM commands. The VM translator takes a collection of .vm files as input and produces a single Hack assembly language .asm file as output (see figure 7.7). Each VM command is translated by the VM translator into Hack assembly code. The order of the functions within the .vm files does not matter.

RAM Usage   The data memory of the Hack computer consists of 32K 16-bit words. The first 16K serve as general-purpose RAM. The next 16K contain memory maps of I/O devices. The VM implementation should use this space as follows:

RAM addresses	*Usage*
0–15	Sixteen virtual registers, usage described below
16–255	Static variables (of all the VM functions in the VM program)
256–2047	Stack
2048–16383	Heap (used to store objects and arrays)
16384–24575	Memory mapped I/O
24575–32767	Unused memory space

Recall that according to the *Hack Machine Language Specification*, RAM addresses 0 to 15 can be referred to by any assembly program using the symbols R0 to R15, respectively. In addition, the specification states that assembly programs can refer to RAM addresses 0 to 4 (i.e., R0 to R4) using the symbols SP, LCL, ARG, THIS, and THAT. This convention was introduced into the assembly language with foresight, in order to promote readable VM implementations. The expected use of these registers in the VM context is described as follows:

Register	Name	Usage
RAM[0]	SP	Stack pointer: points to the next topmost location in the stack;
RAM[1]	LCL	Points to the base of the current VM function's local segment;
RAM[2]	ARG	Points to the base of the current VM function's argument segment;
RAM[3]	THIS	Points to the base of the current this segment (within the heap);
RAM[4]	THAT	Points to the base of the current that segment (within the heap);
RAM[5–12]		Hold the contents of the temp segment;
RAM[13–15]		Can be used by the VM implementation as general-purpose registers.

Memory Segments Mapping

local, argument, this, that: Each one of these segments is mapped directly on the RAM, and its location is maintained by keeping its physical base address in a dedicated register (LCL, ARG, THIS, and THAT, respectively). Thus any access to the ith entry of any one of these segments should be translated to assembly code that accesses address $(base + i)$ in the RAM, where $base$ is the current value stored in the register dedicated to the respective segment.

pointer, temp: These segments are each mapped directly onto a fixed area in the RAM. The pointer segment is mapped on RAM locations 3–4 (also called THIS and THAT) and the temp segment on locations 5–12 (also called R5, R6, ..., R12). Thus access to pointer i should be translated to assembly code that accesses RAM location $3 + i$, and access to temp i should be translated to assembly code that accesses RAM location $5 + i$.

constant: This segment is truly virtual, as it does not occupy any physical space on the target architecture. Instead, the VM implementation handles any VM access to ⟨constant i⟩ by simply supplying the constant i.

`static`:   According to the Hack machine language specification, when a new symbol is encountered for the first time in an assembly program, the assembler allocates a new RAM address to it, starting at address 16. This convention can be exploited to represent each static variable number `j` in a VM file `f` as the assembly language symbol `f.j`. For example, suppose that the file `Xxx.vm` contains the command `push static 3`. This command can be translated to the Hack assembly commands `@Xxx.3` and `D=M`, followed by additional assembly code that pushes `D`'s value to the stack. This implementation of the `static` segment is somewhat tricky, but it works.

Assembly Language Symbols   We recap all the assembly language symbols used by VM implementations that conform to the standard mapping.

Symbol	*Usage*
`SP`, `LCL`, `ARG`, `THIS`, `THAT`	These predefined symbols point, respectively, to the stack top and to the base addresses of the virtual segments `local`, `argument`, `this`, and `that`.
`R13-R15`	These predefined symbols can be used for any purpose.
`Xxx.j` symbols	Each static variable `j` in file `Xxx.vm` is translated into the assembly symbol `Xxx.j`. In the subsequent assembly process, these symbolic variables will be allocated RAM space by the Hack assembler.
Flow of control symbols	The implementation of the VM commands `function`, `call`, and `label` involves generating special label symbols, to be discussed in chapter 8.

7.3.2   Design Suggestion for the VM Implementation

The VM translator should accept a single command line parameter, as follows:

```
prompt> VMtranslator source
```

Where *source* is either a file name of the form `Xxx.vm` (the extension is mandatory) or a directory name containing one or more `.vm` files (in which case there is no extension). The result of the translation is always a single assembly language file named `Xxx.asm`, created in the same directory as the input `Xxx`. The translated code must conform to the standard VM mapping on the Hack platform.

7.3.3   Program Structure

We propose implementing the VM translator using a main program and two modules: *parser* and *code writer*.

The *Parser* Module

Parser: Handles the parsing of a single .vm file, and encapsulates access to the input code. It reads VM commands, parses them, and provides convenient access to their components. In addition, it removes all white space and comments.

Routine	Arguments	Returns	Function
Constructor	Input file/ stream	—	Opens the input file/stream and gets ready to parse it.
hasMoreCommands	—	Boolean	Are there more commands in the input?
advance	—	—	Reads the next command from the input and makes it the current command. Should be called only if hasMoreCommands() is true. Initially there is no current command.
commandType	—	C_ARITHMETIC, C_PUSH, C_POP, C_LABEL, C_GOTO, C_IF, C_FUNCTION, C_RETURN, C_CALL	Returns the type of the current VM command. C_ARITHMETIC is returned for all the arithmetic commands.
arg1	—	string	Returns the first argument of the current command. In the case of C_ARITHMETIC, the command itself (add, sub, etc.) is returned. Should not be called if the current command is C_RETURN.

Routine	Arguments	Returns	Function
arg2	—	int	Returns the second argument of the current command. Should be called only if the current command is C_PUSH, C_POP, C_FUNCTION, or C_CALL.

The *CodeWriter* Module

CodeWriter: Translates VM commands into Hack assembly code.

Routine	Arguments	Returns	Function
Constructor	Output file/stream	—	Opens the output file/ stream and gets ready to write into it.
setFileName	fileName (string)	—	Informs the code writer that the translation of a new VM file is started.
writeArithmetic	command (string)	—	Writes the assembly code that is the translation of the given arithmetic command.
WritePushPop	command (C_PUSH or C_POP), segment (string), index (int)	—	Writes the assembly code that is the translation of the given command, where command is either C_PUSH or C_POP.
Close	—	—	Closes the output file.

Comment: More routines will be added to this module in chapter 8.

Main Program   The main program should construct a `Parser` to parse the VM input file and a `CodeWriter` to generate code into the corresponding output file. It should then march through the VM commands in the input file and generate assembly code for each one of them.

If the program's argument is a directory name rather than a file name, the main program should process all the `.vm` files in this directory. In doing so, it should use a separate `Parser` for handling each input file and a single `CodeWriter` for handling the output.

7.4   Perspective

In this chapter we began the process of developing a compiler for a high-level language. Following modern software engineering practices, we have chosen to base the compiler on a two-tier compilation model. In the *frontend* tier, covered in chapters 10 and 11, the high-level code is translated into an intermediate code, running on a virtual machine. In the *backend* tier, covered in this and in the next chapter, the intermediate code is translated into the machine language of a target hardware platform (see figures 7.1 and 7.9).

The idea of formulating the intermediate code as the explicit language of a virtual machine goes back to the late 1970s, when it was used by several popular Pascal compilers. These compilers generated an intermediate "p-code" that could execute on any computer that implemented it. Following the wide spread use of the World Wide Web in the mid-1990s, cross-platform compatibility became a universally vexing issue. In order to address the problem, the Sun Microsystems company (later acquired by Oracle) sought to develop a new programming language that could potentially run on any computer and digital device connected to the Internet. The language that emerged from this initiative—*Java*—is also founded on an intermediate code execution model called the *Java Virtual Machine*, on JVM.

The JVM is a specification that describes an intermediate language called *bytecode*—the target language of Java compilers. Files written in bytecode are then used for dynamic code distribution of Java programs over the Internet, most notably as applets embedded in web pages. Of course in order to execute these programs, the client computers must be equipped with suitable JVM implementations. These programs, also called *Java Run-time Environments* (JREs), are widely available for numerous processor/OS combinations, including game consoles and cell phones.

In the early 2000s, Microsoft entered the fray with its .NET infrastructure. The centerpiece of .NET is a virtual machine model called *Common Language Runtime* (CLR). According to the Microsoft vision, many programming languages (including

C++, C#, Visual Basic, and J#—a Java variant) could be compiled into intermediate code running on the CLR. This enables code written in different languages to interoperate and share the software libraries of a common run-time environment.

We note in closing that a crucial ingredient that must be added to the virtual machine model before its full potential of interoperability is unleashed is a common software library. Indeed the Java virtual machine comes with the *standard Java libraries*, and the Microsoft virtual machine comes with the *Common Language Runtime*. These software libraries can be viewed as small operating systems, providing the languages that run on top of the VM with unified services like memory management, GUI utilities, string functions, math functions, and so on. One such library will be described and built in chapter 12.

7.5   Project

This section describes how to build the VM translator presented in the chapter. In the next chapter we will extend this basic translator with additional functionality, leading to a full-scale VM implementation. Before you get started, two comments are in order. First, section 7.2.6 is irrelevant to this project. Second, since the VM translator is designed to generate Hack assembly code, it is recommended to refresh your memory about the Hack assembly programming (section 4.2). This can be done by reviewing Figure 4.2 and the programs you wrote in Project 4.

Objective   Build the first part of the VM translator (the second part is implemented in Project 8), focusing on the implementation of the *stack arithmetic* and *memory access* commands of the VM language.

Resources   You will need two tools: the programming language in which you will implement your VM translator, and the CPU emulator supplied with the book. This emulator will allow you to execute the machine code generated by your VM translator—an indirect way to test the correctness of the latter. Another tool that may come in handy in this project is the visual VM emulator supplied with the book. This program allows experimenting with a working VM implementation before you set out to build one yourself. For more information about this tool, refer to the VM emulator tutorial.

Contract   Write a VM-to-Hack translator, conforming to the VM Specification, Part I (section 7.2) and to the Standard VM Mapping on the Hack Platform, Part I (section 7.3.1). Use it to translate the test VM programs supplied here, yielding corresponding programs written in the Hack assembly language. When executed on the supplied CPU emulator, the assembly programs generated by your translator should deliver the results mandated by the supplied test scripts and compare files.

Proposed Implementation Stages

We recommend building the translator in two stages. This will allow you to unit-test your implementation incrementally, using the test programs supplied here.

Stage I: Stack Arithmetic Commands   The first version of your VM translator should implement the nine stack arithmetic and logical commands of the VM language as well as the push constant *x* command (which, among other things, will help in testing the nine former commands). Note that the latter is the generic push command for the special case where the first argument is constant and the second argument is some decimal constant.

Stage II: Memory Access Commands   The next version of your translator should include a full implementation of the VM language's push and pop commands, handling all eight memory segments. We suggest breaking this stage into the following substages:

0.   You have already handled the constant segment.

1.   Next, handle the segments local, argument, this, and that.

2.   Next, handle the pointer and temp segments, in particular allowing modification of the bases of the this and that segments.

3.   Finally, handle the static segment.

Test Programs

The five VM programs listed here are designed to unit-test the proposed implementation stages just described.

Stage I: Stack Arithmetic

- SimpleAdd: Pushes and adds two constants.

- StackTest: Executes a sequence of arithmetic and logical operations on the stack.

Stage II: Memory Access

- `BasicTest`: Executes `pop` and `push` operations using the virtual memory segments.

- `PointerTest`: Executes `pop` and `push` operations using the `pointer`, `this`, and `that` segments.

- `StaticTest`: Executes `pop` and `push` operations using the `static` segment.

For each program `Xxx` we supply four files, beginning with the program's code in `Xxx.vm`. The `XxxVME.tst` script allows running the program on the supplied VM emulator, so that you can gain familiarity with the program's intended operation. After translating the program using your VM translator, the supplied `Xxx.tst` and `Xxx.cmp` scripts allow testing the translated assembly code on the CPU emulator.

Tips

Initialization   In order for any translated VM program to start running, it must include a preamble startup code that forces the VM implementation to start executing it on the host platform. In addition, in order for any VM code to operate properly, the VM implementation must anchor the base addresses of the virtual segments in selected RAM locations. Both issues—startup code and segments initializations—are implemented in the next project. The difficulty of course is that we need these initializations in place in order to execute the test programs given in this project. The good news is that you should not worry about these issues at all, since the supplied test scripts carry out all the necessary initializations in a manual fashion (for the purpose of this project only).

Testing/Debugging   For each one of the five test programs, follow these steps:

1. Run the `Xxx.vm` program on the supplied VM emulator, using the `XxxVME.tst` test script, to get acquainted with the intended program's behavior.

2. Use your partial translator to translate the `.vm` file. The result should be a text file containing a translated `.asm` program, written in the Hack assembly language.

3. Inspect the translated `.asm` program. If there are visible syntax (or any other) errors, debug and fix your translator.

4.   Use the supplied `.tst` and `.cmp` files to run your translated `.asm` program on the CPU emulator. If there are run-time errors, debug and fix your translator.

The supplied test programs were carefully planned to test the specific features of each stage in your VM implementation. Therefore, it's important to implement your translator in the proposed order and to test it using the appropriate test programs at each stage. Implementing a later stage before an early one may cause the test programs to fail.

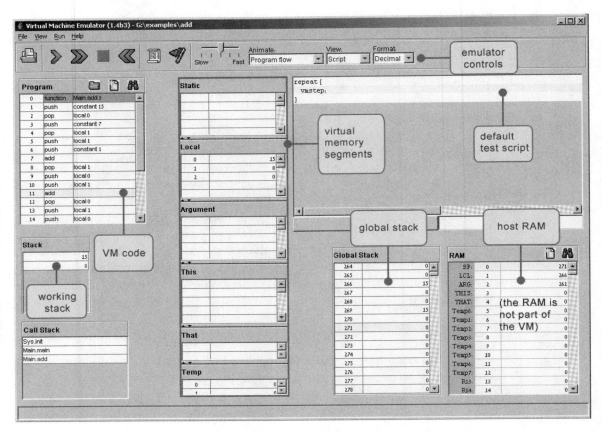

Figure 7.12   The VM emulator supplied with the book.

Tools

The VM Emulator   The book's software suite includes a Java-based VM implementation. This VM emulator allows executing VM programs directly, without having to translate them first into machine language. This practice enables experimentation with the VM environment before you set out to implement one yourself. Figure 7.12 is a typical screen shot of the VM emulator in action.

8 Virtual Machine II: Program Control

If everything seems under control, you're just not going fast enough.
—Mario Andretti (b. 1940), race car champion

Chapter 7 introduced the notion of a virtual machine (VM) and ended with the construction of a basic VM implementation over the Hack platform. In this chapter we continue to develop the VM abstraction, language, and implementation. In particular, we design stack-based mechanisms for handling nested subroutine calls (procedures, functions, methods) of procedural or object-oriented languages. As the chapter progresses, we extend the previously built basic VM implementation, ending with a full-scale VM translator. This translator will serve as the backend of the compiler that we will build in chapters 10 and 11, following the introduction of a high-level object-based language in chapter 9.

In any Great Gems in Computer Science contest, *stack processing* will be a strong finalist. The previous chapter showed how arithmetic and Boolean expressions can be calculated by elementary stack operations. This chapter goes on to show how this remarkably simple data structure can also support remarkably complex tasks like nested subroutine calling, parameter passing, recursion, and the associated memory allocation techniques. Most programmers tend to take these capabilities for granted, expecting the compiler to deliver them, one way or another. We are now in a position to open this black box and see how these fundamental programming mechanisms are actually implemented by a stack-based virtual machine.

8.1 Background

High-level languages allow writing programs in high-level terms. For example, $x = -b + \sqrt{b^2 - 4 \cdot a \cdot c}$ can be expressed as `x=-b+sqrt(power(b,2)-4*a*c)`, which is almost as descriptive as the real thing. High-level languages support this power of expression through three conventions. First, one is allowed to freely define high-level operations like `sqrt` and `power`, as needed. Second, one is allowed to freely use (call) these subroutines as if they were elementary operations like + and *. Third, one is allowed to assume that each called subroutine will get executed—somehow—and that following its termination control will return—somehow—to the next command in one's code. Flow of control commands take this freedom one step further, allowing writing, say, `if ~(a=0) {x=(-b+sqrt(power(b,2)-4*a*c))/(2*a)} else {x=-c/b}`.

The ability to compose such expressions freely permits us to write abstract code, closer to the world of algorithmic thought than to that of machine execution. Of course the more abstract the high level, the more work someone has to do at the low level. In particular, the low level must manage the delicate interplay between the calling subroutine (the *caller*) and the *called* subroutines—the program units that implement system- and user-defined operations like `sqrt` and `power`. For each subroutine call during runtime, the low level must handle the following details behind the scene:

- Passing parameters from the caller to the called subroutine
- Saving the state of the caller before switching to execute the called subroutine
- Allocating space for the local variables of the called subroutine
- Jumping to execute the called subroutine
- Returning values from the called subroutine back to the caller
- Recycling the memory space occupied by the called subroutine, when it returns
- Reinstating the state of the caller
- Jumping to execute the code of the caller immediately following the spot where we left it

Taking care of these housekeeping chores is a major headache, and high-level programmers are fortunate that the compiler relieves them from this duty. So how does the compiler do it? Well, if we choose to base our low level implementation on a *stack machine*, the job will be surprisingly manageable. In fact, the stack structure lends itself perfectly well to supporting all the housekeeping tasks mentioned above.

With that in mind, the remainder of this section describes how *program flow* and *subroutine calling* commands can be implemented on a stack machine. We begin with the implementation of program flow commands, which is rather simple and requires no memory management, and continue to describe the more challenging implementation of subroutine calling commands.

8.1.1   Program Flow

The default execution of computer programs is linear, one command after the other. This sequential flow is occasionally broken by branching commands, for example, embarking on a new iteration in a loop. In low-level programming, the branching logic is accomplished by instructing the machine to continue execution at some destination in the program other than the next instruction, using a *goto destination* command. The destination specification can take several forms, the most primitive being the physical address of the instruction that should be executed next. A slightly more abstract redirection command is established by describing the jump destination using a symbolic *label*. This variation requires that the language be equipped with some *labeling* directive, designed to assign symbols to selected points in the code.

This basic *goto* mechanism can easily be altered to effect conditional branching as well. For example, an *if-goto destination* command can instruct the machine to take the jump only if a given Boolean condition is true; if the condition is false, the regular program flow should continue, executing the next command in the code. How should we introduce the Boolean condition into the language? In a stack machine paradigm, the most natural approach is conditioning the jump on the value of the stack's topmost element: if it's not zero, jump to the specified destination; otherwise, execute the next command in the program.

In chapter 7 we saw how primitive VM operations can be used to compute any Boolean expression, leaving its truth-value at the stack's topmost element. This power of expression, combined with the *goto* and *if-goto* commands just described, can be used to express any flow of control structure found in any programming language. Two typical examples appear in figure 8.1.

The low-level implementation of the VM commands *label*, *goto label*, and *if-goto label* is straightforward. All programming languages, including the "lowest" ones, feature branching commands of some sort. For example, if our low-level implementation is based on translating the VM commands into assembly code, all we have to do is reexpress these *goto* commands using the branching logic of the assembly language.

8.1.2   Subroutine Calling

Each programming language is characterized by a fixed set of built-in commands. The key abstraction mechanism provided by modern languages is the freedom to extend this basic repertoire with high-level, programmer-defined operations. In procedural languages, the high-level operations are called *subroutines,*

Flow of control structure	Pseudo VM code
| ```
if (cond)
   s1
else
   s2
...
``` | ```
VM code for computing ~(cond)
   if-goto L1
   VM code for executing s1
   goto L2
label L1
   VM code for executing s2
label L2
   ...
``` |
| ```
while (cond)
   s1
...
``` | ```
label L1
   VM code for computing ~(cond)
   if-goto L2
   VM code for executing s1
   goto L1
label L2
   ...
``` |

Figure 8.1   Low-level flow of control using *goto* commands.

procedures, or *functions*, and in object-oriented languages they are usually called *methods*. Throughout this chapter, all these high-level program units are referred to as *subroutines*.

In well-designed programming languages, the use of a high-level operation (implemented by a subroutine) has the same "look and feel" as that of built-in commands. For example, consider the functions *add* and *raise to a power*. Most languages feature the former as a built-in operation, while the latter may be written as a subroutine. In spite of these different implementations, both functions should ideally look alike from the caller's perspective. This would allow the caller to weave the two operations together naturally, yielding consistent and readable code. A stack language implementation of this principle is illustrated in figure 8.2.

We see that the only difference between invoking a built-in command and calling a user-defined subroutine is the keyword `call` preceding the latter. Everything else is exactly the same: Both operations require the caller to set up their arguments, both operations are expected to remove their arguments from the stack, and both operations are expected to return a value which becomes the topmost stack element. The uniformity of this protocol has a subtle elegance that, we hope, is not lost on the reader.

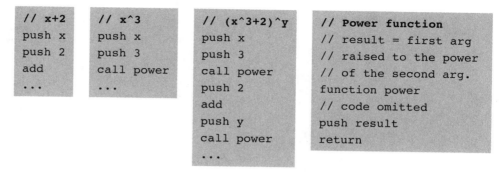

```
// x+2          // x^3          // (x^3+2)^y       // Power function
push x          push x          push x             // result = first arg
push 2          push 3          push 3             // raised to the power
add             call power      call power         // of the second arg.
...             ...             push 2             function power
                                add                // code omitted
                                push y             push result
                                call power         return
                                ...
```

Figure 8.2 Subroutine calling. Elementary commands (like add) and high-level operations (like power) have the same look and feel in terms of argument handling and return values.

Subroutines like `power` usually use local variables for temporary storage. These local variables must be represented in memory during the subroutine's lifetime, namely, from the point the subroutine starts executing until a `return` command is encountered. At this point, the memory space occupied by the subroutine's local variables can be freed. This scheme is complicated by allowing subroutines to be arbitrarily nested: One subroutine may call another subroutine, which may then call another one, and so on. Further, subroutines should be allowed to call themselves recursively; each recursive call must be executed independently of all the other calls and maintain its own set of local and argument variables. How can we implement this nesting mechanism and the memory management tasks implied by it?

The property that makes this housekeeping task tractable is the hierarchical nature of the call-and-return logic. Although the subroutine calling chain may be arbitrarily deep as well as recursive, at any given point in time only one subroutine executes at the chain's end, while all the other subroutines up the calling chain are waiting for it to terminate. This *Last-In-First-Out* (LIFO) processing model lends itself perfectly well to a *stack* data structure, which is also LIFO. When subroutine xxx calls subroutine yyy, we can push (save) xxx's world on the stack and branch to execute yyy. When yyy returns, we can pop (reinstate) xxx's world off the stack, and continue executing xxx as if nothing happened. This execution model is illustrated in figure 8.3.

We use the term *frame* to refer, conceptually, to the subroutine's local variables, the arguments on which it operates, its working stack, and the other memory segments that support its operation. In chapter 7, the term *stack* referred to the working memory that supports operations like *pop, push, add,* and so on. From now on, when we say *stack* we mean *global stack*—the memory area containing the frames of the

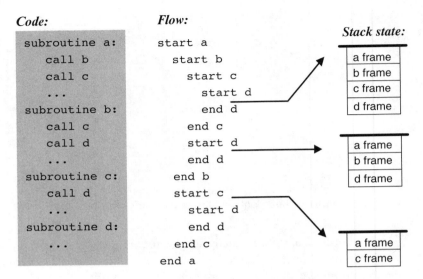

Code: *Flow:*   *Stack state:*

Figure 8.3   Subroutine calls and stack states associated with three representative points in the program's life cycle. All the layers in the stack are waiting for the current layer to complete its execution, at which point the stack becomes shorter and execution resumes at the level just below the current layer. (Following convention, the stack is drawn as if it grows downward.)

current subroutine and all the subroutines waiting for it to return. These two stack notions are closely related, since the working stack of the current subroutine is located at the very tip of the global stack.

To recap, the low-level implementation of the `call xxx` operation entails saving the caller's frame on the stack, allocating stack space for the local variables of the called subroutine (`xxx`), then jumping to execute its code. This last "mega jump" is not hard to implement. Since the name of the target subroutine is specified in the `call` command, the implementation can resolve the symbolic name to a memory address, then jump to execute the code starting at that address. Returning from the called subroutine via a `return` command is trickier, since the command specifies no return address. Indeed, the caller's anonymity is inherent in the very notion of a subroutine call. For example, subroutines like `power(x,y)` or `sqrt(x)` are designed to serve *any* caller, implying that the return address cannot be specified in the caller's code. Instead, a `return` command should be interpreted as follows: Redirect the program's execution to the command following the `call` command that called the current subroutine, wherever this command may be. The memory location of this command is called *return address*.

A glance at figure 8.3 suggests a stack-based solution to implementing this return logic. When we encounter a `call xxx` operation, we know exactly what the return address should be: It's the address of the next command in the caller's code. Thus, we can push this return address on the stack and proceed to execute the code of the called subroutine. When we later encounter a `return` command, we can pop the saved return address and simply *goto* it. In other words, the return address can also be placed in the caller's frame.

8.2   VM Specification, Part II

This section extends the basic VM specification from chapter 7 with *program flow* and *function calling* commands, thereby completing the overall VM specification.

8.2.1   Program Flow Commands

The VM language features three program flow commands:

■ `label` *label*   This command labels the current location in the function's code. Only labeled locations can be jumped to from other parts of the program. The scope of the label is the function in which it is defined. The *label* is an arbitrary string composed of any sequence of letters, digits, underscore (_), dot (.), and colon (:) that does not begin with a digit.

■ `goto` *label*   This command effects an *unconditional goto* operation, causing execution to continue from the location marked by the *label*. The jump destination must be located in the same function.

■ `if-goto` *label*   This command effects a *conditional goto* operation. The stack's topmost value is popped; if the value is not zero, execution continues from the location marked by the *label*; otherwise, execution continues from the next command in the program. The jump destination must be located in the same function.

8.2.2   Function Calling Commands

Different high-level languages have different names for program units including *functions*, *procedures*, *methods*, and *subroutines*. In our overall compilation model (elaborated in chapters 10–11), each such high-level program unit is translated into a low-level program unit called *VM function*, or simply *function*.

A function has a symbolic name that is used globally to call it. The function name is an arbitrary string composed of any sequence of letters, digits, underscore (_), dot (.), and colon (:) that does not begin with a digit. (We expect that a method `bar` in class `Foo` in some high-level language will be translated by the compiler to a VM function named `Foo.bar`). The scope of the function name is global: At the VM level, all functions in all files are seen by each other and may call each other using the function name.

The VM language features three function-related commands:

- `function` *f n* Here starts the code of a function named *f* that has *n* local variables;

- `call` *f m* Call function *f*, stating that *m* arguments have already been pushed onto the stack by the caller;

- `return` Return to the calling function.

8.2.3 The Function Calling Protocol

The events of calling a function and returning from a function can be viewed from two different perspectives: that of the calling function and that of the called function.

The calling function view:

- Before calling the function, the caller must push as many arguments as necessary onto the stack;

- Next, the caller invokes the function using the `call` command;

- After the called function returns, the arguments that the caller has pushed before the call have disappeared from the stack, and a *return value* (that always exists) appears at the top of the stack;

- After the called function returns, the caller's memory segments `argument`, `local`, `static`, `this`, `that`, and `pointer` are the same as before the call, and the `temp` segment is undefined.

The called function view:

- When the called function starts executing, its `argument` segment has been initialized with actual argument values passed by the caller and its `local` variables segment has been allocated and initialized to zeros. The `static` segment that the called function sees has been set to the `static` segment of the VM file to which it belongs, and the working stack that it sees is empty. The segments `this`, `that`, `pointer`, and `temp` are undefined upon entry.

- Before returning, the called function must push a value onto the stack.

To repeat an observation made in the previous chapter, we see that when a VM function starts running (or resumes its previous execution), it assumes that it is surrounded by a private world, all of its own, consisting of its memory segments and stack, waiting to be manipulated by its commands. The agent responsible for building this virtual worldview for every VM function is the VM implementation, as we elaborate in section 8.3.

8.2.4   Initialization

A VM program is a collection of related VM functions, typically resulting from the compilation of some high-level program. When the VM implementation starts running (or is reset), the convention is that it always executes an argument-less VM function called `Sys.init`. Typically, this function then calls the main function in the user's program. Thus, compilers that generate VM code must ensure that each translated program will have one such `Sys.init` function.

8.3   Implementation

This section describes how to complete the VM implementation that we started building in chapter 7, leading to a full-scale virtual machine implementation. Section 8.3.1 describes the stack structure that must be maintained, along with its standard mapping over the Hack platform. Section 8.3.2 gives an example, and section 8.3.3 provides design suggestions and a proposed API for actually building the VM implementation.

Some of the implementation details are rather technical, and dwelling on them may distract attention from the overall VM operation. This big picture is restored in section 8.3.2, which illustrates the VM implementation in action. Therefore, one may want to consult 8.3.2 for motivation while reading 8.3.1.

8.3.1   Standard VM Mapping on the Hack Platform, Part II

The Global Stack   The memory resources of the VM are implemented by maintaining a global stack. Each time a function is called, a new block is added to the global stack. The block consists of the *arguments* that were set by the calling function for the called function, the *pointers* used by the VM implementation to save the state of the calling function, the *local variables* of the called function (initialized to 0), and an empty *working stack* for the called function. Figure 8.4 shows this generic stack structure.

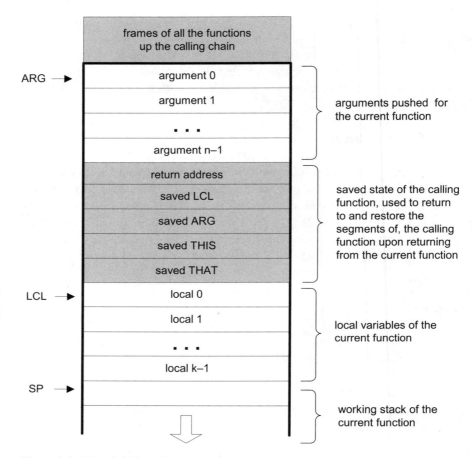

Figure 8.4   The global stack structure.

Note that the shaded areas in figure 8.4 as well as the ARG, LCL, and SP pointers are never seen by VM functions. Rather, they are created and used by the VM implementation to implement the function call-and-return protocol behind the scene.

How can we implement this model on the Hack platform? First, it's important to remember that the VM implementation is a *translator* program, written in some high level language. It accepts VM code as input, and emits assembly code as output. Now, according to the standard VM-on-Hack mapping, the stack should start at RAM[256]. Therefore, the VM implementation should start by generating assembly code that sets SP=256. From this point onward, when the VM implementation encounters commands like pop, push, add, etc. in the input VM code, it can emit assembly code that affects these operations by manipulating SP and relevant words in the host RAM. This was already done in chapter 7. In a similar fashion, when the VM implementation encounters function calling commands like `call`, `function`, and `return` in the input VM code, it can emit assembly code that maintains, on the host RAM, the stack structure shown in figure 8.5. This translation task is described next.

Function Calling Protocol Implementation   The function calling protocol and the global stack structure implied by it can be implemented on the Hack platform by affecting—in Hack assembly—the pseudo code given in figure 8.5. In particular, each pseudo operation described in the right column of figure 8.5 is implemented by

VM command	*Generated (pseudo)code emitted by the VM implementation*	

call f n
 	
(calling a function f after n arguments have been pushed onto the stack)
	`push return-address`
	`push LCL`
	`push ARG`
	`push THIS`
	`push THAT`
	`ARG = SP-n-5`
	`LCL = SP`
	`goto f`
	`(return-address)`
		// (Using the label declared below)
		// Save LCL of the calling function
		// Save ARG of the calling function
		// Save THIS of the calling function
		// Save THAT of the calling function
		// Reposition ARG (n = number of args.)
		// Reposition LCL
		// Transfer control
		// Declare a label for the return-address

function f k
 	
(declaring a function f that has k local variables)
	`(f)`
	   `repeat k times:`
	   `push 0`
		// Declare a label for the function entry
		// k = number of local variables
		// Initialize all of them to 0

return
 	
(from a function)
	`FRAME = LCL`
	`RET = *(FRAME-5)`
	`*ARG = pop()`
	`SP = ARG+1`
	`THAT = *(FRAME-1)`
	`THIS = *(FRAME-2)`
	`ARG = *(FRAME-3)`
	`LCL = *(FRAME-4)`
	`goto RET`
		// FRAME is a temporary variable
		// Put the return-address in a temp. var.
		// Reposition the return value for the caller
		// Restore SP of the caller
		// Restore THAT of the caller
		// Restore THIS of the caller
		// Restore ARG of the caller
		// Restore LCL of the caller
		// Goto return-address (in the caller's code)

Figure 8.5   VM implementation of the three *function calling* commands of the VM language. The parenthetical (return address) and (f) are label declarations, using Hack assembly syntax convention.

emitting code that effects the operation using assembly language instructions. Note that some of these "instructions" entail planting label declarations in the generated code stream.

Assembly Language Symbols   As we have seen earlier, the implementation of *program flow* and *function calling* commands requires the VM implementation to create and use special symbols at the assembly level. These symbols are summarized in figure 8.6. For completeness of presentation, the first three rows of the table document the symbols described and implemented in chapter 7.

Symbol	*Usage*
SP, LCL, ARG, THIS, THAT	These predefined symbols point, respectively, to the stack top and to the base addresses of the virtual segments local, argument, this, and that.
R13-R15	These predefined symbols can be used for any purpose.
Xxx.j	Each static variable j in a VM file Xxx.vm is translated into the assembly symbol Xxx.j. In the subsequent assembly process, these symbolic variables will be allocated RAM space by the Hack assembler.
functionName$label	Each label b command in a VM function f should cause the VM implementation to generate a globally unique symbol "f$b" where "f" is the function name and "b" is the label symbol within the VM function's code. When translating goto b and if-goto b VM commands into the target language, the full label specification "f$b" must be used instead of "b".
(FunctionName)	Each VM function f should cause the VM implementation to generate a symbol "f" that refers to its entry point in the instruction memory of the target computer.
return-address	Each VM function call should cause the VM implementation to generate and insert into the translated code stream a unique symbol that serves as a return address, namely the memory location (in the target platform's memory) of the command following the function call.

Figure 8.6 All the special assembly symbols prescribed by the VM-on-Hack standard mapping.

Bootstrap Code   When applied to a VM program (a collection of one or more .vm files), the VM-to-Hack translator produces a single .asm file, written in the Hack assembly language. This file must conform to certain conventions. Specifically, the standard mapping specifies that (i) the VM stack should be mapped on location RAM[256] onward, and (ii) the first VM function that starts executing should be Sys.init (see section 8.2.4).

How can we effect this initialization in the .asm file produced by the VM translator? Well, when we built the Hack computer hardware in chapter 5, we wired it in such a way that upon reset, it will fetch and execute the word located in ROM[0]. Thus, the code segment that starts at ROM address 0, called *bootstrap code*, is the first thing that gets executed when the computer "boots up." Therefore, in view of the previous paragraph, the computer's bootstrap code should effect the following operations (in machine language):

```
SP=256          // Initialize the stack pointer to 0x0100
call Sys.init   // Start executing (the translated code of) Sys.init
```

Sys.init is then expected to call the main function of the main program and then enter an infinite loop. This action should cause the translated VM program to start running.

The notions of "program," "main program," and "main function" are compilation-specific and vary from one high-level language to another. For example, in the Jack language, the default is that the first program unit that starts running automatically is the main method of a class named Main. In a similar fashion, when we tell the JVM to execute a given Java class, say Foo, it looks for, and executes, the Foo.main method. Each language compiler can effect such "automatic" startup routines by programming Sys.init appropriately.

8.3.2   Example

The factorial of a positive number *n* can be computed by the iterative formula $n! = 1 \cdot 2 \cdot \ldots \cdot (n-1) \cdot n$. This algorithm is implemented in figure 8.7.

Let us focus on the call mult command highlighted in the fact function code from figure 8.7. Figure 8.8 shows three stack states related to this call, illustrating the function calling protocol in action.

If we ignore the middle stack instance in figure 8.8, we observe that fact has set up some arguments and called mult to operate on them (left stack instance). When mult returns (right stack instance), the arguments of the called function have been replaced with the function's return value. In other words, when the dust clears from

```
function p
...
// Compute 4!
push constant 4
call fact 1 // 1 arg
...
```

```
function fact 2 // 2 local variables
// Returns the factorial of a given argument
    push constant 1
    pop local 0     // result=1
    push constant 1
    pop local 1     // j=1
label loop
    push constant 1
    push local 1
    add
    pop local 1     // j=j+1
    push local 1
    push argument 0
    gt
    if-goto end     // if j>n goto end
    push local 0
    push local 1
    call mult 2     // 2 arguments were pushed
    pop local 0     // result=mult(result,j)
    goto loop
label end
    push local 0
    return
```

```
function mult 2
// (2 local variables)
// Multiplies argument 0
// times argument 1.
// Code appears in
// figure 7.9.
...
// Return the result:
push local 0
return
```

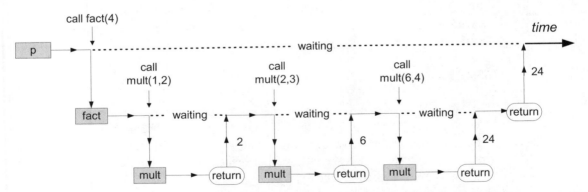

Figure 8.7 The life cycle of function calls. An arbitrary function p calls function fact, which then calls mult several times. Vertical arrows depict transfer of control from one function to another. At any given point in time, only one function is running, while all the functions up the calling chain are waiting for it to return. When a function returns, the function that called it resumes its execution.

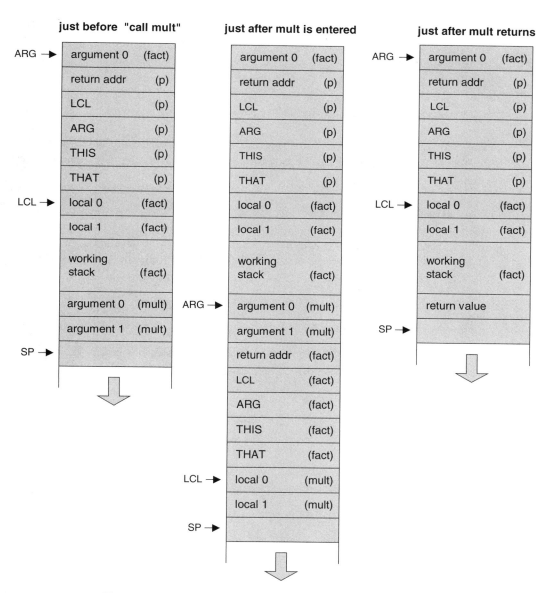

Figure 8.8 Global stack dynamics corresponding to figure 8.7, focusing on the `call mult` event. The pointers SP, ARG, and LCL are not part of the VM abstraction and are used by the VM implementation to map the stack on the host RAM.

the function call, the calling function has received the service that it has requested, and processing resumes as if nothing happened: The drama of mult's processing (middle stack instance) has left no trace whatsoever on the stack, except for the return value.

8.3.3   Design Suggestions for the VM Implementation

The basic VM translator built in Project 7 was based on two modules: *parser* and *code writer*. This translator can be extended into a full-scale VM implementation by extending these modules with the functionality described here.

The *Parser* Module   If the basic parser that you built in Project 7 does not already parse the six VM commands specified in this chapter, then add their parsing now. Specifically, make sure that the commandType method developed in Project 7 also returns the constants corresponding to the six VM commands described in this chapter: C_LABEL, C_GOTO, C_IF, C_FUNCTION, C_RETURN, and C_CALL.

The *CodeWriter* Module   The basic CodeWriter specified in chapter 7 should be augmented with the following functionality.

CodeWriter: Translates VM commands into Hack assembly code. The routines listed here should be added to the CodeWriter module API given in chapter 7.

Routine	Arguments	Returns	Function
writeInit	—	—	Writes assembly code that effects the VM initialization, also called *bootstrap code*. This code must be placed at the beginning of the output file.
writeLabel	label (string)	—	Writes assembly code that effects the label command.
writeGoto	label (string)	—	Writes assembly code that effects the goto command.

Routine	Arguments	Returns	Function
writeIf	label (string)	—	Writes assembly code that effects the if-goto command.
writeCall	functionName (string) numArgs (int)	—	Writes assembly code that effects the call command.
writeReturn	—	—	Writes assembly code that effects the return command.
writeFunction	functionName (string) numLocals (int)	—	Writes assembly code that effects the function command.

8.4   Perspective

The notions of subroutine calling and program flow are fundamental to all high-level languages. This means that somewhere down the translation path to binary code, someone must take care of the intricate housekeeping chores related to their implementation. In Java, C#, and Jack, this burden falls on the VM level. And if the VM is *stack-based*, it lends itself nicely to the job, as we have seen throughout this chapter. In general then, virtual machines that implement subroutine calls and recursion as a primitive feature deliver a significant and useful abstraction.

Of course this is just one implementation option. Some compilers handle the details of subroutine calling directly, without using a VM at all. Other compilers use various forms of VMs, but not necessarily for managing subroutine calling. Finally, in some architectures most of the subroutine calling functionality is handled directly by the hardware.

In the next two chapters we will develop a Jack-to-VM compiler. Since the back-end of this compiler was already developed—it is the VM implementation built in chapters 7–8—the compiler's development will be a relatively easy task.

8.5   Project

Objective   Extend the basic VM translator built in Project 7 into a full-scale VM translator. In particular, add the ability to handle the program flow and function calling commands of the VM language.

Resources (same as Project 7)   You will need two tools: the programming language in which you will implement your VM translator, and the CPU emulator supplied with the book. This emulator will allow you to execute the machine code generated by your VM translator—an indirect way to test the correctness of the latter. Another tool that may come in handy in this project is the visual VM emulator supplied with the book. This program allows experimenting with a working VM implementation before you set out to build one yourself. For more information about this tool, refer to the VM emulator tutorial.

Contract   Write a full-scale VM-to-Hack translator, extending the translator developed in Project 7, and conforming to the VM Specification, Part II (section 8.2) and to the Standard VM Mapping on the Hack Platform (section 8.3.1). Use it to translate the VM programs supplied below, yielding corresponding programs written in the Hack assembly language. When executed on the supplied CPU emulator, these assembly programs should deliver the results mandated by the supplied test scripts and compare files.

Testing Programs

We recommend completing the implementation of the translator in two stages. First implement the *program flow* commands, then the *function calling* commands. This will allow you to unit-test your implementation incrementally, using the test programs supplied here.

For each program Xxx, the XxxVME.tst script allows running the program on the supplied VM emulator, so that you can gain familiarity with the program's intended operation. After translating the program using your VM translator, the supplied Xxx.tst and Xxx.cmp scripts allow testing the translated assembly code on the CPU emulator.

Test Programs for Program Flow Commands

■ `BasicLoop:` computes $1 + 2 + \cdots + n$ and pushes the result onto the stack. This program tests the implementation of the VM language's `goto` and `if-goto` commands.

■ `Fibonacci:` computes and stores in memory the first n elements of the Fibonacci series. This typical array manipulation program provides a more challenging test of the VM's branching commands.

Test Programs for Function Calling Commands

■ `SimpleFunction:` performs a simple calculation and returns the result. This program provides a basic test of the implementation of the `function` and `return` commands.

■ `FibonacciElement:` This program provides a full test of the implementation of the VM's function calling commands, the bootstrap section, and most of the other VM commands.

The program directory consists of two `.vm` files:

• `Main.vm` contains one function called `fibonacci`. This recursive function returns the n-th element of the Fibonacci series;

• `Sys.vm` contains one function called `init`. This function calls the `Main.fibonacci` function with $n = 4$, then loops infinitely.

Since the overall program consists of two `.vm` files, the entire directory must be compiled in order to produce a single `FibonacciElement.asm` file. (Compiling each `.vm` file separately will yield two separate `.asm` files, which is not desired here.)

■ `StaticsTest:` A full test of the VM implementation's handling of static variables. Consists of two `.vm` files, each representing the compilation of a stand-alone class file, plus a `Sys.vm` file. The entire directory should be compiled in order to produce a single `StaticsTest.asm` file.

(Recall that according to the VM Specification, the bootstrap code generated by the VM implementation must include a call to the `Sys.init` function).

Tips

Initialization   In order for any translated VM program to start running, it must include a preamble startup code that forces the VM implementation to start executing it on the host platform. In addition, in order for any VM code to operate properly, the VM implementation must store the base addresses of the virtual segments in selected locations in the host RAM. The first three test programs in this project assume that the startup code was not yet implemented and include test scripts that effect the necessary initializations "manually." The last two programs assume that the startup code is already part of the VM implementation.

Testing/Debugging   For each one of the five test programs, follow these steps:

1.   Run the program on the supplied VM emulator, using the XxxVME.tst test script, to get acquainted with the intended program's behavior.

2.   Use your translator to translate the .vm file(s), yielding a single .asm text file that contains a translated program written in the Hack assembly language.

3.   Inspect the translated .asm program. If there are visible syntax (or any other) errors, debug and fix your translator.

4.   Use the supplied .tst and .cmp files to run your translated .asm program on the CPU emulator. If there are run-time errors, debug and fix your translator.

Note: The supplied test programs were carefully planned to unit-test the specific features of each stage in your VM implementation. Therefore, it's important to implement your translator in the proposed order and to test it using the appropriate test programs at each stage. Implementing a later stage before an early one may cause the test programs to fail.

Tools   Same as in Project 7.

9 High-Level Language

High thoughts need a high language.
—Aristophanes (448–380 BC)

All the hardware and software systems presented so far in the book were low-level, meaning that humans are not expected to read and write them directly. In this chapter we present a high-level language, called Jack, designed to enable human programmers write high-level programs.

Jack is a simple object-based language. It has the basic features and flavor of modern languages like Java and C#, with a much simpler syntax and no support for inheritance. In spite of this simplicity, Jack is a general-purpose language that can be used to create numerous applications. In particular, it lends itself nicely to simple interactive games like Snake, Tetris, and Pong—a program whose complete Jack code is included in the book's software suite.

The introduction of Jack marks the beginning of the end of our journey. In chapters 10 and 11 we will write a compiler that translates Jack programs into VM code, and in chapter 12 we will develop a simple operating system for the Jack/Hack platform, written in Jack. This will complete the computer's construction. With that in mind, it's important to say at the outset that the goal of this chapter is not to turn you into a Jack programmer. Instead, our hidden agenda is to prepare you to develop the compiler and operating system that lie ahead.

If you have any experience with a modern object-oriented programming language, you will immediately feel at home with Jack. Therefore, the Background section starts the chapter with some typical programming examples, and the Specification section proceeds with a full functional description of the language and its standard library. The Implementation section gives some screen shots of typical Jack applications and offers general guidelines on how to write similar programs over the Hack platform. The final Project section provides additional details about compiling and debugging Jack programs.

All the programs shown in the chapter can be compiled by the Jack compiler supplied with the book. The resulting VM code can then run as is on the supplied VM emulator. Alternatively, one can further translate the compiled VM code into binary code, using the VM translator and the assembler built in chapters 7–8 and 6, respectively. The resulting machine code can then be executed as is on the hardware platform that we built in chapters 1–5.

It's important to reiterate that in and by itself, Jack is a rather uninteresting and simple-minded language. However, this simplicity has a purpose. First, you can learn (and unlearn) Jack very quickly—in about an hour. Second, the Jack language was carefully planned to lend itself nicely to simple compilation techniques. As a result, one can write an elegant *Jack compiler* with relative ease, as we will do in chapters 10 and 11. In other words, the deliberately simple structure of Jack is designed to help uncover the software engineering principles underlying modern languages like Java and C#. Rather than taking the compilers and run-time environments of these languages for granted, we will build a Jack compiler and a run-time environment ourselves, beginning in the next chapter. For now, let's take Jack out of the box.

9.1   Background

Jack is mostly self-explanatory. Therefore, we defer the language specification to the next section, starting with some examples. We begin with the inevitable *Hello World* program. The second example illustrates procedural programming and array processing. The third example illustrates how the basic language can be extended with abstract data types. The fourth example illustrates a linked list implementation using the language's object handling capabilities.

9.1.1   Example 1: Hello World

When we tell the Jack run-time environment to run a given program, execution always starts with the Main.main function. Thus, each Jack program must include a class named Main, and this class must include a function named main. This convention is illustrated in figure 9.1.

Jack is equipped with a *standard library* whose complete API is given in section 9.2.7. This library extends the basic language with various abstractions and services such as arrays, strings, mathematical functions, memory management, and input/output functions. Two such functions are invoked by the program in figure

```
/** Hello World program. */
class Main {
  function void main() {
    /* Prints some text using the standard library. */
    do Output.printString("Hello World");
    do Output.println();      // New line
    return;
  }
}
```

Figure 9.1 Hello World.

9.1, effecting the "Hello world" printout. The program also demonstrates the three comment formats supported by Jack.

9.1.2 Example 2: Procedural Programming and Array Handling

Jack is equipped with typical language constructs for procedural programming. It also includes basic commands for declaring and manipulating arrays. Figure 9.2 illustrates both of these features, in the context of inputting and computing the average of a series of numbers.

Jack programs declare and construct arrays using the built-in Array class, which is part of the standard Jack library. Note that Jack arrays are not typed and can include anything—integers, objects, and so forth.

9.1.3 Example 3: Abstract Data Types

Every programming language has a fixed set of primitive data types, of which Jack supports three: int, char, and boolean. Programmers can extend this basic repertoire by creating new classes that represent abstract data types, as needed. For example, suppose we wish to endow Jack with the ability to handle *rational numbers*, namely, objects of the form n/m where n and m are integers. This can be done by creating a stand-alone class, designed to provide a fraction abstraction for Jack programs. Let us call this class Fraction.

Defining a Class Interface A reasonable way to get started is to specify the set of properties and services expected from a fraction abstraction. One such *Application Program Interface* (API), is given in figure 9.3a.

```
/** Computes the average of a sequence of integers. */
class Main {
  function void main() {
    var Array a;
    var int length;
    var int i, sum;

    let length = Keyboard.readInt("How many numbers? ");
    let a = Array.new(length); // Constructs the array
    let i = 0;

    while (i < length) {
      let a[i] = Keyboard.readInt("Enter the next number: ");
      let sum = sum + a[i];
      let i = i + 1;
    }

    do Output.printString("The average is: ");
    do Output.printInt(sum / length);
    do Output.println();
    return;
  }
}
```

Figure 9.2   Procedural programming and array handling.

In Jack, operations on the current object (referred to as this) are represented by
methods, whereas class-level operations (equivalent to *static methods* in Java) are
represented by *functions*. Operations that create new objects are called *constructors*.

Using Classes   APIs mean different things to different people. If you are the
programmer who has to *implement* the fraction class, you can view its API as a contract that must be implemented, one way or another. Alternatively, if you are a
programmer who needs to *use* fractions in your work, you can view the API as a
documentation of a fraction server, designed to generate fraction objects and supply
fraction-related operations. Taking this latter view, consider the Jack code listed in
figure 9.3b.

Figure 9.3b illustrates an important software engineering principle: Users of any
given abstraction don't have to know anything about its underlying *implementation*.

```
// A Fraction is an object representation of n/m where n and m are integers.
field int numerator, denominator        // Fraction object properties
constructor Fraction new(int a, int b)   // Returns a new Fraction object
method int getNumerator()                // Returns the numerator of this
                                         // fraction
method int getDenominator()              // Returns the denominator of this
                                         // fraction
method Fraction plus(Fraction other)     // Returns the sum of this fraction
                                         // and another fraction, as a
                                         // fraction
method void print()                      // Prints this fraction in the
                                         // format "numerator/denominator"
// Additional fraction-related services are specified here, as needed.
```

Figure 9.3a   Fraction class API.

```
// Computes the sum of 2/3 and 1/5.
class Main {
  function void main() {
    var Fraction a, b, c;
    let a = Fraction.new(2,3);
    let b = Fraction.new(1,5);
    let c = a.plus(b);   // Compute c = a + b
    do c.print();   // Should print the text "13/15"
    return;
  }
}
```

Figure 9.3b   Using the Fraction abstraction.

```
/** Provides the Fraction type and related services. */
class Fraction {
  field int numerator, denominator;

  /** Constructs a new (and reduced) fraction from given
   *  numerator and denominator. */
  constructor Fraction new(int a, int b) {
    let numerator = a;   let denominator = b;
    do reduce();  // If a/b is not reduced, reduce it
    return this;
  }

  /** Reduces this fraction. */
  method void reduce() {
    var int g;
    let g = Fraction.gcd(numerator, denominator);
    if (g > 1) {
      let numerator = numerator / g;
      let denominator = denominator / g; }
    return;
  }

  /** Computes the greatest common denominator of a and b. */
  function int gcd(int a, int b) {
    var int r;
    while (~(b = 0)) {                 // Apply Euclid's algorithm.
      let r = a - (b * (a / b));  // r=remainder of a/b
      let a = b; let b = r; }
    return a;
  }

  /** Accessors. */
  method int getNumerator() { return numerator; }
  method int getDenominator() { return denominator; }
```

Figure 9.3c   A possible Fraction class implementation.

```
/** Returns the sum of this fraction and another one. */
method Fraction plus(Fraction other) {
  var int sum;
  let sum = (numerator * other.getDenominator()) +
            (other.getNumerator() * denominator);
  return Fraction.new(sum, denominator *
          other.getDenominator());
}

// More fraction-related methods: minus, times, div, etc.

/** Prints this fraction. */
method void print() {
  do Output.printInt(numerator);
  do Output.printString("/");
  do Output.printInt(denominator);
  return;
}
} // Fraction class
```

Figure 9.3c (continued)

Rather, they can be given access only to the abstraction's *interface*, or class API, and then use it as a black box server of abstraction-related operations.

Implementing the Class   We now turn to the other player in our story—the programmer who has to actually implement the fraction abstraction. A possible Jack implementation is given in figure 9.3c.

Figure 9.3c illustrates the typical Jack program structures: *classes, methods, constructors*, and *functions*. It also demonstrates all the statement types available in the language: let, do, if, while, and return.

9.1.4   Example 4: Linked List Implementation

A *linked list* (or simply *list*) is a chain of objects, each consisting of a data element and a reference (pointer) to the rest of the list. Figure 9.4 shows a possible Jack class implementation of the linked list abstraction. The purpose of this example is to illustrate typical object handling in the Jack language.

```
/** The List class provides a linked list abstraction. */
class List {
  field int data;
  field List next;

  /* Creates a new List object. */
  constructor List new(int car, List cdr) {
    let data = car;
    let next = cdr;
    return this;
  }

  /* Disposes this List by recursively disposing its tail. */
  method void dispose() {
    if (~(next = null)) {
       do next.dispose();
    }
    // Use an OS routine to recycle the memory held by this
    // object.
    do Memory.deAlloc(this);
    return;
  }

  // More List-related methods come here

} // class List
```

```
/* Creates a list holding the numbers (2,3,5).
   (this code can appear in any class). */
function void create235() {
  var List v;
  let v = List.new(5,null);
  let v = List.new(2,List.new(3,v));
  ... // Does something with the list
  do v.dispose();
  return;
}
```

Figure 9.4   Object handling in a linked list context.

9.2   The Jack Language Specification

We now turn to a formal and complete description of the Jack language, organized by its syntactic elements, program structure, variables, expressions, and statements. This language specification should be viewed as a technical reference, to be consulted as needed.

9.2.1   Syntactic Elements

A Jack program is a sequence of tokens separated by an arbitrary amount of white space and comments, which are ignored. Tokens can be *symbols, reserved words, constants,* and *identifiers,* as listed in figure 9.5.

9.2.2   Program Structure

The basic programming unit in Jack is a *class.* Each class resides in a separate file and can be compiled separately. Class declarations have the following format:

```
class name {
    Field and static variable declarations  // Must precede subroutine declarations.
    Subroutine declarations  // Constructor, method and function declarations.
}
```

Each class declaration specifies a name through which the class can be globally accessed. Next comes a sequence of zero or more *field* and *static variable* declarations. Then comes a sequence of one or more *subroutine* declarations, each defining a *method,* a *function,* or a *constructor.* Methods "belong to" objects and provide their functionality, while functions "belong to" the class in general and are not associated with a particular object (similar to Java's *static methods*). A constructor "belongs to" the class and, when called, generates object instances of this class.

All subroutine declarations have the following format:

```
subroutine type name (parameter-list) {
    local variable declarations
    statements
}
```

where *subroutine* is either `constructor`, `method`, or `function`. Each subroutine has a *name* through which it can be accessed, and a *type* describing the value returned by

White space and comments	Space characters, newline characters, and comments are ignored.
	
	The following comment formats are supported:
	
	`//  Comment to end of line`
	`/*  Comment until closing */`
	`/** API documentation comment */`

Symbols	`( )` Used for grouping arithmetic expressions and for enclosing parameter-lists and argument-lists `[ ]` Used for array indexing `{ }` Used for grouping program units and statements `,` Variable list separator `;` Statement terminator `=` Assignment and comparison operator `.` Class membership `+ - * / & | ~ < >` Operators
Reserved words	`class, constructor, method, function` Program components `int, boolean, char, void` Primitive types `var, static, field` Variable declarations `let, do, if, else, while, return` Statements `true, false, null` Constant values `this` Object reference
Constants	*Integer* constants must be positive and in standard decimal notation, e.g., `1984`. Negative integers like `-13` are not constants but rather expressions consisting of a unary minus operator applied to an integer constant. *String* constants are enclosed within two quote (") characters and may contain any characters except *newline* or *double-quote*. (These characters are supplied by the functions `String.newLine()` and `String.doubleQuote()` from the standard library.) *Boolean* constants can be `true` or `false`. The constant `null` signifies a null reference.
Identifiers	Identifiers are composed from arbitrarily long sequences of letters (`A-Z, a-z`), digits (`0-9`), and "_". The first character must be a letter or "_". The language is case sensitive. Thus `x` and `X` are treated as different identifiers.

Figure 9.5   Jack syntactic elements.

the subroutine. If the subroutine returns no value, the type is declared `void`; otherwise, it can be any of the primitive data types supported by the language, or any of the class types supplied by the standard library, or any of the class types supplied by other classes in the application. Constructors may have arbitrary names, but they must return an object of the class type. Therefore the type of a constructor must always be the name of the class to which it belongs.

Following its header specification, the subroutine declaration contains a sequence of zero or more local variable declarations, then a sequence of zero or more statements.

As in Java, a *Jack program* is a collection of one or more classes. One class must be named `Main`, and this class must include a function named `main`. When instructed to execute a Jack program that resides in some directory, the Jack run-time environment will automatically start running the `Main.main` function.

9.2.3   Variables

Variables in Jack must be explicitly declared before they are used. There are four kinds of variables: *field, static, local,* and *parameter* variables, each with its associated scope. Variables must be typed.

Data Types   Each variable can assume either a *primitive* data type (`int`, `char`, `boolean`), as predefined in the Jack language specification, or an *object* type, which is the name of a class. The class that implements this type can be either part of the Jack standard library (e.g., `String` or `Array`), or it may be any other user-defined class residing in the program directory.

Primitive Types   Jack features three primitive data types:

- `int`:   16-bit 2's complement
- `boolean`:   *false* and *true*
- `char`:   unicode character

Variables of primitive types are allocated to memory when they are declared. For example, the declarations `var int age; var boolean gender;` cause the compiler to create the variables `age` and `gender` and to allocate memory space to them.

Object Types   Every class defines an object type. As in Java, the declaration of an object variable only causes the creation of a reference variable (pointer). Memory

```
// This code assumes the existence of Car and Employee classes.
// Car objects have model and licensePlate fields.
// Employee objects have name and Car fields.
var Employee e, f;  // Creates variables e, f that contain null references
var Car c;          // Creates a variable c that contains a null reference
...
let c = Car.new("Jaguar","007")    // Constructs a new Car object
let e = Employee.new("Bond",c)     // Constructs a new Employee object
// At this point c and e hold the base addresses of the memory segments
// allocated to the two objects.
let f = e;  // Only the reference is copied - no new object is constructed.
```

Figure 9.6   Object types (example).

for storing the object itself is allocated later, if and when the programmer actually *constructs* the object by calling a constructor. Figure 9.6 gives an example.

The Jack standard library provides two built-in object types (classes) that play a role in the language syntax: `Array` and `String`.

Arrays   Arrays are declared using a built-in class called `Array`. Arrays are one-dimensional and the first index is always 0 (multi-dimensional arrays may be obtained as arrays of arrays). Array entries do not have a declared type, and different entries in the same array may have different types. The declaration of an array only creates a reference, while the actual construction of the array is done by calling the `Array.new(length)` constructor. Access to array elements is done using the `a[j]` notation. Figure 9.2 illustrates working with arrays.

Strings   Strings are declared using a built-in class called `String`. The Jack compiler recognizes the syntax `"xxx"` and treats it as the contents of some `String` object. The contents of `String` objects can be accessed and modified using the methods of the `String` class, as documented in its API. Example:

```
var String s;
var char c;
...
let s = "Hello World";
let c = s.charAt(6);       // "W"
```

Type Conversions   The Jack language is weakly typed. The language specification does not define the results of attempted assignment or conversion from one type to another, and different Jack compilers may allow or forbid them. (This under-specification is intentional, allowing the construction of minimal Jack compilers that ignore typing issues.)

Having said that, all Jack compilers are expected to allow, and automatically perform, the following assignments:

- Characters and integers are automatically converted into each other as needed, according to the Unicode specification. Example:

```
var char c;  var String s;
let c = 33;  // 'A'
// Equivalently:
let s = "A"; let c = s.charAt(0);
```

- An integer can be assigned to a reference variable (of any object type), in which case it is treated as an address in memory. Example:

```
var Array a;
let a = 5000;
let a[100] = 77; // Memory address 5100 is set to 77
```

- An object variable (whose type is a class name) may be converted into an `Array` variable, and vice versa. The conversion allows accessing the object fields as array entries, and vice versa. Example:

```
// Assume that class Complex has two int fields: re and im.
var Complex c; var Array a;
let a = Array.new(2);
let a[0] = 7; let a[1] = 8;
let c = a; // c==Complex(7,8)
```

Variable Kinds and Scope   Jack features four kinds of variables. *Static variables* are defined at the class level and are shared by all the objects derived from the class. For example, a `BankAccount` class may have a `totalBalance` static variable holding the sum of balances of all the bank accounts, each account being an object derived from the `BankAccount` class. *Field variables* are used to define the properties of individual objects of the class, for example, account `owner` and `balance`. *Local variables*, used by subroutines, exist only as long as the subroutine is running, and

Variable kind	Definition/Description	Declared in	Scope
Static variables	**static** *type name1*, *name2*, . . . ; Only one copy of each static variable exists, and this copy is shared by all the object instances of the class (like *private static variables* in Java)	Class declaration.	The class in which they are declared.
Field variables	**field** *type name1*, *name2*, . . . ; Every object instance of the class has a private copy of the field variables (like *private object variables* in Java)	Class declaration.	The class in which they are declared, except for functions.
Local variables	**var** *type name1*, *name2*, . . . ; Local variables are allocated on the stack when the subroutine is called and freed when it returns (like *local variables* in Java)	Subroutine declaration.	The subroutine in which they are declared.
Parameter variables	*type name1*, *name2*, . . . Used to specify inputs of subroutines, for example: `function void drive (Car c, int miles)`	Appear in parameter lists as part of subroutine declarations.	The subroutine in which they are declared.

Figure 9.7   Variable kinds in the Jack language (throughout the table, *subroutine* is either a *function*, a *method*, or a *constructor*).

parameter variables are used to pass arguments to subroutines. For example, our `BankAccount` class may include the method signature `method void transfer-(BankAccount from, int sum)`, declaring the two parameters `from` and `sum`. Thus, if `joeAccount` and `janeAccount` were two variables of type `BankAccount`, the command `joeAccount.transfer(janeAccount,100)` will effect a transfer of 100 from Jane to Joe.

Figure 9.7 gives a formal description of all the variable kinds supported by the Jack language. The *scope* of a variable is the region in the program in which the variable name is recognized.

Statement	Syntax	Description
`let`	`let` *variable* = *expression*; or `let` *variable* [*expression*] = *expression*;	An assignment operation (where *variable* is either single-valued or an array). The variable kind may be *static*, *local*, *field*, or *parameter*.

`if`	`if` (*expression*) {
	     statements
	 }
	 `else` {
	     statements
	 }
		Typical *if* statement with an optional *else* clause.
		
		 The curly brackets are mandatory even if *statements* is a single statement.

`while`	`while` (*expression*) {
	     statements
	 }
		Typical *while* statement.
		
		 The curly brackets are mandatory even if *statements* is a single statement.

`do`	`do` *function-or-method-call*;	Used to call a function or a method for its effect, ignoring the returned value.
`return`	`return` *expression*; or `return`;	Used to return a value from a subroutine. The second form must be used by functions and methods that return a void value. Constructors must return the expression `this`.

Figure 9.8 Jack statements.

9.2.4 Statements

The Jack language features five generic statements. They are defined and described in figure 9.8.

9.2.5 Expressions

Jack expressions are defined recursively according to the rules given in figure 9.9.

A *Jack expression* is one of the following:

- A *constant;*

- A *variable name* in scope (the variable may be *static, field, local,* or *parameter*);

- The `this` keyword, denoting the current object (cannot be used in functions);

- An *array element* using the syntax *name*[*expression*], where *name* is a variable name of type `Array` in scope;

- A *subroutine call* that returns a non-void type;

- An expression prefixed by one of the unary operators - or ~:
  - *expression*: arithmetic negation;
  - ~ *expression*: boolean negation (bit-wise for integers);

- An expression of the form *expression operator expression* where *operator* is one of the following binary operators:

+ - * /	Integer arithmetic operators;
& |	Boolean And and Boolean Or (bit-wise for integers) operators;
< > =	Comparison operators;

- (*expression*) An expression in parentheses.

Figure 9.9   Jack expressions.

Operator Priority and Order of Evaluation   Operator priority is *not* defined by the language, except that expressions in parentheses are evaluated first. Thus an expression like `2+3*4` may yield either 20 or 14, whereas `2+(3*4)` is guaranteed to yield 14. The need to use parentheses in such expressions makes Jack programming a bit cumbersome. However, the lack of formal operator priority is intentional, since it simplifies the writing of Jack compilers. Of course, different language implementations (compilers) can specify an operator priority and add it to the language documentation, if so desired.

9.2.6   Subroutine Calls

Subroutine calls invoke methods, functions, and constructors for their effect, using the general syntax *subroutineName*(*argument-list*). The number and type of the arguments must match those of the subroutine's parameters, as defined in its declaration. The parentheses must appear even if the argument list is empty. Each argument may be an expression of unlimited complexity. For example, the `Math` class, which

```
class Foo {
  // Some subroutine declarations - code omitted
  ...
  method void f() {
    var Bar b;        // Declares a local variable of class type Bar
    var int i;        // Declares a local variable of primitive type int
    ...
    do g(5,7);        // Calls method g of class Foo (on this object)
    do Foo.p(2);      // Calls function p of class Foo
    do Bar.h(3);      // Calls function h of class Bar
    let b = Bar.r(4); // Calls constructor or function r of class Bar
    do b.q();         // Calls method q of class Bar (on object b)
    Let i = w(b.s(3), Foo.t());  // Calls method w on this object,
                                 // method s on object b and function
                                 // or constructor t of class Foo
    ...
  }
}
```

Figure 9.10   Subroutine call examples.

is part of Jack's standard library, contains a square root function whose declaration is `function int sqrt(int n)`. Such a function can be invoked using calls like `Math.sqrt(17)`, or `Math.sqrt((a * Math.sqrt(c - 17) + 3)`, and so on.

Within a class, methods are called using the syntax *methodName*(*argument-list*), while functions and constructors must be called using their full names, namely, *className.subroutineName*(*argument-list*). Outside a class, the class functions and constructors are also called using their full names, while methods are called using the syntax *varName.methodName*(*argument-list*), where *varName* is a previously defined object variable. Figure 9.10 gives some examples.

Object Construction and Disposal   Object construction is a two-stage affair. When a program declares a variable of some object type, only a reference (pointer) variable is created and allocated memory. To complete the object's construction (if so desired), the program must call a constructor from the object's class. Thus, a class that implements a type (e.g., `Fraction` from figure 9.3c) must contain at least one constructor. Constructors may have arbitrary names, but it is customary to call one of them `new`. Constructors are called just like any other class function using the format:

`let` *varName* $=$ *className.constructorName*(*argument-list*);

For example, `let c = Circle.new(x,y,50)` where `x`, `y`, and 50 are the screen location of the circle's center and its radius. When a constructor is called, the compiler requests the operating system to allocate enough memory space to hold the new object in memory. The OS returns the base address of the allocated memory segment, and the compiler assigns it to `this` (in the circle example, the value of `this` is assigned to `c`). Next, the constructed object is typically initialized to some valid state, effected by the Jack commands found in the constructor's body.

Jack has no garbage collection. Therefore, when an object is no longer needed in a program, the best practice is to dispose it explicitly. In particular, objects can be de-allocated from memory and their space reclaimed using the `Memory .deAlloc(object)` function from the standard library. Convention calls for every class to contain a `dispose()` method that properly encapsulates this de-allocation. For example, see figure 9.4.

9.2.7   The Jack Standard Library

The Jack language comes with a collection of built-in classes that extend the language's capabilities. This standard library, which can also be viewed as a basic operating system, must be provided in every Jack language implementation. The standard library includes the following classes, all implemented in Jack:

- *Math:*   provides basic mathematical operations;
- *String:*   implements the `String` type and string-related operations;
- *Array:*   implements the `Array` type and array-related operations;
- *Output:*   handles text output to the screen;
- *Screen:*   handles graphic output to the screen;
- *Keyboard:*   handles user input from the keyboard;
- *Memory:*   handles memory operations;
- *Sys:*   provides some execution-related services.

Math   This class enables various mathematical operations.

- function void **init**(): for internal use only;
- function int **abs**(int x): returns the absolute value of x;

- function int **multiply**(int x, int y): returns the product of x and y;
- function int **divide**(int x, int y): returns the integer part of x/y;
- function int **min**(int x, int y): returns the minimum of x and y;
- function int **max**(int x, int y): returns the maximum of x and y;
- function int **sqrt**(int x): returns the integer part of the square root of x.

String   This class implements the String data type and various string-related operations.

- constructor String **new**(int maxLength): constructs a new empty string (of length zero) that can contain at most maxLength characters;
- method void **dispose**(): disposes this string;
- method int **length**(): returns the length of this string;
- method char **charAt**(int j): returns the character at location j of this string;
- method void **setCharAt**(int j, char c): sets the j-th element of this string to c;
- method String **appendChar**(char c): appends c to this string and returns this string;
- method void **eraseLastChar**(): erases the last character from this string;
- method int **intValue**(): returns the integer value of this string (or of the string prefix until a non-digit character is detected);
- method void **setInt**(int j): sets this string to hold a representation of j;
- function char **backSpace**(): returns the backspace character;
- function char **doubleQuote**(): returns the double quote (") character;
- function char **newLine**(): returns the newline character.

Array   This class enables the construction and disposal of arrays.

- function Array **new**(int size): constructs a new array of the given size;
- method void **dispose**(): disposes this array.

Output   This class allows writing text on the screen.

- function void **init**(): for internal use only;
- function void **moveCursor**(int i, int j): moves the cursor to the j-th column of the i-th row, and erases the character displayed there;

- function void **printChar**(char c): prints c at the cursor location and advances the cursor one column forward;
- function void **printString**(String s): prints s starting at the cursor location and advances the cursor appropriately;
- function void **printInt**(int i): prints i starting at the cursor location and advances the cursor appropriately;
- function void **println**( ): advances the cursor to the beginning of the next line;
- function void **backSpace**( ): moves the cursor one column back.

Screen   This class allows drawing graphics on the screen. Column indices start at 0 and are left-to-right. Row indices start at 0 and are top-to-bottom. The screen size is hardware-dependant (in the Hack platform: 256 rows by 512 columns).

- function void **init**( ): for internal use only;
- function void **clearScreen**( ): erases the entire screen;
- function void **setColor**(boolean b): sets a color (white = false, black = true) to be used for all further drawXXX commands;
- function void **drawPixel**(int x, int y): draws the (x,y) pixel;
- function void **drawLine**(int x1, int y1, int x2, int y2): draws a line from pixel (x1,y1) to pixel (x2,y2);
- function void **drawRectangle**(int x1, int y1, int x2, int y2): draws a filled rectangle whose top left corner is (x1,y1) and bottom right corner is (x2,y2);
- function void **drawCircle**(int x, int y, int r): draws a filled circle of radius $r <= 181$ around (x,y).

Keyboard   This class allows reading inputs from a standard keyboard.

- function void **init**( ): for internal use only;
- function char **keyPressed**( ): returns the character of the currently pressed key on the keyboard; if no key is currently pressed, returns 0;
- function char **readChar**( ): waits until a key is pressed on the keyboard and released, then echoes the key to the screen and returns the character of the pressed key;
- function String **readLine**(String message): prints the message on the screen, reads the line (text until a newline character is detected) from the keyboard, echoes the line to the screen, and returns its value. This function also handles user back-spaces;

- function int **readInt**(String message): prints the message on the screen, reads the line (text until a newline character is detected) from the keyboard, echoes the line to the screen, and returns its integer value (until the first nondigit character in the line is detected). This function also handles user backspaces.

Memory This class allows direct access to the main memory of the host platform.

- function void **init**(): for internal use only;
- function int **peek**(int address): returns the value of the main memory at this address;
- function void **poke**(int address, int value): sets the contents of the main memory at this address to value;
- function Array **alloc**(int size): finds and allocates from the heap a memory block of the specified size and returns a reference to its base address;
- function void **deAlloc**(Array o): De-allocates the given object and frees its memory space.

Sys This class supports some execution-related services.

- function void **init**(): calls the init functions of the other OS classes and then calls the Main.main() function. For internal use only;
- function void **halt**(): halts the program execution;
- function void **error**(int errorCode): prints the error code on the screen and halts;
- function void **wait**(int duration): waits approximately duration milliseconds and returns.

9.3   Writing Jack Applications

Jack is a general-purpose programming language that can be implemented over different hardware platforms. In the next two chapters we will develop a *Jack compiler* that ultimately generates binary Hack code, and thus it is natural to discuss Jack applications in the Hack context. This section illustrates briefly three such applications and provides general guidelines about application development on the Jack-Hack platform.

Examples Four sample applications are illustrated in figure 9.11. The *Pong* game, whose Jack code is supplied with the book, provides a good illustration of

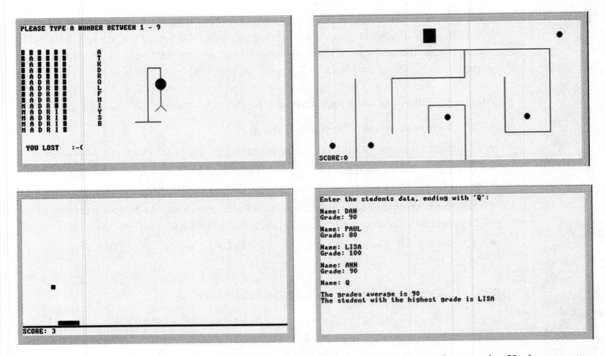

Figure 9.11 Screen shots of sample Jack applications, running on the Hack computer. Hangman, Maze, Pong, and a simple data processing program.

Jack programming over the Hack platform. The Pong program consists of several hundred lines of Jack code, organized in several classes. The program carries out various mathematical calculations in order to compute the direction of the ball's movements, and animates those movements using various drawing methods from the language's standard library. In order to perform these operations quickly, the program's code seeks to minimize the number of real-time calculations and screen drawing operations.

Application Design and Implementation The development of Jack applications over a hardware platform like Hack requires careful planning (as always). First, the application designer must consider the physical limitations of the hardware, and plan accordingly. For example, the dimensions of the computer's screen limit the size of the graphical images that the program can handle. Likewise, one must consider the language's range of input/output commands and the platform's execution speed, to gain a realistic expectation of what can and cannot be done.

As usual, the design process normally starts with a conceptual description of the application's behavior. In the case of graphical and interactive programs, this may take the form of hand-written drawings of typical screens. In simple applications, one can proceed to implementation using procedural programming. In more complex tasks, it is advisable to first create an object-based design of the application. This entails the identification of *classes*, *fields*, and *subroutines*, possibly leading to the creation of some API document (e.g., figure 9.3a).

Next, one can proceed to implement the design in Jack and compile the class files using a Jack compiler. The testing and debugging of the code generated by the compiler depend on the details of the target platform. In the Hack platform supplied with the book, testing and debugging are normally done using the supplied VM emulator. Alternatively, one can translate the Jack program all the way to binary code and run it directly on the Hack hardware, or on the CPU emulator supplied with the book.

The Jack OS   Jack programs make an extensive use of the various abstractions and services supplied by the language's standard library, also called the Jack OS. The chain of command is as follows: the computer is programmed to first run `Sys.init`. This OS function, in turn, is programmed to call your `Main.main` function, which starts running your application. The Jack OS is itself implemented in Jack, and thus its executable version is a set of compiled `.vm` files—just like the application that you will write (following compilation). However, to simplify matters and speed up execution, the supplied VM emulator features a full implementation of all the OS functions. In other words, if your compiled code includes OS function calls, e.g. `call Math.divide`, the supplied VM emulator will know how to service them.

Although the standard library of the Jack language can be extended, readers will perhaps want to hone their programming skills elsewhere. After all, we don't expect Jack to be part of your life beyond this book. Therefore, it is best to view the Jack/Hack platform as a given environment and make the best out of it. That's precisely what programmers do when they write software for embedded devices and dedicated processors that operate in restricted environments. Instead of viewing the constrains imposed by the host platform as a problem, professionals view it as an opportunity to display their resourcefulness and ingenuity. That's why some of the best programmers in the trade were first trained on primitive computers.

9.4   Perspective

Jack is an "object-based" language, meaning that it supports objects and classes, but not inheritance. In this respect it is located somewhere between procedural languages like Pascal or C and object-oriented languages like Java or C++. Jack is certainly more "clunky" than any of these industrial-strength programming languages. However, its basic syntax and semantics are not very different from those of modern languages.

Some features of the Jack language leave much to be desired. For example, its primitive type system is, well, rather primitive. Moreover, it is a weakly typed language, meaning that type conformity in assignments and operations is not strictly enforced. Also, one may wonder why the Jack syntax includes keywords like do and let, why curly brackets must be used even in single statement blocks, and why the language does not enforce a formal operator priority.

Well, all these deviations from normal programming languages were introduced into Jack with one purpose: to allow the development of elegant and simple Jack compilers, as we will do in the next two chapters. For example, when parsing a statement (in any language), it is much easier to handle the code if the first token of the statement indicates which statement we're in. That's why the Jack syntax includes the do and let keywords, and so on. Thus, although Jack's simplicity may be a nuisance when writing a *Jack application*, you will probably be quite grateful for it while writing the *Jack compiler* in the next two chapters.

Most modern languages are deployed with *standard libraries*, and so is Jack. As in Java and C#, this library can also be viewed as an interface to a simple and portable operating system. In the Jack-Hack platform, the services supplied by this OS are minimal. They include no concurrency to support multi-threading or multi-processing, no file system to support permanent storage, and no communication. At the same time, the Jack OS provides some classical OS services like graphic and textual I/O (in very basic forms), standard implementation of strings, and standard memory allocation and de-allocation. Additionally, the Jack OS implements various mathematical functions, including multiplication and division, normally implemented in hardware. We return to these issues in chapter 12, where we will build this simple operating system as the last module in our computer system.

9.5   Project

Objective   The hidden agenda of this project is to get acquainted with the Jack language, for two purposes: writing the Jack compiler in Projects 10 and 11, and writing the Jack operating system in Project 12.

Contract   Adopt or invent an application idea, for example, a simple computer game or some other interactive program. Then design and build the application.

Resources   You will need three tools: the Jack compiler, to translate your program into a set of .vm files, the VM emulator, to run and test your translated program, and the Jack Operating System.

The Jack OS   The Jack Operating System is available as a set of .vm files. These files constitute an implementation of the standard library of the Jack programming language. In order for any Jack program to execute properly, the compiled .vm files of the program must reside in a directory that also contains all the .vm files of the Jack OS. When an OS-oriented error is detected by the Jack OS, it displays a numeric error code (rather than text, which wastes precious memory space). A list of all the currently supported error codes and their textual descriptions can be found in the file projects/09/OSerrors.txt.

Compiling and Running a Jack Program

0.   Each program must be stored in a separate directory, say Xxx. Start by creating this directory, then copy all the files from tools/OS into it.

1.   Write your Jack program—a set of one or more Jack classes—each stored in a separate ClassName.jack text file. Put all these .jack files in the Xxx directory.

2.   Compile your program using the supplied Jack compiler. This is best done by applying the compiler to the name of the program directory (Xxx). This will cause the compiler to translate all the .jack classes found in the directory into corresponding .vm files. If a compilation error is reported, debug the program and recompile Xxx until no error messages are issued.

3.   At this point the program directory should contain three sets of files: (i) your source .jack files, (ii) the compiled .vm files, one for each of your .jack class files, and (iii) additional .vm files, comprising the supplied Jack OS. To test the compiled program, invoke the VM emulator and load the entire Xxx program directory. Then run the program. In case of run-time errors or undesired program behavior, fix the program and go to stage 2.

A Sample Jack Program   The book's software suite includes a complete example of a Jack application, stored in projects/09/Square. This directory contains the source Jack code of three classes comprising a simple interactive game.

10 Compiler I: Syntax Analysis

Neither can embellishments of language be found without arrangement and expression of thoughts, nor can thoughts be made to shine without the light of language.
—Cicero (106–43 BC)

The previous chapter introduced *Jack*—a simple object-based programming language whose syntax resembles that of Java and C#. In this chapter we start building a *compiler* for the Jack language. A compiler is a program that translates programs from a source language into a target language. The translation process, known as *compilation*, is conceptually based on two distinct tasks. First, we have to understand the *syntax* of the source program, and, from it, uncover the program's *semantics*. For example, the parsing of the code can reveal that the program seeks to declare an array or manipulate an object. This information enables us to reconstruct the program's logic using the syntax of the target language. The first task, typically called *syntax analysis*, is described in this chapter; the second task—*code generation*—is taken up in chapter 11.

How can we tell that a compiler is capable of "understanding" the language's syntax? Well, as long as the code generated by the compiler is doing what it is supposed to do, we can optimistically assume that the compiler is operating properly. Yet in this chapter we build only the *syntax analyzer* module of the compiler, with no code generation capabilities. If we wish to unit-test the syntax analyzer in isolation, we have to contrive some passive way to demonstrate that it "understands" the source program. Our solution is to have the syntax analyzer output an XML file whose format reflects the syntactic structure of the input program. By inspecting the generated XML output, we should be able to ascertain that the analyzer is parsing input programs correctly.

The chapter starts with a Background section that surveys the minimal set of concepts necessary for building a syntax analyzer: lexical analysis, context-free grammars, parse trees, and recursive descent algorithms for building them. This sets the stage for a Specification section that presents the formal grammar of the Jack language and the format of the output that a Jack analyzer is expected to generate. The Implementation section proposes a software architecture for constructing a Jack analyzer, along with a suggested API. As usual, the final Project section gives step-by-step instructions and test programs for actually building and testing the syntax analyzer. In the next chapter, this analyzer will be extended into a full-scale compiler.

Writing a compiler from scratch is a task that brings to bear several fundamental topics in computer science. It requires an understanding of language translation and parsing techniques, use of classical data structures like trees and hash tables, and application of sophisticated recursive compilation algorithms. For all these reasons, writing a compiler is also a challenging task. However, by splitting the compiler's construction into two separate projects (or actually *four*, counting the VM projects as well), and by allowing the modular development and unit-testing of each part in isolation, we have turned the compiler's development into a surprisingly manageable and self-contained activity.

Why should you go through the trouble of building a compiler? First, a hands-on grasp of compilation internals will turn you into a significantly better high-level programmer. Second, the same types of rules and grammars used for describing programming languages are also used for specifying the syntax of data sets in diverse applications ranging from computer graphics to database management to communications protocols to bioinformatics. Thus, while most programmers will not have to develop compilers in their careers, it is very likely that they will be required to parse and manipulate files of some complex syntax. These tasks will employ the same concepts and techniques used in the parsing of programming languages, as described in this chapter.

10.1   Background

A typical compiler consists of two main modules: *syntax analysis* and *code generation*. The syntax analysis task is usually divided further into two modules: *tokenizing*, or grouping of input characters into language atoms, and *parsing*, or attempting to match the resulting atoms stream to the syntax rules of the underlying language. Note that these activities are completely independent of the target language into which we seek to translate the source program. Since in this chapter we don't deal with code generation, we have chosen to have the syntax analyzer output the parsed structure of the compiled program as an XML file structured in a pre-defined way.

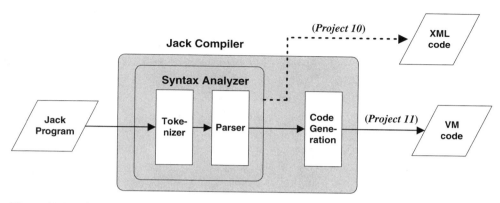

Figure 10.1   The Jack Compiler. The project in chapter 10 is an intermediate step, designed to localize the development and unit-testing of the *syntax analyzer* module.

This decision has two benefits. First, the XML file can be easily viewed in any Web browser, demonstrating that the syntax analyzer is parsing source programs correctly. Second, the requirement to output this file explicitly forces us to write the syntax analyzer in a software architecture that can be later morphed into a full-scale compiler. In particular, in the next chapter we will simply replace the routines that generate the passive XML code with routines that generate executable VM code, leaving the rest of the compiler's architecture intact (see figure 10.1).

In this chapter we focus only on the *syntax analyzer* module of the compiler, whose job is "understanding the structure of a program." This notion needs some explanation. When humans read a computer program, they immediately recognize the program's structure. They can identify where classes and methods begin and end, what are declarations, what are statements, what are expressions and how they are built, and so on. This understanding is not trivial, since it requires an ability to identify and classify nested patterns: In a typical program, classes contain methods that contain statements that contain other statements that contain expressions, and so on. In order to recognize these language constructs correctly, human cognition must recursively map them on the range of textual patterns permitted by the language syntax.

When it comes to understanding a natural language like English, the question of how syntax rules are represented in the human brain and whether they are innate or acquired is a subject of intense debate. However, if we limit our attention to *formal languages*—artifacts whose simplicity hardly justifies the title "language"—we know precisely how to formalize their syntactic structure. In particular, programming languages are usually described using a set of rules called *context-free grammar*. To understand—*parse*—a given program means to determine the exact correspondence between the program's text and the grammar's rules. In order to do so, we first have to transform the program's text into a list of *tokens*, as we now describe.

10.1.1   Lexical Analysis

In its plainest syntactic form, a program is simply a sequence of characters, stored in a text file. The first step in the syntax analysis of a program is to group the characters into *tokens* (as defined by the language syntax), while ignoring white space and comments. This step is usually called *lexical analysis, scanning,* or *tokenizing*. Once a program has been tokenized, the tokens (rather than the characters) are viewed as its basic atoms, and the tokens stream becomes the main input of the compiler. Figure 10.2 illustrates the tokenizing of a typical code fragment, taken from a C or Java program.

As seen in figure 10.2, tokens may be keywords, symbols, user-defined identifiers like variable names, and constants. In general, each programming language specifies the exact tokens it allows, as well as the exact syntax rules for combining them into valid and meaningful programmatic structures. For example, some languages may specify that "++" is a valid operator token, while other languages may not. In the latter case, an expression containing two consecutive "+" characters will be rendered invalid by the compiler.

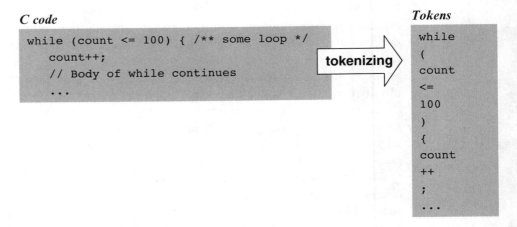

Figure 10.2   Lexical analysis.

10.1.2 Grammars

Once we have lexically analyzed a program into a stream of tokens, we now face the more challenging task of parsing the tokens stream into a formal structure. In other words, we have to figure out how to group the tokens into language constructs like variable declarations, statements, expressions, and so on. These grouping and classification tasks can be done by attempting to match the tokens stream on some pre-defined set of rules known as a *grammar*.

Almost all programming languages, as well as most other formal languages used for describing the syntax of complex file types, can be specified using formalisms known as *context-free grammars*. A context-free grammar is a set of rules specifying how syntactic elements in some language can be formed from simpler ones. For example, the Java grammar allows us to combine the atoms `100`, `count`, and `<=` into the expression `count<=100`. In a similar fashion, the Java grammar allows us to ascertain that the text `count<=100` is a valid Java expression. Indeed, each grammar has a dual perspective. From a declarative standpoint, the grammar specifies allowable ways to combine tokens, also called *terminals*, into higher-level syntactic elements, also called *non-terminals*. From an analytic standpoint, the grammar is a prescription for doing the reverse: parsing a given input (set of tokens resulting from the tokenizing phase) into non-terminals, lower-level non-terminals, and eventually terminals that cannot be decomposed any further. Figure 10.3 gives an example of a typical grammar.

In this chapter we specify grammars using the following notation: Terminal elements appear in bold text enclosed in single quotes, and non-terminal elements in regular font. When there is more than one way to parse a non-terminal, the "|" notation is used to list the alternative possibilities. Thus, figure 10.3 specifies that a *statement* can be either a *whileStatement*, or an *ifStatement*, and so on. Typically, grammar rules are highly recursive, and figure 10.3 is no exception. For example, *statementSequence* is either null, or a single *statement* followed by a semicolon and a *statementSequence*. This recursive definition can accommodate a sequence of 0, 1, 2, or any other number of semicolon-separated statements. As an exercise, the reader may use figure 10.3 to ascertain that the text appearing in the right side of the figure constitutes a valid C code. You may start by trying to match the entire text with *statement*, and work your way from there.

10.1.3 Parsing

The act of checking whether a grammar "accepts" an input text as valid is called *parsing*. As we noted earlier, parsing a given text means determining the exact

```
...
statement: whileStatement
         | ifStatement
         | ... // Other statement possibilities
         | '{' statementSequence '}'

whileStatement: 'while' '(' expression ')'
                    statement

ifStatement: ... // Definition of "if"

statementSequence: ''   // empty sequence (null)
                  | statement ';'
                    statementSequence
expression: ...       // Definition of "expression"
...                   // More definitions follow
```

```
while (expression) {
   statement;
   statement;
   while (expression) {
      while(expression)
           statement;
      statement;
   }
}
```

Figure 10.3 A subset of the C language grammar (left) and a sample code segment accepted by this grammar (right).

correspondence between the text and the rules of a given grammar. Since the grammar rules are hierarchical, the output generated by the parser can be described in a tree-oriented data structure called a *parse tree* or a *derivation tree*. Figure 10.4 gives a typical example.

Note that as a side effect of the parsing process, the entire syntactic structure of the input text is uncovered. Some compilers represent this tree by an explicit data structure that is further used for code generation and error reporting. Other compilers (including the one that we will build) represent the program's structure implicitly, generating code and reporting errors on the fly. Such compilers don't have to hold the entire program structure in memory, but only the subtree associated with the presently parsed element. More about this later.

Recursive Descent Parsing   There are several algorithms for constructing parse trees. The top-down approach, also called *recursive descent parsing*, attempts to parse the tokens stream recursively, using the nested structure prescribed by the language grammar. Let us consider how a *parser program* that implements this strategy can be written. For every rule in the grammar describing a non-terminal, we can equip the parser program with a recursive routine designed to parse that non-terminal. If the non-terminal consists of terminal atoms only, the routine can simply output them in

C code

```
while (count<=100) {
  count++;
  // ...
```

**Tokenized
(parser's input):**

```
while
(
count
<=
100
)
{
count
++
;
...
```

C language grammar (partial)

```
statement:  whileStatement | ifStatement
            | ... |    '{' statementSequence '}'
whileStatement: 'while' '(' expression ')'
                      statement
ifStatement: ... // Definition of "if"
statementSequence: '' // Null
              | statement ';' statementSequence
expression: ... // Definition of "expression"
```

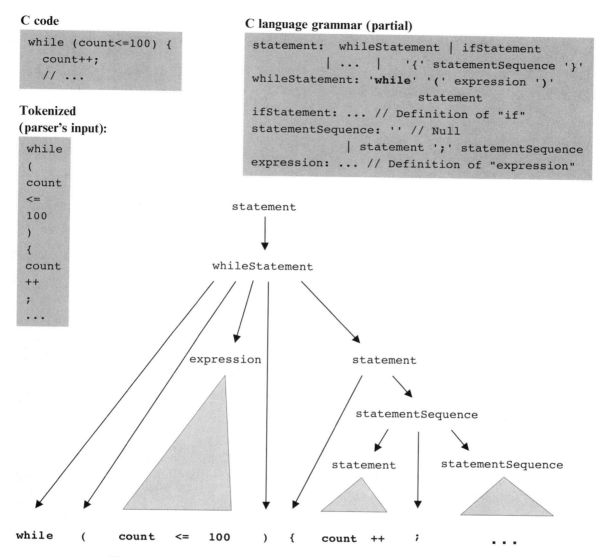

Figure 10.4 Parse tree of a program segment according to a grammar segment. Solid triangles represent lower-level parse trees.

some structured way. Otherwise, for every non-terminal building block in the rule's right-hand side, the routine can recursively call the routine designed to parse this non-terminal. The process will continue recursively, until all the terminal atoms have been reached and processed.

To illustrate, suppose we have to write a recursive descent parser that follows the grammar from figure 10.3. Since the grammar has five derivation rules, the parser implementation can consist of five major routines: `parseStatement()`, `parse-WhileStatement()`, `parseIfStatement()`, `parseStatementSequence()`, and `parseExpression()`. The parsing logic of these routines should follow the syntactic patterns appearing in the right-hand sides of the corresponding grammar rules. Thus `parseStatement()` should probably start its processing by determining what is the first token in the input. Having established the token's identity, the routine could determine which statement we are in, and then call the parsing routine associated with this statement type.

For example, if the input stream were that depicted in figure 10.4, the routine will establish that the first token is `while`, then call the `parseWhileStatement()` routine. According to the corresponding grammar rule, this routine should next attempt to read the terminals "`while`" and "`(`", and then call `parseExpression()` to parse the non-terminal *expression*. After `parseExpression()` would return (having parsed the "`count<=100`" sequence in our example), the grammar dictates that `parseWhileStatement()` should attempt to read the terminal "`)`" and then recursively call `parseStatement()`. This call would continue recursively, until at some point only terminal atoms are read. Clearly, the same logic can also be used for detecting syntax errors in the source program. The better the compiler, the better will be its error diagnostics.

LL(1) Grammars Recursive parsing algorithms are simple and elegant. The only possible complication arises when there are several alternatives for parsing non-terminals. For example, when `parseStatement()` attempts to parse a statement, it does not know in advance whether this statement is a while-statement, an if-statement, or a bunch of statements enclosed in curly brackets. The span of possibilities is determined by the grammar, and in some cases it is easy to tell which alternative we are in. For example, consider figure 10.3. If the first token is "`while`," it is clear that we are faced with a *while statement*, since this is the only alternative in the grammar that starts with a "`while`" token. This observation can be generalized as follows: whenever a non-terminal has several alternative derivation rules, the first token suffices to resolve without ambiguity which rule to use. Grammars that have this property are called LL(1). These grammars can be handled simply and neatly by recursive descent algorithms.

When the first token does not suffice to resolve the element's type, it is possible that a "look ahead" to the next token will settle the dilemma. Such parsing can obviously be done, but as we need to look ahead at more and more tokens down the stream, things start getting complicated. The Jack language grammar, which we now turn to present, is almost LL(1), and thus it can be handled rather simply by a recursive descent parser. The only exception is the parsing of expressions, where just a little look ahead is necessary.

10.2   Specification

This section has two distinct parts. First, we specify the Jack language's *grammar*. Next, we specify a *syntax analyzer* designed to parse programs according to this grammar.

10.2.1   The Jack Language Grammar

The functional specification of the Jack language given in chapter 9 was aimed at Jack programmers. We now turn to giving a formal specification of the language, aimed at Jack compiler developers. Our grammar specification is based on the following conventions:

'xxx':   quoted boldface is used for tokens that appear verbatim ("terminals");

xxx: regular typeface is used for names of language constructs ("non-terminals");

():   parentheses are used for grouping of language constructs;

x|y: indicates that either x or y can appear;

x?:   indicates that x appears 0 or 1 times;

x*:   indicates that x appears 0 or more times.

The Jack language syntax is given in figure 10.5, using the preceding conventions.

10.2.2   A Syntax Analyzer for the Jack Language

The main purpose of the syntax analyzer is to read a Jack program and "understand" its syntactic structure according to the Jack grammar. By understanding, we

Lexical elements:	The Jack language includes five types of terminal elements (tokens):
keyword:	`'class'` | `'constructor'` | `'function'` | `'method'` | `'field'` | `'static'` | `'var'` | `'int'` | `'char'` | `'boolean'` | `'void'` | `'true'` | `'false'` | `'null'` | `'this'` | `'let'` | `'do'` | `'if'` | `'else'` | `'while'` | `'return'`
symbol:	`'{'` | `'}'` | `'('` | `')'` | `'['` | `']'` | `'.'` | `','` | `';'` | `'+'` | `'-'` | `'*'` | `'/'` | `'&'` | `'|'` | `'<'` | `'>'` | `'='` | `'~'`
integerConstant:	A decimal number in the range 0 .. 32767.
StringConstant	`'"'` A sequence of Unicode characters not including double quote or newline `'"'`
identifier:	A sequence of letters, digits, and underscore (`'_'`) not starting with a digit.

Program structure:	A Jack program is a collection of classes, each appearing in a separate file. The compilation unit is a class. A class is a sequence of tokens structured according to the following context free syntax:
class:	`'class'` className `'{'` classVarDec* subroutineDec* `'}'`
classVarDec:	(`'static'` | `'field'`) type varName (`','` varName)* `';'`
type:	`'int'` | `'char'` | `'boolean'` | className
subroutineDec:	(`'constructor'` | `'function'` | `'method'`) (`'void'` | type) subroutineName `'('` parameterList `')'` subroutineBody
parameterList:	((type varName) (`','` type varName)*)?
subroutineBody:	`'{'` varDec* statements `'}'`
varDec:	`'var'` type varName (`','` varName)* `';'`
className:	identifier
subroutineName:	identifier
varName:	identifier

Figure 10.5   Complete grammar of the Jack language.

Statements:

statements:	statement*
statement:	letStatement | ifStatement | whileStatement | doStatement | returnStatement
letStatement:	**'let'** varName (**'['** expression **']'**)? **'='** expression **';'**
ifStatement:	**'if'** **'('** expression **')'** **'{'** statements **'}'** (**'else'** **'{'** statements **'}'**)?
whileStatement:	**'while'** **'('** expression **')'** **'{'** statements **'}'**
doStatement:	**'do'** subroutineCall **';'**
ReturnStatement	**'return'** expression? **';'**

Expressions:

expression:	term (op term)*
term:	integerConstant | stringConstant | keywordConstant | varName | varName **'['** expression **']'** | subroutineCall | **'('** expression **')'** | unaryOp term
subroutineCall:	subroutineName **'('** expressionList **')'** | (className | varName) **'.'** subroutineName **'('** expressionList **')'**
expressionList:	(expression (**','** expression)*)?
op:	**'+'** | **'-'** | **'*'** | **'/'** | **'&'** | **'|'** | **'<'** | **'>'** | **'='**
unaryOp:	**'-'** | **'~'**
KeywordConstant:	**'true'** | **'false'** | **'null'** | **'this'**

Figure 10.5 (continued)

mean that the syntax analyzer must know, at each point in the parsing process, the structural identity of the program element that it is currently reading, namely, whether it is an *expression*, a *statement*, a *variable name*, and so on. The syntax analyzer must possess this syntactic knowledge in a complete recursive sense. Without it, it will be impossible to move on to code generation—the ultimate goal of the overall compiler.

The fact that the syntax analyzer "understands" the programmatic structure of the input can be demonstrated by having it print the processed text in some well-structured and easy-to-read format. One can think of several ways to cook up such a demonstration. In this book, we decided to have the syntax analyzer output an XML file whose marked-up format reflects the syntactic structure of the underlying program. By inspecting this XML output file—a task that can be conveniently done with any Web browser—one should be able to tell right away if the syntax analyzer is doing the job or not.

10.2.3   The Syntax Analyzer's Input

The Jack syntax analyzer accepts a single command line parameter, as follows:

```
prompt> JackAnalyzer source
```

Where *source* is either a file name of the form `Xxx.jack` (the extension is mandatory) or a directory name containing one or more `.jack` files (in which case there is no extension). The syntax analyzer compiles the `Xxx.jack` file into a file named `Xxx.xml`, created in the same directory in which the source file is located. If *source* is a directory name, each `.jack` file located in it is compiled, creating a corresponding `.xml` file in the same directory.

Each `Xxx.jack` file is a stream of characters. This stream should be tokenized into a stream of tokens according to the rules specified by the *lexical elements* of the Jack language (see figure 10.5, top). The tokens may be separated by an arbitrary number of space characters, newline characters, and comments, which are ignored. Comments are of the standard formats `/* comment until closing */`, `/** API comment */`, and `// comment to end of line`.

10.2.4   The Syntax Analyzer's Output

Recall that the development of the Jack compiler is split into two stages (see figure 10.1), starting with the syntax analyzer. In this chapter, we want the syntax analyzer to emit an XML description of the input program, as illustrated in figure 10.6. In order to do so, the syntax analyzer has to recognize two major types of language constructs: terminal and non-terminal elements. These constructs are handled as follows.

Terminals   Whenever a terminal language element of type *xxx* is encountered, the syntax analyzer should generate the following marked-up output:

⟨*xxx*⟩ terminal ⟨/*xxx*⟩

    Where *xxx* is one of the five lexical elements of the Jack language: namely, `keyword`, `symbol`, `integerConstant`, `stringConstant`, or `identifier`.

Non-Terminals   Whenever a non-terminal language element of type *xxx* is encountered, the syntax analyzer should generate marked-up output, using the following pseudo-code:

print ⟨*xxx*⟩
Recursive code for the body of the *xxx* element.
print ⟨/*xxx*⟩

Where *xxx* is one of the following (and only the following) non-terminals of the Jack grammar:

- `class, classVarDec, subroutineDec, parameterList, subroutineBody, varDec;`

- `statements, whileSatement, ifStatement, returnStatement, letStatement, doStatement;`

- `expression, term, expressionList.`

    Figure 10.6, which shows the analyzer's output, should evoke some sense of déjà vu. Earlier in the chapter we noted that the structure of a program can be analyzed into a *parse tree*. And indeed, XML output is simply a textual description of a tree. In particular, note that in a parse tree, the non-terminal nodes form a "super structure" that describes how the tree's terminal nodes (the *tokens*) are grouped into language constructs. This pattern is mirrored in the XML output, where non-terminal XML elements describe how terminal XML items are arranged. In a similar fashion, the tokens generated by the tokenizer form the lowest level of the XML output, just as they form the terminal leaves of the program's parse tree.

Analyzer's input (Jack code)

```
Class Bar {
  method Fraction foo(int y) {
    var int temp; // a variable
    let temp = (xxx+12)*-63;
    ...
```

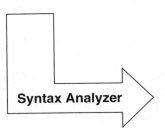

Syntax Analyzer

Analyzer's output (XML code)

```
<class>
  <keyword> class </keyword>
  <identifier> Bar </identifier>
  <symbol> { </symbol>
  <subroutineDec>
    <keyword> method </keyword>
    <identifier> Fraction </identifier>
    <identifier> foo </identifier>
    <symbol> ( </symbol>
    <parameterList>
      <keyword> int </keyword>
      <identifier> y </identifier>
    </parameterList>
    <symbol> ) </symbol>
    <subroutineBody>
      <symbol> { </symbol>
      <varDec>
        <keyword> var </keyword>
        <keyword> int </keyword>
        <identifier> temp </identifier>
        <symbol> ; </symbol>
      </varDec>
      <statements>
        <letStatement>
          <keyword> let </keyword>
          <identifier> temp </identifier>
          <symbol> = </symbol>
          <expression>
          ...
          </expression>
          <symbol> ; </symbol>
          ...
```

Figure 10.6   Jack Analyzer in action.

Code Generation   We have just finished specifying the analyzer's XML output. In the next chapter we'll replace the software that generates this output with software that generates executable VM code, leading to a full-scale Jack compiler.

10.3   Implementation

Section 10.2 described how to build a *syntax analyzer* for the Jack language, without any implementation details. This section describes a proposed software architecture for the syntax analyzer. We suggest arranging the implementation in three modules:

- `JackAnalyzer`:   top-level driver that sets up and invokes the other modules;
- `JackTokenizer`:   tokenizer;
- `CompilationEngine`:   recursive top-down parser.

These modules are designed to handle the language's syntax. In the next chapter we extend this architecture with two additional modules that handle the language's semantics: a *symbol table* and a *VM-code writer*. This will complete the construction of a full-scale compiler for the Jack language. Since the module that drives the parsing process in this project will also drive the overall compilation in the next project, we call it `CompilationEngine`.

10.3.1   *The JackAnalyzer* Module

The analyzer program operates on a given *source*, where *source* is either a file name of the form `Xxx.jack` or a directory name containing one or more such files. For each source `Xxx.jack` file, the analyzer goes through the following logic:

1.   Create a *JackTokenizer* from the `Xxx.jack` input file.

2.   Create an *output file* called `Xxx.xml` and prepare it for writing.

3.   Use the *CompilationEngine* to compile the input *JackTokenizer* into the *output file*.

10.3.2   The *JackTokenizer* Module

JackTokenizer: Removes all comments and white space from the input stream and breaks it into Jack-language tokens, as specified by the Jack grammar.

Routine	Arguments	Returns	Function
Constructor	input file/ stream	—	Opens the input file/stream and gets ready to tokenize it.
hasMoreTokens	—	Boolean	Do we have more tokens in the input?
advance	—	—	Gets the next token from the input and makes it the current token. This method should only be called if *hasMoreTokens( )* is true. Initially there is no current token.
tokenType	—	KEYWORD, SYMBOL, IDENTIFIER, INT_CONST, STRING_CONST	Returns the type of the current token.
keyWord	—	CLASS, METHOD, FUNCTION, CONSTRUCTOR, INT, BOOLEAN, CHAR, VOID, VAR, STATIC, FIELD, LET, DO, IF, ELSE, WHILE, RETURN, TRUE, FALSE, NULL, THIS	Returns the keyword which is the current token. Should be called only when tokenType( ) is KEYWORD.
symbol	—	Char	Returns the character which is the current token. Should be called only when tokenType( ) is SYMBOL.
identifier	—	String	Returns the identifier which is the current token. Should be called only when tokenType( ) is IDENTIFIER.
intVal		Int	Returns the integer value of the current token. Should be called only when tokenType( ) is INT_CONST.

Routine	Arguments	Returns	Function
`stringVal`		String	Returns the string value of the current token, without the double quotes. Should be called only when `tokenType()` is STRING_CONST.

10.3.3 The *CompilationEngine* Module

CompilationEngine: Effects the actual compilation output. Gets its input from a `JackTokenizer` and emits its parsed structure into an output file/stream. The output is generated by a series of `compilexxx()` routines, one for every syntactic element `xxx` of the Jack grammar. The contract between these routines is that each `compilexxx()` routine should read the syntactic construct `xxx` from the input, `advance()` the tokenizer exactly beyond `xxx`, and output the parsing of `xxx`. Thus, `compilexxx()` may only be called if indeed `xxx` is the next syntactic element of the input.

In the first version of the compiler, described in this chapter, this module emits a structured printout of the code, wrapped in XML tags. In the final version of the compiler, described in chapter 11, this module generates executable VM code. In both cases, the parsing logic and module API are exactly the same.

Routine	Arguments	Returns	Function
Constructor	Input stream/file Output stream/file	—	Creates a new compilation engine with the given input and output. The next routine called must be `compileClass()`.
`CompileClass`	—	—	Compiles a complete class.
`CompileClassVarDec`	—	—	Compiles a static declaration or a field declaration.
`CompileSubroutine`	—	—	Compiles a complete method, function, or constructor.
`compileParameterList`	—	—	Compiles a (possibly empty) parameter list, not including the enclosing "`()`".

Routine	Arguments	Returns	Function
compileVarDec	—	—	Compiles a var declaration.
compileStatements	—	—	Compiles a sequence of statements, not including the enclosing "{}".
compileDo	—	—	Compiles a do statement.
compileLet	—	—	Compiles a let statement.
compileWhile	—	—	Compiles a while statement.
compileReturn	—	—	Compiles a return statement.
compileIf	—	—	Compiles an if statement, possibly with a trailing else clause.
CompileExpression	—	—	Compiles an expression.
CompileTerm	—	—	Compiles a *term*. This routine is faced with a slight difficulty when trying to decide between some of the alternative parsing rules. Specifically, if the current token is an identifier, the routine must distinguish between a variable, an array entry, and a subroutine call. A single look-ahead token, which may be one of "[", "(", or "." suffices to distinguish between the three possibilities. Any other token is not part of this term and should not be advanced over.
CompileExpressionList	—	—	Compiles a (possibly empty) comma-separated list of expressions.

10.4 Perspective

Although it is convenient to describe the structure of computer programs using parse trees and XML files, it's important to understand that compilers don't necessarily have to maintain such data structures explicitly. For example, the parsing algorithm described in this chapter runs "on-line," meaning that it parses the input as it reads it and does not keep the entire input program in memory. There are essentially two types of strategies for doing such parsing. The simpler strategy works top-down, and this is the one presented in this chapter. The more advanced algorithms, which work bottom-up, are not described here since they require some elaboration of theory.

Indeed, in this chapter we have sidestepped almost all the formal language theory studied in typical compilation courses. We were able to do so by choosing a very simple syntax for the Jack language—a syntax that can be easily compiled using recursive descent techniques. For example, the Jack grammar does not mandate the usual operator precedence in expressions evaluation (multiplication before addition, and so on). This has enabled us to avoid parsing algorithms that are more powerful yet much more technical than the elegant top-down parsing techniques presented in the chapter.

Another topic that was hardly mentioned in the chapter is how the syntax of languages is specified in general. There is a rich theory called *formal languages* that discusses properties of classes of languages, as well as metalanguages and formalisms for specifying them. This is also the point where computer science meets the study of human languages, leading to the vibrant area of research known as *computational linguistics*.

Finally, it is worth mentioning that syntax analyzers are not stand-alone programs, and are rarely written from scratch. Instead, programmers usually build tokenizers and parsers using a variety of "compiler generator" tools like *LEX* (for *lexical analysis*) and *YACC* (for *Yet Another Compiler Compiler*). These utilities receive as input a context-free grammar, and produce as output syntax analysis code capable of tokenizing and parsing programs written in that grammar. The generated code can then be customized to fit the specific compilation needs of the application at hand. Following the "show me" spirit of this book, we have chosen not to use such black boxes in the implementation of our compiler, but rather to build everything from the ground up.

10.5   Project

The compiler construction spans two projects: 10 and 11. This section describes how to build the syntax analyzer described in this chapter. In the next chapter we extend this analyzer into a full-scale Jack compiler.

Objective   Build a syntax analyzer that parses Jack programs according to the Jack grammar. The analyzer's output should be written in XML, as defined in the specification section.

Resources   The main tool in this project is the programming language in which you will implement the syntax analyzer. You will also need the supplied `TextComparer` utility, which allows comparing the output files generated by your analyzer to the compare files supplied by us. You may also want to inspect the generated and supplied output files using an XML viewer (any standard Web browser should do the job).

Contract   Write the syntax analyzer program in two stages: tokenizing and parsing. Use it to parse all the `.jack` files mentioned here. For each source `.jack` file, your analyzer should generate an `.xml` output file. The generated files should be identical to the `.xml` compare-files supplied by us.

Test Programs

The syntax analyzer's job is to parse programs written in the Jack language. Thus, a reasonable way to test your analyzer it is to have it parse several representative Jack programs. We supply two such test programs, called *Square Dance* and *Array Test*. The former includes all the features of the Jack language except for array processing, which appears in the latter. We also provide a *simpler version* of the *Square Dance* program, as explained in what follows.

For each one of the three programs, we supply all the Jack source files comprising the program. For each such `Xxx.jack` file, we supply two compare files named `XxxT.xml` and `Xxx.xml`. These files contain, respectively, the output that should be produced by a *tokenizer* and by a *parser* applied to `Xxx.jack`.

■   *Square Dance* (`projects/10/Square`): A trivial interactive "game" that enables moving a black square around the screen using the keyboard's four arrow keys.

▪ *Expressionless Square Dance* (`projects/10/ExpressionlessSquare`): An identical copy of *Square Dance*, except that each expression in the original program is replaced with a single identifier (some variable name in scope). For example, the `Square` class has a method that increases the size of the graphical square object by 2 pixels, as long as the new size does not cause the square image to spill over the screen's boundaries. The code of this method is as follows.

Square Class Code

```
method void incSize() {
  if (((y + size) < 254) &
      ((x + size) < 510)) {
    do erase();
    let size = size + 2;
    do draw();
  }
  return;
}
```

ExpressionlessSquare Class Code

```
method void incSize() {
  if (x) {
    do erase();
    let size=size;
    do draw();
  }
  return;
}
```

Note that the replacement of expressions with variables has resulted in a nonsensical program that cannot be compiled by the supplied Jack compiler. Still, it follows all the Jack grammar rules. The expressionless class files have the same names as those of the original files, but they are located in a separate directory.

▪ *Array test* (`projects/10/ArrayTest`): A single-class Jack program that computes the average of a user-supplied sequence of integers using array notation and array manipulation.

Experimenting with the Test Programs   If you want, you can compile the *Square Dance* and *ArrayTest* programs using the supplied Jack compiler, then use the supplied VM emulator to run the compiled code. These activities are completely irrelevant to this project, but they serve to highlight the fact that the test programs are not just plain text (although this is perhaps the best way to think about them in the context of this project).

Stage 1: Tokenizer

First, implement the `JackTokenizer` module specified in section 10.3. When applied to a text file containing Jack code, the tokenizer should produce a list of tokens, each printed in a separate line along with its classification: *symbol, keyword, identifier, integer constant*, or *string constant*. The classification should be recorded using XML tags. Here is an example:

Source Code

```
if (x < 153)
   {let city="Paris";}
```

Tokenizer Output

```
<tokens>
  <keyword> if </keyword>
  <symbol> ( </symbol>
  <identifier> x </identifier>
  <symbol> &lt; </symbol>
  <integerConstant> 153
  </integerConstant>
  <symbol> ) </symbol>
  <symbol> { </symbol>
  <keyword> let </keyword>
  <identifier> city </identifier>
  <symbol> = </symbol>
  <stringConstant> Paris
  </stringConstant>
  <symbol> ; </symbol>
  <symbol> } </symbol>
</tokens>
```

Note that in the case of *string constants*, the tokenizer throws away the double quote characters. That's intentional.

The tokenizer's output has two "peculiarities" dictated by XML conventions. First, an XML file must be enclosed in some begin and end tags, and that's why the `<tokens>` and `</tokens>` tags were added to the output. Second, three of the symbols used in the Jack language (<, >, &) are also used for XML markup, and thus they cannot appear as data in XML files. To solve the problem, we require the tokenizer to output these tokens as `&lt;`, `&gt;`, and `&amp;`, respectively. For example, in order for the text "`<symbol> < </symbol>`" to be displayed properly in a Web browser, the source XML should be written as "`<symbol> &lt; </symbol>`."

Testing Your Tokenizer

■ Test your tokenizer on the *Square Dance* and *Test Array* programs. There is no need to test it on the expressionless version of the former.

- For each source file `Xxx.jack`, have your tokenizer give the output file the name `XxxT.xml`. Apply your tokenizer to every class file in the test programs, then use the supplied `TextComparer` utility to compare the generated output to the supplied `.xml` compare files.

- Since the output files generated by your tokenizer will have the same names and extensions as those of the supplied compare files, we suggest putting them in separate directories.

Stage 2: Parser

Next, implement the `CompilationEngine` module specified in section 10.3. Write each method of the engine, as specified in the API, and make sure that it emits the correct XML output. We recommend to start by writing a compilation engine that handles everything except expressions, and test it on the *expressionless Square Dance* program only. Next, extend the parser to handle expressions as well, and proceed to test it on the *Square Dance* and *Array Test* programs.

Testing Your Parser

- Apply your `CompilationEngine` to the supplied test programs, then use the supplied `TextComparer` utility to compare the generated output to the supplied `.xml` compare files.

- Since the output files generated by your analyzer will have the same names and extensions as those of the supplied compare files, we suggest putting them in separate directories.

- Note that the indentation of the XML output is only for readability. Web browsers and the supplied *TextComparer* utility ignore white space.

11   Compiler II: Code Generation

The syntactic component of a grammar must specify, for each sentence, a deep structure that determines its semantic interpretation.
—Noam Chomsky (b. 1928), mathematical linguist

Most programmers take compilers for granted. But if you'll stop to think about it for a moment, the ability to translate a high-level program into binary code is almost like magic. In this book we demystify this transformation by writing a compiler for *Jack*—a simple yet modern object-based language. As with Java and C#, the overall Jack compiler is based on two tiers: a virtual machine *back-end*, developed in chapters 7–8, and a typical *front-end* module, designed to bridge the gap between the high-level language and the VM language. The compiler's front-end module consists of a *syntax analyzer*, developed in chapter 10, and a *code generator*—the subject of this chapter.

Although the compiler's front-end comprises two conceptual modules, they are usually combined into a single program, as we will do here. Specifically, in chapter 10 we built a syntax analyzer capable of "understanding"—parsing—source Jack programs. In this chapter we extend the analyzer into a full-scale compiler that converts each "understood" high-level construct into an equivalent series of VM operations. This approach follows the modular *analysis-synthesis* paradigm underlying the construction of most compilers.

Modern high-level programming languages are rich and powerful. They allow defining and using elaborate abstractions such as objects and functions, implementing algorithms using elegant flow of control statements, and building data structures of unlimited complexity. In contrast, the target platforms on which these programs eventually run are spartan and minimal. Typically, they offer nothing more than a vector of registers for storage and a primitive instruction set for processing. Thus, the translation of programs from high-level to low-level is an interesting brain teaser.

If the target platform is a virtual machine, life is somewhat easier, but still the gap between the expressiveness of a high-level language and that of a virtual machine is wide and challenging.

The chapter begins with a Background section covering the minimal set of topics necessary for completing the compiler's development: managing a symbol table; representing and generating code for variables, objects, and arrays; and translating control flow commands into low-level instructions. The Specification section defines how to map the semantics of Jack programs on the VM platform and language, and the Implementation section proposes an API for a code generation module that performs this transformation. The chapter ends with the usual Project section, providing step-by-step guidelines and test programs for completing the compiler's construction.

So what's in it for *you?* Typically, students who don't take a formal compilation course don't have an opportunity to develop a full-scale compiler. Thus readers who follow our instructions and build the Jack compiler from scratch will gain an important lesson for a relatively small effort (of course, their knowledge of compilation theory will remain limited unless they take a course on the subject). Further, some of the tricks and techniques used in the code generation part of the compiler are rather clever. Seeing these tricks in action leads one to marvel, once again, at how human ingenuity can dress up a primitive switching machine to look like something approaching magic.

11.1   Background

A program is essentially a series of operations that manipulate data. Thus, the compilation of high-level programs into a low-level language focuses on two main issues: *data translation* and *command translation*.

The overall compilation task entails translation all the way to binary code. However, since we are focusing on a two-tier compiler architecture, we assume throughout this chapter that the compiler generates VM code. Therefore, we do not touch low-level issues that have already been dealt with at the Virtual Machine level (chapters 7 and 8).

11.1.1   Data Translation

Programs manipulate many *types* of variables, including simple types like integers and booleans and complex types like arrays and objects. Another dimension of interest is the variables' *kind* of life cycle and *scope*—namely, whether it is local, global, an argument, an object field, and so forth.

For each variable encountered in the program, the compiler must map the variable on an equivalent representation suitable to accommodate its *type* in the target platform. In addition, the compiler must manage the variable's life cycle and scope, as implied by its *kind*. This section describes how compilers handle these tasks, beginning with the notion of a *symbol table*.

Symbol Table   High-level programs introduce and manipulate many *identifiers*. Whenever the compiler encounters an identifier, say xxx, it needs to know what xxx stands for. Is it a variable name, a class name, or a function name? If it's a variable, is xxx a field of an object, or an argument of a function? What type of variable is it—an integer, a boolean, a char, or perhaps some class type? The compiler must resolve these questions before it can represent xxx's semantics in the target language. Further, all these questions must be answered (for code generation) each time xxx is encountered in the source code.

Clearly, there is a need to keep track of all the identifiers introduced by the program, and, for each one, to record what the identifier stands for in the source program and on which construct it is mapped in the target language. Most compilers maintain this information using a *symbol table* abstraction. Whenever a new identifier is encountered in the source code for the first time (e.g., in a variable declaration), the compiler adds its description to the table. Whenever an identifier is encountered elsewhere in the code, the compiler looks it up in the symbol table and gets all the necessary information about it. Here is a typical example:

Symbol table (of some hypothetical subroutine)

Name	Type	Kind	#
nAccounts	int	static	0
id	int	field	0
name	String	field	1
balance	int	field	2
sum	int	argument	0
status	boolean	local	0

The symbol table is the "Rosetta stone" that the compiler uses when translating high-level code involving identifiers. For example, consider the statement balance=

`balance+sum`. Using the symbol table, the compiler can translate this statement into code reflecting the facts that `balance` is field number 2 of the current object, while `sum` is argument number 0 of the running subroutine. Other details of this translation will depend on the target language.

The basic symbol table abstraction is complicated slightly due to the fact that most languages permit different program units to use the same identifiers to represent completely different things. In order to enable this freedom of expression, each identifier is implicitly associated with a *scope*, namely, the region of the program in which the identifier is recognized. The scopes are typically nested, the convention being that inner-scoped definitions hide outer ones. For example, if the statement x++ appears in some C function, the C compiler first checks whether the identifier x is declared locally in the current function, and if so, generates code that increments the local variable. Otherwise, the compiler checks whether x is declared globally in the file, and if so, generates code that increments the global variable. The depth of this scoping convention is potentially unlimited, since some languages permit defining variables which are local only to the block of code in which they are declared.

Thus, we see that in addition to all the relevant information that must be kept about each identifier, the symbol table must also record in some way the identifier's *scope*. The classic data structure for this purpose is a *list of hash tables*, each reflecting a single scope nested within the next one in the list. When the compiler fails to find the identifier in the table associated with the current scope, it looks it up in the next table in the list, from inner scopes outward. Thus if x appears undeclared in a certain code segment (e.g., a method), it may be that x is declared in the code segment that owns the current segment (e.g., a class), and so on.

Handling Variables   One of the basic challenges faced by every compiler is how to map the various types of variables declared in the source program onto the memory of the target platform. This is not a trivial task. First, different *types* of variables require different sizes of memory chunks, so the mapping is not one-to-one. Second, different *kinds* of variables have different life cycles. For example, a single copy of each static variable should be kept alive during the complete duration of the program's run-time. In contrast, each object instance of a class should have a different copy of all its instance variables (*fields*), and, when disposed, the object's memory should be recycled. Also, each time a subroutine is being called, new copies of its local and argument variables must be created—a need that is clearly seen in recursion.

That's the bad news. The good news is that we have already handled all these difficulties. In our two-tier compiler architecture, memory allocation of variables was delegated to the VM back-end. In particular, the virtual machine that we built in chapters 7–8 includes built-in mechanisms for accommodating the standard kinds of variables needed by most high-level languages: *static*, *local*, and *argument* variables, as well as *fields* of objects. All the allocation and de-allocation details of these variables were already handled at the VM level, using the global stack and the virtual memory segments.

Recall that this functionality was not achieved easily. In fact, we had to work rather hard to build a VM implementation that maps the global stack and the virtual memory segments on the ultimate hardware platform. Yet this effort was worth our while: For any given language L, any L-to-VM compiler is now completely relieved from low-level memory management. The only thing required from the compiler is mapping the variables found in the source program on the virtual memory segments and expressing the high-level commands that manipulate them using VM commands—a rather simple translation task.

Handling Arrays   *Arrays* are almost always stored as sequences of consecutive memory locations (multi-dimensional arrays are flattened into one-dimensional ones). The array name is usually treated as a pointer to the base address of the RAM block allocated to store the array in memory. In some languages like Pascal, the entire memory space necessary to represent the array is allocated when the array is declared. In other languages like Java, the array declaration results in the allocation of a single pointer only, which, eventually, may point to the array's base address. The array proper is created in memory later, if and when the array is actually constructed at run-time. This type of *dynamic memory allocation* is done from the heap, using the memory management services of the operating system. Typically, the OS has an `alloc(size)` function that knows how to find an available memory block of size `size` and return its base address to the caller. Thus, when compiling a high-level statement like `bar=new int[10]`, the compiler generates low-level code that effects the operation `bar=alloc(10)`. This results in assigning the base-address of the array's memory block to `bar`, which is exactly what we want. Figure 11.1 offers a snapshot of this practice.

Let us consider how the compiler translates the statement `bar[k]=19`. Since the symbol `bar` points to the array's base-address, this statement can be also expressed using the C-language notation `*(bar+k)=19`, that is, "store 19 in the memory cell whose address is `bar+k`." In order to implement this operation, the target language must be equipped with some sort of an indirect addressing mechanism. Specifically, instead of storing a value in some memory location y, we need to be able to store the value in the memory location whose address is the current contents of y. Different

Java code

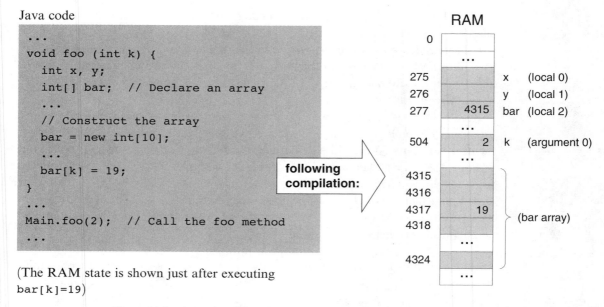

(The RAM state is shown just after executing
`bar[k]=19`)

Figure 11.1 Array handling. Since memory allocations are run-time dependent, all the shown addresses are arbitrary examples.

languages have different means to carry out this pointer arithmetic, and figure 11.2 shows two possibilities.

Handling Objects   Object instances of a certain class, say *Employee*, are said to encapsulate data items like *name* and *salary*, as well as a set of operations (methods) that manipulate them. The data and the operations are handled quite differently by the compiler. Let's start with the data.

The low-level handling of object data is quite similar to that of arrays, storing the fields of each object instance in consecutive memory locations. In most object-oriented languages, when a class-type variable is declared, the compiler only allocates a pointer variable. The memory space for the object proper is allocated later, if and when the object is actually created via a call to a class constructor. Thus, when compiling a constructor of some class xxx, the compiler first uses the number and type of the class fields to determine how many words—say *n*—are necessary to represent an object instance of type xxx on the host RAM. Next, the compiler generates the code necessary for allocating memory for the newly constructed object, for example, `this=alloc(n)`. This operation sets the `this` pointer to the base address of

Pseudo VM code

```
// bar[k]=19, or *(bar+k)=19
push bar
push k
add
// Use a pointer to access x[k]
pop addr // addr points to bar[k]
push 19
pop *addr // Set bar[k] to 19
```

Final VM code

```
// bar[k]=19, or *(bar+k)=19
push local 2
push argument 0
add
// Use the that segment to access x[k]
pop pointer 1
push constant 19
pop that 0
```

Figure 11.2   Array processing. The Hack VM code (right) follows the conventions described in section 7.2.6.

the memory block that represents the new object, which is exactly what we want. Figure 11.3 illustrates these operations in a Java context.

Since each object is represented by a pointer variable that contains its base-address, the data encapsulated by the object can be accessed linearly, using an index relative to its base. For example, suppose that the Complex class includes the following method:

```
public void mult (int c) {
  re = re * c;
  im = im * c;
}
```

How should the compiler handle the statement im = im * c? Well, an inspection of the symbol table will tell the compiler that im is the second field of this object and that c is the first argument of the mult method. Using this information, the compiler can translate im = im * c into code effecting the operation *(this + 1) = *(this + 1) times (argument 0). Of course, the generated code will have to accomplish this operation using the target language.

Suppose now that we wish to apply the mult method to the b object, using a method call like b.mult(5). How should the compiler handle this method call? Unlike the fields data (e.g., re and im), of which *different copies* are kept for each object instance, only *one copy* of each method (e.g., mult) is actually kept at the target code level for *all* the object instances derived from this class. In order to make it look as if each object encapsulates its own code, the compiler must force this single method to always operate on the desired object. The standard compilation

Java code

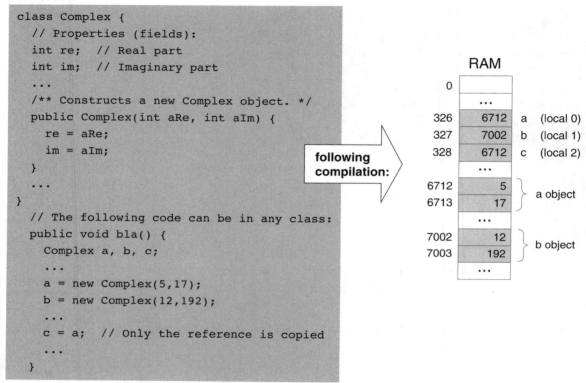

```
class Complex {
  // Properties (fields):
  int re;  // Real part
  int im;  // Imaginary part
  ...
  /** Constructs a new Complex object. */
  public Complex(int aRe, int aIm) {
    re = aRe;
    im = aIm;
  }
  ...
}
  // The following code can be in any class:
  public void bla() {
    Complex a, b, c;
    ...
    a = new Complex(5,17);
    b = new Complex(12,192);
    ...
    c = a;  // Only the reference is copied
    ...
  }
```

following compilation:

RAM

0	
	...
326	6712	a (local 0)
327	7002	b (local 1)
328	6712	c (local 2)
	...
6712	5	} a object
6713	17	
	...
7002	12	} b object
7003	192	
	...

Figure 11.3 Objects handling. Since memory allocations are run-time dependent, all the shown addresses are arbitrary examples.

trick that accomplishes this abstraction is to pass a reference to the manipulated object as a hidden argument of the called method, compiling b.mult(5) as if it were written as mult(b,5). In general then, each object-based method call foo.bar(v1,v2,...) is translated into the VM code push foo, push v1, push v2, ..., call bar. This way, the compiler can force the same method to operate on any desired object for instance, creating the high-level perception that each object encapsulates its own code.

However, the compiler's job is not done yet. Since the language allows different methods in different classes to have the same name, the compiler must ensure that the right method is applied to the right object. Further, due to the possibility of method overriding in a subclass, compilers of object-oriented languages must do this determination at run-time. When run-time typing is out of the picture, for example, in languages like Jack, this determination can be done at compile-time. Specifically, in each method call like `x.m(y)`, the compiler must ensure that the called method `m()` belongs to the class from which the `x` object was derived.

11.1.2   Commands Translation

We now describe how high-level commands are translated into the target language. Since we have already discussed the handling of variables, objects, and arrays, there are only two more issues to consider: *expression evaluation* and *flow control*.

Evaluating Expressions   How should we generate code for evaluating high-level expressions like `x+g(2,y,-z)*5`? First, we must "understand" the syntactic structure of the expression, for example, convert it into a parse tree like the one depicted in figure 11.4. This parsing was already handled by the *syntax analyzer* described in chapter 10. Next, as seen in the figure, we can traverse the parse tree and generate from it the equivalent VM code.

The choice of the code generation algorithm depends on the target language into which we are translating. For a stack-based target platform, we simply need to print the tree in *postfix* notation, also known as *Reverse Polish Notation* (RPN). In RPN

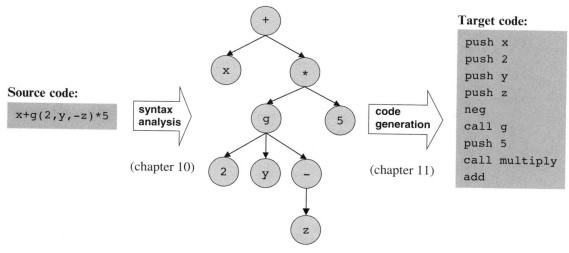

Figure 11.4   Code generation.

syntax, an operation like $f(x, y)$ is expressed as x, y, f (or, in the VM language syntax, push x, push y, call f). Likewise, an operation like $x + y$, which is $+(x, y)$ in prefix notation, is stated as x, y, $+$ (i.e., push x, push y, add). The strategy for translating expressions into stack-based VM code is straightforward and is based on recursive post-order traversal of the underlying parse tree, as follows:

codeWrite(exp):
if *exp* is a number *n*	then output "push n"
if *exp* is a variable *v*	then output "push v"
if *exp* = (*exp1 op exp2*)	then codeWrite(*exp1*), codeWrite(*exp2*), output "op"
if *exp* = *op*(*exp1*)	then codeWrite(*exp1*), output "op"
if *exp* = *f*(*exp1* ... *expN*)	then codeWrite(*exp1*), ..., codeWrite(*expN*), output "call f"

The reader can verify that when applied to the tree in figure 11.4, this algorithm generates the stack-machine code shown in the figure.

Translating Flow Control High-level programming languages are equipped with a variety of control flow structures like if, while, for, switch, and so on. In contrast, low-level languages typically offer two basic control primitives: *conditional goto* and *unconditional goto*. Therefore, one of the challenges faced by the compiler writer is to translate structured code segments into target code utilizing these primitives only. As shown in figure 11.5, the translation logic is rather simple.

Two features of high-level languages make the compilation of control structures slightly more challenging than that shown in figure 11.5. First, a program normally contains multiple instances of if and while statements. The compiler can handle this multiplicity by generating and using unique label names. Second, control structures can be nested, for example, if within while within another while and so on. This complexity can be dealt with easily using a recursive compilation strategy.

11.2 Specification

Usage The Jack compiler accepts a single command line parameter, as follows:

```
prompt> JackCompiler source
```

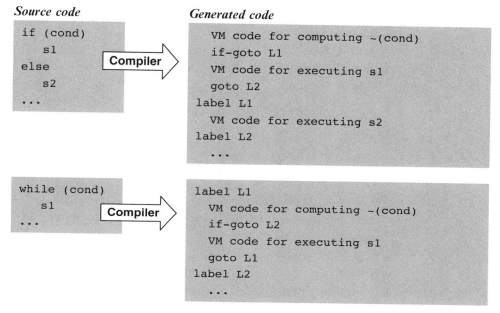

Figure 11.5   Compilation of control structures.

Where *source* is either a file name of the form `Xxx.jack` (the extension is mandatory) or a directory name containing one or more `.jack` files (in which case there is no extension). The compiler compiles each `Xxx.jack` file into a file named `Xxx.vm`, created in the same directory in which the source file is located. If *source* is a directory name, each `.jack` file located in it is compiled, creating a corresponding `.vm` file in the same directory.

11.2.1   Standard Mapping over the Virtual Machine

The compiler translates each `.jack` file into a `.vm` file containing one VM function for each constructor, function, and method found in the `.jack` file (see figure 7.8). In doing so, every Jack-to-VM compiler must follow the following code generation conventions.

File and Function Naming   Each `.jack` class file is compiled into a separate `.vm` file. The Jack subroutines (functions, methods, and constructors) are compiled into VM functions as follows:

- A Jack subroutine `xxx()` in a Jack class `Yyy` is compiled into a VM function called `Yyy.xxx`.

- A Jack *function* or *constructor* with k arguments is compiled into a VM function that operates on k arguments.

- A Jack *method* with k arguments is compiled into a VM function that operates on $k + 1$ arguments. The first argument (argument number 0) always refers to the `this` object.

Memory Allocation and Access

- The *local variables* of a Jack subroutine are allocated to, and accessed via, the virtual `local` segment.

- The *argument variables* of a Jack subroutine are allocated to, and accessed via, the virtual `argument` segment.

- The *static variables* of a `.jack` class file are allocated to, and accessed via, the virtual `static` segment of the corresponding `.vm` file.

- Within a VM function corresponding to a Jack *method* or a Jack *constructor*, access to the fields of the `this` object is obtained by first pointing the virtual `this` segment to the current object (using `pointer 0`) and then accessing individual fields via `this` *index* references, where *index* is an non-negative integer.

- Within a VM function, access to array entries is obtained by first pointing the virtual `that` segment (using `pointer 1`) to the address of the desired array entry and then accessing the array entry via `that 0` references.

Subroutine Calling

- Before calling a VM function, the caller (itself a VM function) must push the function's arguments onto the stack. If the called VM function corresponds to a Jack *method*, the first pushed argument must be a reference to the object on which the method is supposed to operate.

- When compiling a Jack *method* into a VM function, the compiler must insert VM code that sets the base of the `this` segment properly. Similarly, when compiling a Jack *constructor*, the compiler must insert VM code that allocates a memory block for the new object and then sets the base of the `this` segment to point at its base.

Returning from Void Methods and Functions High-level void subroutines don't return values. This abstraction is handled as follows:

- VM functions corresponding to *void* Jack methods and functions must return the constant 0 as their return value.

- When translating a do sub statement where sub is a void method or function, the caller of the corresponding VM function must pop (and ignore) the returned value (which is always the constant 0).

Constants

- null and false are mapped to the constant 0. True is mapped to the constant −1 (this constant can be obtained via push constant 1 followed by neg).

Use of Operating System Services The basic Jack OS is implemented as a set of VM files named Math.vm, Array.vm, Output.vm, Screen.vm, Keyboard.vm, Memory.vm, and Sys.vm (the API of these compiled class files was given in chapter 9). All these files must reside alongside the VM files generated by the compiler. This way, any VM function can call any OS VM function for its effect. In particular, when needed, the compiler should generate code that uses the following OS functions:

- Multiplication and division are handled using the OS functions Math.multiply() and Math.divide().

- String constants are created using the OS constructor String.new(length). String assignments like x="cc...c" are handled using a series of calls to the OS routine String.appendChar(nextChar).

- Constructors allocate space for new objects using the OS function Memory.alloc(size).

11.2.2 Compilation Example

Compiling a Jack program (one or more .jack class files) involves two main tasks: parsing the code using the compilation engine developed in the previous chapter, and generating code according to the guidelines and specifications given above. Figure 11.6 gives a "live example" of many of the code generation issues mentioned in this chapter.

High-level code (*BankAccount.jack* class file)

```
/* Some common sense was sacrificed in this banking example in order to
   create a nontrivial and easy-to-follow compilation example. */
class BankAccount {
    // Class variables
    static int nAccounts;
    static int bankCommission;  // As a percentage, e.g., 10 for 10 percent
    // account properties
    field int id;
    field String owner;
    field int balance;

    method int commission(int x) { /* Code omitted */ }

    method void transfer(int sum, BankAccount from, Date when) {
        var int i, j;  // Some local variables
        var Date due;  // Date is a user-defined type
        let balance = (balance + sum) - commission(sum * 5);
        // More code ...
        return;

    }
    // More methods ...
}
```

Class-scope symbol table

Name	Type	Kind	#
nAccounts	int	static	0
bankCommission	int	static	1
id	int	field	0
owner	String	field	1
balance	int	field	2

Method-scope (transfer) symbol table

Name	Type	Kind	#
this	BankAccount	argument	0
sum	int	argument	1
from	BankAccount	argument	2
when	Date	argument	3
i	int	var	0
j	int	var	1
due	Date	var	2

Figure 11.6 Code generation example focusing on the translation of the statement `let balance = (balance + sum) – commission(sum * 5)`.

Pseudo VM code

```
function BankAccount.commission
  // Code omitted
function BankAccount.transfer
  // Code for setting "this" to point
  // to the passed object (omitted)
  push balance
  push sum
  add
  push this
  push sum
  push 5
  call multiply
  call commission
  sub
  pop balance
  // More code ...
  push 0
  return
```

Final VM code

```
function BankAccount.commission 0
  // Code omitted
function BankAccount.transfer 3
  push argument 0
  pop pointer 0
  push this 2
  push argument 1
  add
  push argument 0
  push argument 1
  push constant 5
  call Math.multiply 2
  call BankAccount.commission 2
  sub
  pop this 2
  // More code ...
  push 0
  return
```

Figure 11.6 (continued)

11.3 Implementation

We now turn to propose a software architecture for the overall compiler. This architecture builds upon the *syntax analyzer* described in chapter 10. In fact, the current architecture is based on gradually evolving the syntax analyzer into a full-scale compiler. The overall compiler can thus be constructed using five modules:

- `JackCompiler`: top-level driver that sets up and invokes the other modules;
- `JackTokenizer`: tokenizer;
- `SymbolTable`: symbol table;
- `VMWriter`: output module for generating VM code;
- `CompilationEngine`: recursive top-down compilation engine.

11.3.1   The *JackCompiler* Module

The compiler operates on a given *source*, where *source* is either a file name of the form xxx.jack or a directory name containing one or more such files. For each xxx.jack input file, the compiler creates a *JackTokenizer* and an output xxx.vm file. Next, the compiler uses the *CompilationEngine*, *SymbolTable*, and *VMWriter* modules to write the output file.

11.3.2   The *JackTokenizer* Module

The tokenizer API was given in section 10.3.2.

11.3.3   The *SymbolTable* Module

This module provides services for creating and using a *symbol table*. Recall that each symbol has a scope from which it is visible in the source code. The symbol table implements this abstraction by giving each symbol a running number (index) within the scope. The index starts at 0, increments by 1 each time an identifier is added to the table, and resets to 0 when starting a new scope. The following kinds of identifiers may appear in the symbol table:

Static: Scope: class.

Field: Scope: class.

Argument: Scope: subroutine (method/function/constructor).

Var: Scope: subroutine (method/function/constructor).

When compiling error-free Jack code, any identifier not found in the symbol table may be assumed to be a subroutine name or a class name. Since the Jack language syntax rules suffice for distinguishing between these two possibilities, and since no "linking" needs to be done by the compiler, there is no need to keep these identifiers in the symbol table.

SymbolTable: Provides a symbol table abstraction. The symbol table associates the identifier names found in the program with identifier properties needed for compilation: *type*, *kind*, and running index. The symbol table for Jack programs has two nested scopes (class/subroutine).

Routine	Arguments	Returns	Function
`Constructor`	—	—	Creates a new empty symbol table.
`startSubroutine`	—	—	Starts a new subroutine scope (i.e., resets the subroutine's symbol table).
`Define`	name (String) type (String) kind (`STATIC`, `FIELD`, `ARG`, or `VAR`)	—	Defines a new identifier of a given *name*, *type*, and *kind* and assigns it a running index. `STATIC` and `FIELD` identifiers have a class scope, while `ARG` and `VAR` identifiers have a subroutine scope.
`VarCount`	kind (`STATIC`, `FIELD`, `ARG`, or `VAR`)	int	Returns the number of variables of the given *kind* already defined in the current scope.
`KindOf`	name (String)	(`STATIC`, `FIELD`, `ARG`, `VAR`, `NONE`)	Returns the *kind* of the named identifier in the current scope. If the identifier is unknown in the current scope, returns `NONE`.
`TypeOf`	name (String)	String	Returns the *type* of the named identifier in the current scope.
`IndexOf`	name (String)	int	Returns the *index* assigned to the named identifier.

Implementation Tip   The symbol table abstraction and API can be implemented using two separate hash tables: one for the class scope and another one for the subroutine scope. When a new subroutine is started, the subroutine scope table can be cleared.

11.3.4 The *VMWriter* Module

VMWriter: Emits VM commands into a file, using the VM command syntax.

Routine	Arguments	Returns	Function
Constructor	Output file/stream	—	Creates a new file and prepares it for writing.
writePush	Segment (CONST, ARG, LOCAL, STATIC, THIS, THAT, POINTER, TEMP) Index (int)	—	Writes a VM push command.
writePop	Segment (CONST, ARG, LOCAL, STATIC, THIS, THAT, POINTER, TEMP) Index (int)	—	Writes a VM pop command.
WriteArithmetic	command (ADD, SUB, NEG, EQ, GT, LT, AND, OR, NOT)	—	Writes a VM arithmetic command.
WriteLabel	label (String)	—	Writes a VM label command.
WriteGoto	label (String)	—	Writes a VM goto command.
WriteIf	label (String)		Writes a VM If-goto command.
writeCall	name (String) nArgs (int)	—	Writes a VM call command.
writeFunction	name (String) nLocals (int)	—	Writes a VM function command.
writeReturn	—	—	Writes a VM return command.
close	—	—	Closes the output file.

11.3.5   The *CompilationEngine* Module

This class does the compilation itself. It reads its input from a `JackTokenizer` and writes its output into a `VMWriter`. It is organized as a series of `compilexxx()` routines, where `xxx` is a syntactic element of the Jack language. The contract between these routines is that each `compilexxx()` routine should read the syntactic construct `xxx` from the input, `advance()` the tokenizer exactly beyond `xxx`, and emit to the output VM code effecting the semantics of `xxx`. Thus `compilexxx()` may only be called if indeed `xxx` is the next syntactic element of the input. If `xxx` is a part of an expression and thus has a value, the emitted code should compute this value and leave it at the top of the VM stack.

The API of this module is identical to that of the syntax analyzer's *Compilation-Engine* module from chapter 10, and thus we suggest gradually morphing the syntax analyzer into a full compiler. Section 11.5 provides step-by-step instructions and test programs for this construction.

11.4   Perspective

The fact that Jack is a relatively simple language permitted us to sidestep several thorny compilation issues. For example, while Jack looks like a typed language, this is hardly the case. All of Jack's data types are 16-bits long, and the language semantics allows Jack compilers to ignore almost all type information. As a result, when compiling and evaluating expressions, Jack compilers need not determine their types (with the single exception that compiling a method call `x.m()` requires determining the class type of `x`). Likewise, array entries in Jack are not typed. In contrast, most programming languages feature rich type systems that have significant implications on their compilers: Different amounts of memory must be allocated for different types of variables; conversion from one type into another requires specific language operations; the compilation of a simple expression like `x+y` depends strongly on the types of `x` and `y`; and so on.

Another significant simplification is that the Jack language does not support inheritance. This implies that all method calls can be handled statically, at compile-time. In contrast, compilers of languages with inheritance must treat methods as virtual, and determine their locations according to the run-time type of the underlying object. For example, consider the method call `x.m()`. If the language supports inheritance, `x` can be derived from more than one class, and we cannot know *which* until run-time. Thus, if the definition of the method m is not found in the class from which x was derived, it may still be found in a class that supersedes it, and so on.

Another common feature of object-oriented languages not supported by Jack is public class fields. For example, if circ is an object of type Circle with a property radius, one cannot write statements like r=circ.radius. Instead, the programmer must equip the Circle class with accessor methods, allowing only statements like r=circ.getRadius() (which is good programming practice anyway).

The lack of real typing, inheritance, and public class fields allows a truly independent compilation of classes. In particular, a Jack class can be compiled without accessing the code of any other class: The fields of other classes are never referred to directly, and all linking to methods of other classes is "late" and done just by name.

Many other simplifications of the Jack language are not significant and can be relaxed with little effort. For example, one may easily extend the language with for and switch statements. Likewise, one can add the capability to assign constants like 'c' to char type variables, which is presently not supported by the language. (To assign the constant 'c' to a Jack char variable x, one must first assign "c" to a String variable, say s, and then use let x=s.charAt(0). Clearly, it would be nicer to simply say let x='c', as in Java).

Finally, as usual, we did not pay any attention to optimization. Consider the high-level statement c++. A naïve compiler may translate it into the series of low-level VM operations push c, push 1, add, pop c. Next, the VM implementation will translate each one of these VM commands into several machine-level instructions, resulting in a considerable chunk of code. At the same time, an optimized compiler will notice that we are dealing with nothing more than a simple increment, and translate it into, say, the two machine instructions @c followed by M=M+1 on the Hack platform. Of course this is just one example of the finesse expected from industrial-strength compilers. Therefore, time and space efficiency play an important role in the code generation part of compilers and compilation courses.

11.5   Project

Objective   Extend the *syntax analyzer* built in chapter 10 into a full-scale Jack compiler. In particular, gradually replace the software modules that generate passive XML code with software modules that generate executable VM code.

Resources   The main tool that you need is the programming language in which you will implement the compiler. You will also need an executable copy of the Jack operating system, as explained below. Finally, you will need the supplied VM Emulator, to test the code generated by your compiler on a set of test programs supplied by us.

Contract   Complete the Jack compiler implementation. The output of the compiler should be VM code designed to run on the virtual machine built in the projects in chapters 7 and 8. Use your compiler to compile all the Jack programs given here. Make sure that each translated program executes according to its documentation.

Stage 1: Symbol Table

We suggest that you start by building the compiler's symbol table module and using it to extend the syntax analyzer built in Project 10. Presently, whenever an *identifier* is encountered in the program, say foo, the syntax analyzer outputs the XML line <identifier> foo </identifier>. Instead, have your analyzer output the following information as part of its XML output (using some format of your choice):

- the identifier category (*var, argument, static, field, class, subroutine*);
- whether the identifier is presently being *defined* (e.g., the identifier stands for a variable declared in a var statement) or *used* (e.g., the identifier stands for a variable in an expression);
- whether the identifier represents a variable of one of the four kinds (*var, argument, static, field*), and the running index assigned to the identifier by the symbol table.

You may test your symbol table module and the preceding capability by running your (extended) syntax analyzer on the test Jack programs supplied in Project 10. Once the output of your extended syntax analyzer includes this information, it means that you have developed a complete executable capability to understand the semantics of Jack programs. At this stage you can make the switch to a full-scale compiler and start generating VM code instead of XML output. This can be done by gradually morphing the code of the extended syntax analyzer into a full compiler.

Stage 2: Code Generation

We don't provide specific guidelines on how to develop the code generation features of the compiler, though the examples spread throughout the chapter are quite instructive. Instead, we provide a set of six application programs designed to unit-test these features incrementally. We strongly suggest to test your compiler on these programs in the given order. This way, you will be implicitly guided to build the compiler's code generation capabilities in stages, according to the demands of each test program.

The Operating System   The Jack OS—the subject of chapter 12—was written in the Jack language. The source OS code was then translated (by an error-free Jack compiler) into a set of VM files, collectively known as the *Jack OS*. Each time we want to run an application program on the VM emulator, we must load into the emulator not only the application's .vm files, but also all the OS .vm files. This way, when an application-level VM function calls some OS-level VM function, they will find each other in the same environment.

Testing Method   Normally, when you compile a program and run into some problems, you conclude that the program is screwed up and proceed to debug it. In this project the setting is exactly the opposite. All the test programs that we supply are error-free. Therefore, if their compilation yields any errors, it's the *compiler* that you have to fix, not the test programs. For each test program, we recommend going through the following routine:

1.   Copy all the supplied OS .vm files from tools/os into the program directory, together with the supplied .jack file(s) comprising the test program.

2.   Compile the program directory using your compiler. This operation should compile only the .jack files in the directory, which is exactly what we want.

3.   If there are any compilation errors, fix your compiler and return to step 2 (note that all the supplied test programs are error-free).

4.   At this point, the program directory should contain one .vm file for each source .jack file, as well as all the supplied OS .vm files. If this is not the case, fix your compiler and return to step 2.

5.   Execute the translated VM program in the VM Emulator, loading the entire directory and using the "no animation" mode. Each one of the six test programs contains specific execution guidelines, as listed here.

6.   If the program behaves unexpectedly or some error message is displayed by the VM emulator, fix your compiler and return to step 2.

Test Programs

We supply six test programs. Each program is designed to gradually unit-test specific language handling capabilities of your compiler.

Seven   This program computes the value of (3*2)+1 and prints the result at the top left of the screen. To test whether your compiler has translated the program correctly, run the translated code in the VM emulator and make sure that it displays 7 correctly. Purpose: Tests how your compiler handles a simple program containing an arithmetic expression with integer constants (without variables), a do statement, and a return statement.

Decimal-to-Binary Conversion   This program converts a 16-bit decimal number into its binary representation. The program takes a decimal number from RAM[8000], converts it to binary, and stores the individual bits in RAM[8001..8016] (each location will contain 0 or 1). Before the conversion starts, the program initializes RAM[8001..8016] to –1. To test whether your compiler has translated the program correctly, load the translated code into the VM emulator and go through the following routine:

- Put (interactively) a 16-bit decimal value in RAM[8000].
- Run the program for a few seconds, then stop its execution.
- Check (interactively) that RAM[8001..8016] contain the correct results, and that none of them contains –1.

Purpose: Tests how your compiler handles all the procedural elements of the Jack language, namely, *expressions* (without arrays or method calls), *functions*, and all the language *statements*. The program does not test the handling of methods, constructors, arrays, strings, static variables, and field variables.

Square Dance   This program is a trivial interactive "game" that enables moving a black square around the screen using the keyboard's four arrow keys. While moving, the size of the square can be increased and decreased by pressing the "z" and "x" keys, respectively. To quit the game, press the "q" key. To test if your compiler has translated the program correctly, run the translated code in the VM emulator and make sure that it works according to this description. Purpose: Tests how your compiler handles the object-oriented constructs of the Jack language: *constructors, methods, fields* and expressions that include *method calls*. It does not test the handling of static variables.

Average   This program computes the average of a user-supplied sequence of integers. To test if your compiler has translated the program correctly, run the translated code in the VM emulator and follow the instructions displayed on the screen. Purpose: Tests how your compiler handles *arrays* and *strings*.

Pong   A ball is moving randomly on the screen, bouncing off the screen "walls." The user can move a small bat horizontally by pressing the keyboard's left and right arrow keys. Each time the bat hits the ball, the user scores a point and the bat shrinks a little, to make the game harder. If the user misses and the ball hits the bottom horizontal line, the game is over. To test whether your compiler has translated this program correctly, run the translated code in the VM emulator and play the game (make sure to score some points, to test the part of the program that displays the score on the screen). Purpose: Provides a complete test of how your compiler handles *objects*, including the handling of *static variables*.

Complex Arrays   Performs five complex calculations using arrays. For each such calculation, the program prints on the screen the expected result versus the actual result (as performed by the compiled program). To test whether your compiler has translated the program correctly, run the translated code in the VM emulator and make sure that the actual results are identical to the expected results. Purpose: Tests how your compiler handles complex *array references* and *expressions*.

12　Operating System

Civilization progresses by extending the number of operations that we can perform without thinking about them.
—Alfred North Whitehead, *Introduction to Mathematics* (1911)

In previous chapters of this book, we described and built the hardware architecture of a computer platform, called *Hack*, and the software hierarchy that makes it usable. In particular, we introduced an object-based language, called *Jack*, and described how to write a compiler for it. Other high-level programming languages can be specified on top of the Hack platform, each requiring its own compiler.

The last major interface missing in this puzzle is an *operating system* (OS). The OS is designed to close gaps between the computer's hardware and software systems, and to make the overall computer more accessible to programmers and users. For example, in order to render the text "Hello World" on our computer's screen, several hundred pixels must be drawn at specific screen locations. This can be done by consulting the hardware specification and writing code that puts the necessary bits in the RAM-resident screen memory map. Obviously, high-level programmers expect something better than that. They want to use a command like printString("Hello World") and let someone else worry about the details. And that's where the operating system enters the picture.

Throughout this chapter, the term *operating system* is used rather loosely. In fact, the OS services that we describe comprise an operating system in a very minimal fashion, aiming at (i) encapsulating various hardware-specific services in a software-friendly way, and (ii) extending high-level languages with various functions and abstract data types. The dividing line between an operating system in this sense and a standard language library is not very clear. Indeed, some modern languages, most notably Java, tend to pack many classic operating system services like GUI management, memory management, and multitasking in its standard software library, along with many language extensions.

Following this pattern, the collection of services that we specify and build in this chapter can be viewed as a combination of a simple OS and a standard library for the Jack language. This OS is packaged as a collection of Jack classes, each providing a set of related services via Jack subroutine calls. The resulting OS has many features resembling those of industrial strength operating systems, but it still lacks numerous OS features such as process handling, disk management, communications, and more.

Operating systems are usually written in a high-level language and compiled into binary form, just like any other program. Our OS is no exception—it can be written completely in Jack. Yet unlike other programs written in high-level languages, the operating system code must be aware of the hardware platform on which it runs. In other words, in order to hide the gory hardware details from the application programmer, the OS programmer must write code that manipulates these details directly (a task that requires access to the hardware documentation). Conveniently, this can be done using the Jack language. As we observe in this chapter, Jack was defined with sufficient "lowness" in it, permitting an intimate closeness to the hardware when needed.

The chapter starts with a relatively long Background section, describing key algorithms normally used to implement basic operating system services. These include mathematical functions, string operations, memory management, handling text and graphics output to the screen, and handling inputs from the keyboard. This algorithmic introduction is followed by a Specification section, providing the complete API of the Jack OS, and an Implementation section, describing how to build the OS using the classic algorithms presented earlier. As usual, the final Project section provides all the necessary project materials for gradual construction and unit-testing the entire OS presented in the chapter.

The chapter provides two key lessons, one in software engineering and one in computer science. First, we complete the construction of the high-level language, compiler, and operating system trio. Second, since operating system services must execute efficiently, we pay attention to running time considerations. The result is an elegant series of algorithms, each being a computer science gem.

12.1 Background

12.1.1 Mathematical Operations

Computer systems must support mathematical operations like addition, multiplication, and division. Normally, addition is implemented in hardware, at the ALU level, as we have done in chapter 3. Other operations like multiplication and division can be handled by either hardware or software, depending on the computer's cost/performance requirements. This section shows how multiplication, division, and square root operations can be implemented efficiently in software, at the OS level. We note in passing that hardware implementations of these mathematical operations can be based on the same algorithms presented here.

Efficiency First   Mathematical algorithms operate on n-bit binary numbers, with typical computer architectures having $n = 16, 32$, or 64. As a rule, we seek algorithms whose running time is proportional (or at least polynomial) in this parameter n. Algorithms whose running time is proportional to the *value* of n-bit numbers are unacceptable, since these values are exponential in n. For example, suppose we implement the multiplication operation $x \cdot y$ using the repeated addition algorithm *for* $i = 1 \ldots y$ $\{result = result + x\}$. Well, the problem is that in a 64-bit computer, y can be greater than 18,000,000,000,000,000,000, implying that this naïve algorithm may run for years even on the fastest computers. In sharp contrast, the running time of the multiplication algorithm that we present below is proportional not to the multipliers' value, which may be as large as 2^n, but rather to n. Therefore, it will require only $c \cdot n$ elementary operations for *any pair of multiplicands*, where c is a small constant representing the number of elementary operations performed in each loop iteration.

We use the standard "Big-Oh" notation, $O(n)$, to describe the running time of algorithms. Readers who are not familiar with this notation can simply read $O(n)$ as "in the order of magnitude of n." With that in mind, we now turn to present an efficient multiplication $x \cdot y$ algorithm for n-bit numbers whose running time is $O(n)$ rather than $O(x)$ or $O(y)$, which are exponentially larger.

Multiplication   Consider the standard multiplication method taught in elementary school. To compute 356 times 27, we line up the two numbers one on top of the other. Next, we multiply each digit of 356 by 7. Next, we "shift to the left" one position, and multiply each digit of 356 by 2. Finally, we sum up the columns and obtain the result. The binary version of this technique—figure 12.1—follows exactly the same logic.

The algorithm in figure 12.1 performs $O(n)$ addition operations on n-bit numbers, where n is the number of bits in x and y. Note that *shiftedX* $* 2$ can be efficiently obtained by either left-shifting its bit representation or by adding *shiftedX* to itself. Both operations can be easily performed using primitive ALU operations. Thus this algorithm lends itself naturally to both software and hardware implementations.

Long multiplication

$$
\begin{array}{cccccccccc}
x & & & 1 & 0 & 1 & 1 & = & 1 & 1 \\
y & * & & & 1 & 0 & 1 & = & & 5 \\
\hline
\end{array}
$$

									j-th bit of *y*

$$
\begin{array}{cccccccc}
 & & 1 & 0 & 1 & 1 & & \qquad 1 \\
 & 0 & 0 & 0 & 0 & & & \qquad 0 \\
1 & 0 & 1 & 1 & & & & \qquad 1 \\
\hline
x \cdot y \quad 1 & 1 & 0 & 1 & 1 & 1 & = & 5 \quad 5
\end{array}
$$

```
multiply (x, y):
   // Where x, y ≥ 0
   sum = 0
   shiftedX = x
   for j = 0 ... (n − 1) do
       if (j-th bit of y) = 1 then
           sum = sum + shiftedX
       shiftedX = shiftedX * 2
```

Figure 12.1   Multiplication of two *n*-bit numbers.

A Comment about Notation   The algorithms in this chapter are written using a self-explanatory pseudocode syntax. The only non-obvious convention is that we use indentation to represent blocks of code (avoiding curly brackets or begin/end keywords). For example, in figure 12.1, $sum = sum + shiftedX$ belongs to the single-statement body of the *if* statement whereas $shiftedX = shiftedX * 2$ ends the two-statement body of the *for* statement.

Division   The naïve way to compute the division of two *n*-bit numbers x/y is to repeatedly subtract *y* from *x* until it is impossible to continue (i.e., until $x < y$). The running time of this algorithm is clearly proportional to the quotient, and may be as large as $O(x)$, that is, exponential in the number of bits *n*. To speed up this algorithm, we can try to subtract large chunks of *y*'s from *x* in each iteration. For example, if $x = 891$ and $y = 5$, we can tell right away that we can deduct a hundred 5's from *x* and the remainder will still be greater than 5, thus shaving 100 iterations from the naïve approach. Indeed, this is the rationale behind the school method for long division x/y. Formally, in each iteration we try to subtract from *x* the largest possible shift of *y*, namely, $y \cdot T$ where *T* is the largest power of 10 such that $y \cdot T \le x$.

```
divide (x, y):
    // Integer part of x/y, where x ≥ 0 and y > 0
    if y > x return 0
    q = divide(x, 2 * y)
    if (x − 2 * q * y) < y
        return 2 * q
    else
        return 2 * q + 1
```

Figure 12.2   Division.

The binary version of this opportunistic algorithm is identical, except that T is a power of 2 instead of 10.

Writing down this long division algorithm as we have done for multiplication is an easy exercise. We find it more illuminating to formulate the same logic as a recursive program that is probably easier to implement, shown in figure 12.2.

The running time of this algorithm is determined by the depth of the recursion. Since in each level of recursion the value of y is multiplied by 2, and since we terminate once $y > x$, it follows that the recursion depth is bounded by n, the number of bits in x. Each recursion level involves a constant number of addition, subtraction, and multiplication operations, implying a total running time of $O(n)$ such operations.

This algorithm may be considered suboptimal since each multiplication operation also requires $O(n)$ addition and subtraction operations. However, careful inspection reveals that the product $2 \cdot q \cdot y$ can be computed without any multiplication. Instead, we can rely on the value of this product in the previous recursion level, and use addition to establish its current value.

Square Root   Square roots can be computed efficiently in a number of different ways, for example, by using the Newton-Raphson method or a Taylor series expansion. For our purpose though, a simpler algorithm will suffice. The square root function $y = \sqrt{x}$ has two convenient properties. First, it is monotonically increasing. Second, its inverse function, $x = y^2$, is something that we already know how to compute (multiplication). Taken together, these properties imply that we have all we need to compute square roots using *binary search*. Figure 12.3 gives the details.

Note that each loop iteration takes a constant number of arithmetic operations. Since the number of iterations is bound by $n/2$, the algorithm's running time is $O(n)$ arithmetic operations.

```
sqrt (x):
    // Compute the integer part of y = √x. Strategy:
    // Find an integer y such that y² ≤ x < (y + 1)² (for 0 ≤ x < 2ⁿ)
    // by performing a binary search in the range 0 ... 2^(n/2) − 1.
    y = 0
    for j = n/2 − 1 ... 0 do
        if (y + 2ʲ)² ≤ x then y = y + 2ʲ
    return y
```

Figure 12.3   Square root computation using binary search.

12.1.2   String Representation of Numbers

Computers represent numbers internally using binary codes. Yet humans are used to dealing with numbers in a decimal notation. Thus, when humans have to read or input numbers, and only then, a conversion to or from decimal notation must be performed. Typically, this service is implicit in the character handling routines supplied by the operating system. We now turn to describe how these OS services are actually implemented.

Of course the only subset of characters which is of interest here are the ten digit symbols that represent actual numbers. The ASCII codes of these characters are as follows:

Character:	'0'	'1'	'2'	'3'	'4'	'5'	'6'	'7'	'8'	'9'
ASCII code:	48	49	50	51	52	53	54	55	56	57

As gleaned from the ASCII code, single digit characters can be easily converted into their numeric representation, and vice versa, as follows. To compute the ASCII code of a given digit $0 \leq x \leq 9$, we can simply add x to 48 — the code of '0'. Conversely, the numeric value represented by an ASCII code $48 \leq c \leq 57$ is obtained by $c - 48$. And once we know how to convert single digits, we can proceed to convert any given integer. These conversion algorithms can be based on either recursive or iterative logic, so we present one of each in figures 12.4 and 12.5, respectively.

12.1.3   Memory Management

Dynamic Memory Allocation   Computer programs declare and use all sorts of variables, including simple data items like integers and booleans and complex ones like arrays and objects. One of the greatest virtues of high-level languages is that pro-

```
// Convert a non-negative number to a string
int2String (n):
    lastDigit = n % 10
    c = character representing lastDigit
    if n < 10
        return c (as a string)
    else
        return int2String(n/10).append(c)
```

```
// Convert a string to a non-negative number
string2Int (s):
    v = 0
    for i = 1 ... length of s do
        d = integer value of the digit s[i]
        v = v * 10 + d
    return v
    // (Assuming that s[1] is the most
    //  significant digit character of s.)
```

Figures 12.4 and 12.5   String-numeric conversions.

grammers don't have to worry about the details of allocating RAM space to these variables and recycling the space when it is no longer needed. Instead, all these memory management chores are done behind the scene by the compiler, the operating system, and the virtual machine implementation. This section describes the role of the operating system in this joint effort.

Different variables are allocated memory at different points of time during the program's life cycle. For example, *static variables* may be allocated by the compiler at compile time, while *local variables* are allocated on the stack each time a subroutine starts running. Other memory is dynamically allocated during the program's execution, and that's where the OS enters the picture. For example, each time a Java program creates a new array or a new object, a memory block whose size can be determined only during run-time should be allocated. And when the array or the object is no longer needed, its RAM space may be recycled. In some languages like C++ and Jack, de-allocation of un-needed space is the responsibility of the programmer, while in others, like Java, "garbage collection" occurs automatically. The RAM segment from which memory is dynamically allocated is called *heap*, and the agent responsible for managing this resource is the operating system.

Operating systems use various techniques for handling dynamic memory allocation and de-allocation. These techniques are implemented in two functions traditionally called `alloc()` and `deAlloc()`. We present two versions of these algorithms: a basic one and an improved one.

Basic Memory Allocation Algorithm   The data structure that this algorithm manages is a single pointer, called *free*, which points to the beginning of the heap segment that was not yet allocated. Figure 12.6a gives the details.

Initialization: *free = heapBase*

// Allocate a memory block of *size* words.
alloc(*size*):
  pointer = free
  free = free + size
  return *pointer*

// De-allocate the memory space of a given *object*.
deAlloc(*object*):
  do nothing

Figure 12.6a Basic memory allocation scheme (wasteful).

This algorithm is clearly wasteful, as it does not reclaim the space of decommissioned objects.

Improved Memory Allocation Algorithm This algorithm manages a linked list of available memory segments, called *freeList*. Each segment contains two housekeeping fields: the segment's length and a pointer to the next segment in the list. These fields can be physically kept in the segment's first two memory locations. For example, the implementation can use the convention `segment.length==segment[0]` and `segment.next==segment[1]`. Figure 12.6b (top left) illustrates a typical *freeList* state.

When asked to allocate a memory block of some given size, the algorithm has to search the *freeList* for a suitable segment. There are two well-known heuristics for doing this search. *Best-fit* finds the segment whose length is the closest (from above) to the required size, while *first-fit* finds the first segment that is long enough. Once a suitable segment has been found, the required memory block is taken from it (the location just before the beginning of the returned block, `block[-1]`, is reserved to hold its length, to be used during de-allocation). Next, this segment is updated in the *freeList*, becoming the part that remained after the allocation. If no memory was left in the segment, or if the remaining part is practically too small, the entire segment is eliminated from the *freeList*.

When asked to reclaim the memory block of an unused object, the algorithm appends the de-allocated block to the *freeList*. The details are given in figure 12.6b.

After a while, dynamic memory allocation schemes like the algorithm in figure 12.6b may create a block fragmentation problem. Hence, some kind of "defrag" op-

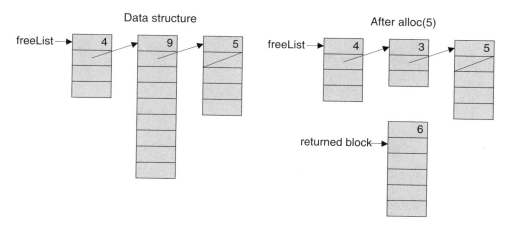

Initialization:
  freeList = *heapBase*
  freeList.length = *heapLength*
  freeList.next = null

// Allocate a memory space of *size* words.
alloc(*size*):
  Search *freeList* using best-fit or first-fit heuristics
    to obtain a segment with *segment.length* > *size*
  If no such segment is found, return failure
    (or attempt defragmentation)
  block = needed part of the found segment
    (or all of it, if the segment remainder is too small)
  Update *freeList* to reflect the allocation
  block[−1] = *size* + 1   // Remember block size, for de-allocation
  Return *block*

// Deallocate a decommissioned *object*.
deAlloc(*object*):
  segment = *object* − 1
  segment.length = *object*[−1]
  Insert *segment* into the *freeList*

Figure 12.6b   Improved memory allocation scheme (with recycling).

eration should be considered, namely, merging memory areas that are physically consecutive in memory but logically split into different segments in the *freeList*. The defragmentation operation can be done each time an object is de-allocated, or when `alloc()` fails to find an appropriate block, or according to some other intermediate or ad-hoc condition.

12.1.4   Variable-length Arrays and Strings

Suppose we want to use high-level operations like `s1="New York"` or `s2=readLine("enter a city")`. How can we implement these variable-length abstractions? The common approach in modern languages is to use a `String` class that supplies services for creating and manipulating string objects. The string object can be physically realized using an array. Normally, when the string is created, this array is allocated to hold some maximum possible length. The actual length of the string at each point of time may be shorter than this maximum, and must be maintained throughout the string object's life cycle. For example, if we issue a command like `s1.eraseLastChar()`, the actual length of `s1` should decrease from 8 to 7 (although the length of the initially created array does not change). In general then, array locations beyond the current length are not considered part of the string contents.

Most programming languages feature string types, as well as other data types of variable lengths. The string objects are usually provided by the language's standard library, for example, the `String` and `StringBuffer` classes in Java or the `strXXX` functions in C.

12.1.5   Input/Output Management

Computers are typically connected to a variety of input/output devices such as keyboard, screen, mouse, disk, network card, etc. Each of these I/O devices has its own electromechanical and physical idiosyncrasies, and thus reading and writing data on them involves many technical details. High-level languages abstract these details away from the programmer using high-level operations like `c=readChar()` and `printChar(c)`. These operations are implemented by OS routines that carry out the actual I/O.

Hence, an important function of the operating system is handling the various I/O devices connected to the computer. This is done by encapsulating the details of interfacing the device and by providing convenient access to its basic functionality, using a set of OS routines collectively known as the *device driver*. In this book we describe the basic elements of handling the two most prevalent I/O devices: a screen and a keyboard. We divide the handling of the screen into two logically separate modules: handling *graphics output* and handling *character output*.

Graphics Output

Pixel Drawing   Most computers today use *raster*, also called *bitmap*, display technologies. The only primitive operation that can be physically performed in a bitmap screen is drawing an individual *pixel*—a single "dot" on the screen specified by (*column*, *row*) coordinates. The usual convention is that columns are numbered from left to right (like the conventional *x*-axis) while rows are numbered from the top down (opposite of the conventional *y*-axis). Thus the screen coordinates of the top left pixel are (0,0).

The low-level drawing of a single pixel is a hardware-specific operation that depends on the particular interface of the screen and the underlying graphics card. If the screen interface is based on a RAM-resident *memory map*, as in Hack, then drawing a pixel is achieved by writing the proper binary value into the RAM location that represents the required pixel in memory (see figure 12.7).

The memory map interface of the Hack screen was described in section 5.2.4. Formulating a `drawPixel` algorithm that follows this contract is a simple task left to the reader as an exercise. So, now that we know how to draw a single pixel, let us turn to describing how to draw lines and circles.

Line Drawing   When asked to draw a line between two locations on a bitmap screen, the best that we can possibly do is approximate the line by drawing a series of pixels along the imaginary line connecting the two points. Note that the "pen" that we use can move in four directions only: up, down, left, and right. Thus the drawn line is bound to be jagged, and the only way to make it look good is to use a high-resolution screen. Since the receptor cells in the human eye's retina also form a grid of "input pixels," there is a limit to the image granularity that the human eye can resolve anyway. Thus, high-resolution screens and printers can fool the human eye to

---

drawPixel (*x*, *y*):
 // Hardware-specific.
 // Assuming a memory mapped screen:
 Write a predetermined value in the RAM location corresponding to screen location (*x*, *y*).

Figure 12.7   Drawing a pixel.

believe that the lines drawn by pixels or printed dots are visibly smooth. In fact they are always jagged.

The procedure for drawing a line from location $(x1, y1)$ to location $(x2, y2)$ starts by drawing the $(x1, y1)$ pixel and then zigzagging in the direction of $(x2, y2)$, until this pixel is reached. See figure 12.8a for the details.

To extend this algorithm to a general-purpose line drawing routine, one also has to take care of the possibilities $dx, dy < 0$, $dx > 0$, $dy < 0$, and $dx < 0$, $dy > 0$. To complete the picture, note that the special cases $dx = 0$ or $dy = 0$, required for drawing vertical and horizontal lines, are not handled by this algorithm. These widely used cases should probably benefit from a separate and optimized treatment anyway.

An annoying feature of the algorithm in figure 12.8a is the use of division operations in each loop iteration. Not only are these division operations time-consuming, but they also require floating point operations rather than simple integer arithmetic. The first obvious solution is to replace the $a/dx < b/dy$ condition with the equivalent $a \cdot dy < b \cdot dx$, which requires only integer multiplication. Further, careful inspection of the algebraic structure of the latter condition reveals that it may be checked

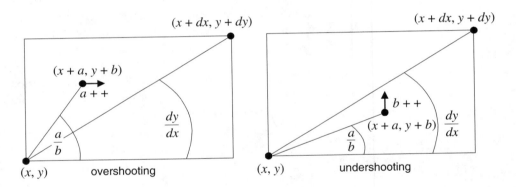

```
drawLine(x, y, x + dx, y + dy):
    // Assuming dx, dy > 0
    initialize (a, b) = (0, 0)
    while a ≤ dx and b ≤ dy do
        drawPixel(x + a, y + b)
        if a/dx < b/dy then a++ else b++
```

Figure 12.8a Line drawing.

// To test whether $a/dx < b/dy$, maintain a variable $adyMinusbdx$,
// and test if it becomes negative.
   Initialization: set $adyMinusbdx = 0$
   When $a{+}{+}$ is performed: set $adyMinusbdx = adyMinusbdx + dy$
   When $b{+}{+}$ is performed: set $adyMinusbdx = adyMinusbdx - dx$

Figure 12.8b   Efficient testing using addition operations only.

without using any multiplication at all. As shown in figure 12.8b, this may be done efficiently by maintaining a variable that updates the value of $a \cdot dy - b \cdot dx$ each time either a or b are modified.

Circle Drawing   There are several ways to draw a circle on a bitmap screen. We present an algorithm (figure 12.9) that uses three routines already implemented in this chapter: *multiplication, square root*, and *line drawing*.

The algorithm is based on drawing a series of horizontal lines (like the typical line *ab* in figure 12.9), one for each row in the range $y - r$ to $y + r$. Since r is specified in pixels, the algorithm ends up drawing a line in every screen row along the circle's north-south axis, resulting in a completely filled circle. A trivial tweaking of this algorithm can yield an empty circle as well.

Note that the algorithm is somewhat inefficient, since the square root computation in each iteration is an expensive operation. There exist many more efficient circle-drawing algorithms, including ones that involve addition operations only, in the same spirit of our line-drawing algorithm.

Character Output   All the output that we have described so far is graphical: pixels, lines, and circles. We now describe how *characters* are printed on the screen, pixel by pixel, using the good services of the operating system. Here are the details.

To develop a capability to write text on a bitmap screen, we first have to divide the physical pixel-oriented screen into a logical, character-oriented screen suitable for writing complete characters. For example, consider a screen that is 256 rows by 512 columns. If we allocate a grid of $11 * 8$ pixels for drawing a single character (11 rows, 8 columns), then our screen can show 23 lines of 64 characters each (with 3 extra rows of pixels left unused).

Next, for each character that we want to display on the screen, we can design a good-looking *font*, and then implement the font using a series of character bitmaps. For example, figure 12.10 gives a possible bitmap for the letter 'A'.

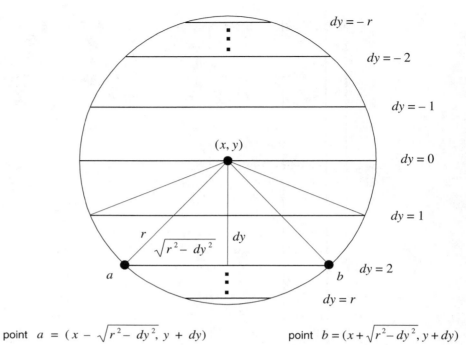

$$\text{point } a = (x - \sqrt{r^2 - dy^2}, y + dy) \qquad \text{point } b = (x + \sqrt{r^2 - dy^2}, y + dy)$$

drawCircle(x, y, r):
  for each $dy \in -r \dots r$ do
    drawLine from $(x - \sqrt{r^2 - dy^2}, y + dy)$ to $(x + \sqrt{r^2 - dy^2}, y + dy)$

Figure 12.9   Circle drawing.

Note that in order for our display scheme to account for the requisite inter-character spacing, we must make sure that the $11 * 8$ bitmap of each character includes at least a 1-pixel space before the next character and at least a 1-pixel space between adjacent lines (the exact spacing may vary with the size of the individual characters).

Characters are usually drawn on the screen one after the other, from left to right. For example, the two commands print("a") and print("b") probably mean that the programmer wants to see the image "ab" drawn on the screen. Thus the character-writing package must maintain a "cursor" object that keeps track of the screen location where the next character should be drawn. The cursor information

Figure 12.10   Character bitmap of the letter "A".

consists of *line* and *column* counts. For example, the character screen described at the section's beginning is characterized (excuse the pun) by $0 \leq line \leq 22$ and $0 \leq column \leq 63$. Drawing a single character at location (*line, column*) is achieved by writing the character's bitmap onto the box of pixels at rows $line \cdot 11 \ldots line \cdot 11 + 10$ and columns $column \cdot 8 \ldots column \cdot 8 + 7$. After the character has been drawn, the cursor should be moved one step to the right (i.e., $column = column + 1$), and, when a new line is requested, *row* should be increased by 1 and *column* reset to 0. When the bottom of the screen is reached, there is a question of what to do next, the common solution being to effect a "scrolling" operation. Another possibility is starting over at the top left corner, namely, setting the cursor to (0,0).

To conclude, we know how to write characters on the screen. Writing other types of data follows naturally from this basic capability: *strings* are written character by character, *numbers* are first converted to strings and then written as strings, and so on.

Keyboard Handling   Handling user-supplied text input is more involved than meets the eye. For example, consider the command `name=readLine("enter your name:")`. The low-level implementation of this command is not trivial, since it involves an unpredictable event: A human user is supposed to press some keys on the keyboard before this code can terminate properly. And the problem, of course, is that human users press keyboard keys for variable durations of time. Hence, the trick is to encapsulate the handling of all these messy low-level details in OS routines like `readLine`, freeing high-level programs from this tedium.

```
keyPressed( ):
    // Depends on the specifics of the keyboard interface
    if a key is presently pressed on the keyboard
        return the ASCII value of the key
    else
        return 0
```

Figure 12.11   Capturing "raw" keyboard input.

This section describes how the operating system manages text-oriented input in three increasing levels of abstraction: (i) detecting which key is currently pressed on the keyboard, (ii) capturing single-character inputs, and (iii) capturing multi-character inputs, that is, strings.

Detecting Keyboard Input   In the lowest-level form of capturing keyboard input, the program gets data directly from the hardware, indicating which key is currently pressed by the user. The access to this raw data depends on the specifics of the keyboard interface. For example, if the interface is a *memory map* that is continuously refreshed from the keyboard, as in Hack, we can simply inspect the contents of the relevant RAM area to determine which key is presently pressed. The details of this inspection can then be incorporated into the implementation of the algorithm in figure 12.11.

For example, if you know the RAM address of the keyboard memory map in the host computer, the implementation of this algorithm entails nothing more than a memory lookup.

Reading a Single Character   The elapsed time between "key pressed" and "key released" events is unpredictable. Hence, we have to write code that neutralizes this variation. Also, when users press keys on the keyboard, we usually want to give a visual feedback as to which keys have been pressed (something that you have probably grown to take for granted). Typically, we want to display some graphical cursor at the screen location where the next input "goes" and, after some key has been pressed, we typically want to echo the inputted character by displaying its bitmap on the screen at the cursor location. This logic is implemented in figure 12.12.

Reading a String   Usually, a multi-key input typed by the user is considered final only after the enter key has been pressed, yielding the *newline* character. And, until

```
readChar( ):
    // Read and echo a single character
    display the cursor
    while no key is pressed on the keyboard
        do nothing // wait till a key is pressed
    c = code of currently pressed key
    while a key is pressed
        do nothing // wait for the user to let go
    print c at the current cursor location
    move the cursor one position to the right
    return c
```

```
readLine( ):
    // Read and echo a "line" (until newline)
    s = empty string
    repeat
        c = readChar( )
        if c = newline character
            print newline
            return s
        else if c = backspace character
            remove last character from s
            move the cursor 1 position back
        else
            s = s.append(c)
```

Figures 12.12 and 12.13   Capturing "cooked" keyboard input.

the `enter` key is pressed, the user should be allowed to backspace and erase previously typed characters. The code that implements this logic and renders its visual effect is given in figure 12.13.

As usual, our input handling solutions are based on a cascading series of abstractions: The high-level program relies on the `readLine` abstraction, which relies on the `readChar` abstraction, which relies on the `keyPressed` abstraction, which relies on the hardware.

12.2   The Jack OS Specification

The previous section presented a series of algorithms that address some classic operating system tasks. In this section we turn to formally specify one particular operating system—the Jack OS—in API form. Since the Jack OS can also be viewed as an extension of the Jack programming language, this documentation duplicates exactly "The Jack Standard Library" from section 9.2.7. In chapter 9, the OS specification was intended for programmers who want to use its abstract services; in this chapter, the OS specification is intended for programmers who have to implement these services. Technical information and implementation tips follow in section 12.3.

The operating system is divided into eight classes:

- *Math:*   provides basic mathematical operations;
- *String:*   implements the String type and string-related operations;
- *Array:*   implements the Array type and array-related operations;
- *Output:*   handles text output to the screen;
- *Screen:*   handles graphic output to the screen;
- *Keyboard:*   handles user input from the keyboard;
- *Memory:*   handles memory operations;
- *Sys:*   provides some execution-related services.

12.2.1   Math

This class enables various mathematical operations.

- function void **init**( ): for internal use only;
- function int **abs**(int x): returns the absolute value of x;
- function int **multiply**(int x, int y): returns the product of x and y;
- function int **divide**(int x, int y): returns the integer part of x/y;
- function int **min**(int x, int y): returns the minimum of x and y;
- function int **max**(int x, int y): returns the maximum of x and y;
- function int **sqrt**(int x): returns the integer part of the square root of x.

12.2.2   String

This class implements the String data type and various string-related operations.

- constructor String **new**(int maxLength): constructs a new empty string (of length zero) that can contain at most maxLength characters;
- method void **dispose**( ): disposes this string;
- method int **length**( ): returns the length of this string;
- method char **charAt**(int j): returns the character at location j of this string;
- method void **setCharAt**(int j, char c): sets the j-th element of this string to c;
- method String **appendChar**(char c): appends c to this string and returns this string;

- method void **eraseLastChar**(): erases the last character from this string;
- method int **intValue**(): returns the integer value of this string (or the string prefix until a non-digit character is detected);
- method void **setInt**(int j): sets this string to hold a representation of j;
- function char **backSpace**(): returns the backspace character;
- function char **doubleQuote**(): returns the double quote (") character;
- function char **newLine**(): returns the newline character.

12.2.3   Array

This class enables the construction and disposal of arrays.

- function Array **new**(int size): constructs a new array of the given size;
- method void **dispose**(): disposes this array.

12.2.4   Output

This class allows writing text on the screen.

- function void **init**(): for internal use only;
- function void **moveCursor**(int i, int j): moves the cursor to the j-th column of the i-th row, and erases the character displayed there;
- function void **printChar**(char c): prints c at the cursor location and advances the cursor one column forward;
- function void **printString**(String s): prints s starting at the cursor location and advances the cursor appropriately;
- function void **printInt**(int i): prints i starting at the cursor location and advances the cursor appropriately;
- function void **println**(): advances the cursor to the beginning of the next line;
- function void **backSpace**(): moves the cursor one column back.

12.2.5   Screen

This class allows drawing graphics on the screen. Column indices start at 0 and are left to right. Row indices start at 0 and are top to bottom. The screen size is hardware-dependant (in the Hack platform: 256 rows by 512 columns).

- function void **init**(): for internal use only;
- function void **clearScreen**(): erases the entire screen;
- function void **setColor**(boolean b): sets a color (white = false, black = true) to be used for all further drawXXX commands;
- function void **drawPixel**(int x, int y): draws the (x,y) pixel;
- function void **drawLine**(int x1, int y1, int x2, int y2): draws a line from pixel (x1,y1) to pixel (x2,y2);
- function void **drawRectangle**(int x1, int y1, int x2, int y2): draws a filled rectangle whose top left corner is (x1,y1) and whose bottom right corner is (x2,y2);
- function void **drawCircle**(int x, int y, int r): draws a filled circle of radius r <= 181 around (x,y).

12.2.6   Keyboard

This class allows reading inputs from a standard keyboard.

- function void **init**(): for internal use only;
- function char **keyPressed**(): returns the character of the currently pressed key on the keyboard; if no key is currently pressed, returns 0;
- function char **readChar**(): waits until a key is pressed on the keyboard and released, then echoes the key to the screen and returns the character of the pressed key;
- function String **readLine**(String message): prints the message on the screen, reads the line (text until a newline character is detected) from the keyboard, echoes the line to the screen, and returns its value. This function also handles user backspaces;
- function int **readInt**(String message): prints the message on the screen, reads the line (text until a newline character is detected) from the keyboard, echoes the line to the screen, and returns its integer value (until the first non-digit character in the line is detected). This function also handles user backspaces.

12.2.7   Memory

This class allows direct access to the main memory of the host platform.

- function void **init**(): for internal use only;
- function int **peek**(int address): returns the value of the main memory at this address;

- function void **poke**(int address, int value): sets the contents of the main memory at this address to value;
- function Array **alloc**(int size): finds and allocates from the heap a memory block of the specified size and returns a reference to its base address;
- function void **deAlloc**(Array o): De-allocates the given object and frees its memory space.

12.2.8 Sys

This class supports some execution-related services.

- function void **init**(): calls the init functions of the other OS classes and then calls the Main.main() function. For internal use only;
- function void **halt**(): halts the program execution;
- function void **error**(int errorCode): prints the error code on the screen and halts;
- function void **wait**(int duration): waits approximately *duration* milliseconds and returns.

12.3   Implementation

The operating system described in the previous section can be implemented as a collection of Jack classes. Each OS subroutine can be implemented as a Jack constructor, function, or method. The API of all these subroutines was given in section 12.2, and key algorithms were presented in section 12.1. This section provides some additional hints and suggestions for completing this implementation. Final technical details and test programs for unit-testing all the OS services are given in section 12.5. Note that most of the subroutines specified in the OS API are rather simple, requiring straightforward Jack programming. Thus we focus here only on the implementation of selected OS subroutines.

Some OS classes require class-level initialization. For example, some mathematical functions can run more quickly if they can use previously calculated values, kept in some static array, constructed once and for all in the Math class. As a rule, when an OS class Xxx needs some initialization code, this code should be embedded in a single function called Xxx.init(). Later in this section we explain how these init() functions are activated when the computer boots up and the OS starts running.

12.3.1   Math

`Math.multiply()`, `Math.divide()`:   The algorithms in figures 12.1 and 12.2 are designed to operate on non-negative integers only. A simple way of handling negative numbers is applying the algorithms on absolute values and then setting the sign appropriately. For the multiplication algorithm, this is not really needed: it turns out that if the multiplicands are given in 2's complement, their product will be correct with no further ado.

Note that in each iteration j of the algorithm in figure 12.1, the j-th bit of the second number is extracted. We suggest encapsulating this operation in the following function:

`bit(x,j)`:   Returns true if the j-th bit of the integer x is 1 and false otherwise.

The `bit(x,j)` function can be easily implemented using shifting operations. Alas, Jack does not support shifting. Instead, to speed up this function implementation in Jack, it may be convenient to define a fixed static array of length 16, say `twoToThe[j]`, whose j-th location holds the value 2 to the power of j. This array may be initialized once (in `Math.init`), and then used, via bitwise Boolean operations, in the implementation of `bit(x,j)`.

In figure 12.2, y is multiplied by a factor of 2 until $y > x$. A detail that needs to be taken into account is that y can overflow. The overflow can be detected by noting when y becomes negative.

`Math.sqrt()`:   Since the calculation of $(y + 2^j)^2$ in figure 12.3 can overflow, the result may be an abnormally negative number. This problem can be addressed by (efficiently) changing the algorithm's *if* logic to

$$\text{if } ((y + 2^j)^2 \leq x) \quad \text{and} \quad ((y + 2^j)^2 > 0) \quad \text{then } y = y + 2^j$$

12.3.2   String

As explained in section 12.1.4, string objects can be implemented as arrays. In a similar vein, all the string related services can be implemented as operations on arrays. An important implementation detail is that the actual length of the string must be maintained throughout these operations and that array entries beyond this length are not considered part of the string.

`String.intValue`, `String.setInt`:   These functions can be implemented using the algorithms from figures 12.4 and 12.5, respectively. Note that both algorithms don't handle negative numbers—a detail that must be handled by the implementation.

All other subroutines in this class are straightforward. Note that the ASCII codes of `newline`, `backspace`, and `doubleQuote` are 128, 129, and 34, respectively.

12.3.3 Array

Note that `Array.new()` is not a constructor, but rather a function (despite its name). Therefore, memory space for a new array should be explicitly allocated using a call to `Memory.alloc()`. Similarly, de-allocation of arrays must be done explicitly using `Memory.deAlloc()`.

12.3.4 Output

Character Bitmaps We suggest using character bitmaps of 11 rows by 8 columns, leading to 23 lines of 64 characters each. Since designing and building bitmaps for all the printable ASCII characters is quite a burden, we supply predefined bitmaps (except for one or two characters, left to you as an exercise). Specifically, we supply a skeletal `Output` class containing Jack code that defines, for each printable ASCII character, an array that holds its bitmap (implementing a font that we created). The array consists of 11 entries, each corresponding to a row of pixels. In particular, the value of entry j is a binary number whose bits represent the 8 pixels that render the character's image in the j-th row of its bitmap.

12.3.5 Screen

`Screen.drawPixel()`: Drawing a pixel on the screen is done by directly accessing the screen's memory map using `Memory.peek()` and `Memory.poke()`. Recall that the memory map of the screen on the Hack platform specifies that the pixel at column c and row r ($0 \leq c \leq 511, 0 \leq r \leq 255$) is mapped to the $c\%16$ bit of memory location $16384 + r \cdot 32 + c/16$. Notice that drawing a single pixel requires changing a single bit in the accessed word, a task that can be achieved in Jack using bit-wise operations.

`Screen.drawLine()`: The algorithm from figure 12.8a can potentially lead to overflow. However, the efficiency improvement suggested in figure 12.8b also eliminates the overflow problem.

`Screen.drawCircle()`: Likewise, the algorithm from figure 12.9 can potentially lead to overflow. Limiting circle radii to be at most 181 avoids this problem.

12.3.6 Keyboard

In the Hack platform, the memory map of the keyboard is a single 16-bit word located at memory address 24576.

Keyboard.keyPressed(): This function provides "raw" (direct) access to this memory location and can be implemented easily using `Memory.peek()`.

Keyboard.readChar, **Keyboard.readString**: These functions provide "cooked" access to single character inputs and to string inputs, respectively. Proposed cooking instructions appear in figures 12.12 and 12.13.

12.3.7 Memory

Memory.peek(), **Memory.poke()**: These functions are supposed to provide direct access to the underlying memory. How can this be accomplished in a high-level language? As it turns out, the Jack language includes a trapdoor that enables programmers to gain complete control of the computer's memory. This hacking trick can be exploited to implement `peek` and `poke` using plain Jack programming.

The trick is based on an anomalous use of reference variables (pointers). Specifically, the Jack language does not prevent the programmer from assigning a constant to a reference variable. This constant can then be treated as an absolute memory address. In particular, when the reference variable happens to be an array, this trick can give convenient and direct access to the entire computer memory. Figure 12.4 gives the details.

Following the first two lines of figure 12.14, the base of the `memory` array points to the first address in the computer's RAM. To set or get the value of the RAM location whose physical address is j, all we have to do is manipulate the array entry

```
// To create a Jack-level "proxy" of the RAM:
var Array memory;
let memory = 0;
// From this point on we can use code like:
let x = memory[j]   // Where j is any RAM address
let memory[j] = y   // Where j is any RAM address
```

Figure 12.14   A trapdoor enabling complete control of the RAM from Jack.

`memory[j]`. This will cause the compiler to manipulate the RAM location whose address is `0+j`, which is precisely what is desired.

As we have pointed out earlier, Jack arrays are not allocated space on the heap at compile-time, but rather at run-time, when the array's new function is called. Here, however, a new initialization will defeat the purpose, since the whole idea is to anchor the array in a selected address rather then let the OS allocate it to an address in the heap that we don't control. In short, this hacking trick works because we use the array variable without allocating it "properly," as we would do in normal usage of arrays.

`Memory.alloc()`, `Memory.deAlloc()`: These functions can be implemented by either the basic algorithm from figure 12.6a or the improved algorithm from figure 12.6b using either *best-fit* or *first-fit*. Recall that the standard implementation of the VM over the Hack platform specifies that the heap resides at RAM locations 2048-16383.

12.3.8 Sys

`Sys.init`: An application program written in Jack is a set of classes. One class must be named `Main`, and this class must include a function named `main`. In order to start running the application program, the `Main.main()` function should be invoked. Now, it should be understood that the operating system is itself a program (set of classes). Thus, when the computer boots up, we want to start running the operating system program first, and then we want the OS to start running the main program.

With that in mind, the chain of command is implemented as follows. First, the VM (chapter 8) includes bootstrap code that automatically invokes a function called `Sys.init()`. This function, which is assumed to exist in the OS's `Sys` class, should then call all the `init()` functions of the other OS classes, and then call `Main.main()`. This latter function is assumed to exist in the application program.

`Sys.wait`: This function can be implemented pragmatically, under the limitations of the simulated Hack platform. In particular, you can use a loop that runs approximately *n* milliseconds before it (and the function) returns. You will have to time your specific computer to obtain a one millisecond wait, as this constant varies from one CPU to another. As a result, your `Sys.wait()` function will not be portable, but that's life.

`Sys.halt`: This function can be implemented by entering an infinite loop.

12.4   Perspective

The software library presented in this chapter includes some basic services found in most operating systems, for example, managing memory, driving I/O, handling initialization, supplying mathematical functions not implemented in hardware, and implementing data types like the *string* abstraction. We have chosen to call this standard software library an "operating system" to reflect its main function: encapsulating the gory hardware details, omissions, and idiosyncrasies in a transparent software packaging, enabling other programs to use its services via a clean interface. However, the gap between what we have called here an OS and industrial-strength operating systems remains wide.

For starters, our OS lacks some of the very basic components most closely associated with operating systems. For example, our OS supports neither multi-threading nor multi-processing; in contrast, the very kernel of most operating systems is devoted to exactly that. Our OS has no mass storage devices; in contrast, the main data store kept and handled by operating systems is a file system abstraction. Our OS has neither a "command line" interface (as in a Unix shell or a DOS window) nor a graphical one (windows, mouse, icons, etc.); in contrast, this is the operating system aspect that users expect to see and interact with. Numerous other services commonly found in operating systems are not present in our OS, for example, security, communication, and more.

Another major difference lies in the interplay between the OS code and the user code. In most computers, the OS code is considered "privileged"—the hardware platform forbids the user code from performing various operations allowed exclusively to OS code. Consequently, access to operating system services requires a mechanism that is more elaborate than a simple function call. Further, programming languages usually wrap these OS services in regular functions or methods. In contrast, in the Hack platform there is no difference between OS code and user code, and operating system services run in the same "user mode" as that of application programs.

In terms of efficiency, the algorithms that we presented for multiplication and division were standard. These algorithms, or variants thereof, are typically implemented in hardware rather than in software. The running time of these algorithms is $O(n)$ addition operations. Since adding two n-bit numbers requires $O(n)$-bit operations (gates in hardware), these algorithms end up requiring $O(n^2)$-bit operations. There exist multiplication and division algorithms whose running time is asymptotically significantly faster than $O(n^2)$, and, for a large number of bits, these algorithms are more efficient. In a similar fashion, optimized versions of the geometric operations that we presented (e.g., line- and circle-drawing) are often also implemented in special graphics acceleration hardware.

Readers who wish to extend the OS functionality are welcome to do so, as we comment on in chapter 13.

12.5   Project

Objective   Implement the operating system described in the chapter. Each of the OS classes can be implemented and unit-tested in isolation, and in any particular order.

Resources   The main tool that you need in this project is Jack—the language in which you will develop the OS. In addition, you will need the supplied Jack compiler, to compile your OS implementation, the supplied test programs, and the supplied VM emulator, which will serve as the testing platform. In particular, recall that the supplied VM emulator features a full implementation of all the OS functions. However, if the VM emulator finds compiled versions of OS functions in the VM code stream, it uses them instead of the built-in OS code. This gives rise to the testing strategy described below.

Contract   Write a Jack OS implementation and test it using the programs and testing scenarios described here. Each test program uses a certain subset of OS services.

Testing Strategy

We suggest developing and unit-testing each OS class in isolation. This can be done by putting the OS class that you write and the relevant test programs in the same directory. In particular, it is recommended to use the following procedure:

1.   Put, in the same directory, the OS class Xxx.jack that you are developing, and the relevant supplied test program (a collection of one or more .jack files);
2.   Compile the directory using the supplied Jack compiler. This will result in compiling your Xxx.jack OS class as well as the class files of the test program. In the process, a new Xxx.vm file will be created, which includes your own OS class implementation. That's exactly what we want: when applied to this directory, the VM emulator will support all the OS functions, minus the functions found in the

original Xxx OS class, plus the compiled functions found in your own version of Xxx.vm.

3. Load the directory's code (OS + test program) into the VM emulator.

4. Execute the code and check that the OS services are working properly, according to the guidelines given below.

OS Classes and Test Programs

There are eight OS classes: Memory, Array, Math, String, Output, Screen, Keyboard, and Sys. For each OS class Xxx we supply a skeletal Xxx.jack class file with all the required subroutine signatures, a corresponding test class named Main.jack, and related test scripts.

Memory, Array, Math To test your implementation of every one of these OS classes, compile the relevant directory, execute the supplied test script on the VM emulator, and make sure that the comparison with the compare file ends successfully.

Note that the supplied test programs don't comprise a full test of the Memory.alloc and Memory.deAlloc functions. A complete test of these memory management functions requires inspecting internal implementation details not visible in user-level testing. Thus it is recommended that you test these two functions using step-by-step debugging in the VM emulator.

String Execution of the corresponding test program should yield the following output:

```
new,appendChar: abcde
setInt: 12345
setInt: -32767
length: 5
charAt[2]: 99
setCharAt(2,'-'): ab-de
eraseLastChar: ab-d
intValue: 456
intValue: -32123
backSpace: 129
doubleQuote: 34
newLine: 128
```

Output Execution of the corresponding test program should yield the following output:

```
A                                                                    B
0123456789
ABCDEFGHIJKLMNOPQRSTUVWXYZ abcdefghijklmnopqrstuvwxyz
!#$%&'()*+,-./:;<=>?@[]^_`{|}~"
-12346789




C                                                                    D
```

Screen Execution of the corresponding test program should yield the following output:

Keyboard This OS class is tested using a test program that effects some user-program interaction. For each function in the Keyboard class (keyPressed, readChar, readLine, readInt), the program requests the user to press some keyboard keys. If the function is implemented correctly and the requested keys are pressed, the program prints the text "ok" and proceeds to test the next function. If not, the program repeats the request for the same function. If all requests end successfully, the program prints 'Test ended successfully', at which point the screen may look like this:

```
keyPressed test:
Please press the 'Page Down' key
ok
readChar test:
(Verify that the pressed character is echoed to the screen)
Please press the number '3': 3
ok
readLine test:
(Verify echo and usage of 'backspace')
Please type 'JACK' and press enter: JACK
ok
readInt test:
(Verify echo and usage of 'backspace')
Please type '-32123' and press enter: -32123
ok

Test completed successfully
```

Sys Only two functions in this class can be tested: Sys.init and Sys.wait. The supplied test program tests the Sys.wait function by requesting the user to press any key, then waiting for two seconds (using Sys.wait), and then printing another message on the screen. The time that elapses from the moment the key is released until the next message is printed should be two seconds.

The Sys.init function is not tested explicitly. However, recall that it performs all the necessary OS initializations and then calls the Main.main function of each test program. Therefore, we can assume that nothing would work properly unless Sys.init is implemented correctly. A simple way to test Sys.init in isolation is to run the *Pong* game using your Sys.vm file.

Complete Test After testing successfully each OS class in isolation, test your entire OS implementation using the *Pong* game, whose source code is available in projects/12/Pong. Put all your OS .jack files in the Pong directory, compile the directory, and execute the game in the VM emulator. If the game works, then Mazel Tov! You are the proud owner of an operating system written entirely by you.

13   Postscript: More Fun to Go

We shall not cease from exploration, and at the end we will arrive where we started, and know the place for the first time.
—T. S. Eliot (1888–1965)

Congratulations! You have finished the construction of a complete computing system. We hope that you enjoyed this journey. Let us, the authors of this book, share a secret with you: We suspect that we enjoyed writing the book even more. After all, we got to *design* this computing system, and design is often the "funnest" part of every project. We are sure that some of you, adventurous readers, would like to get in on some of that design action. Maybe you would like to improve the architecture; maybe you have ideas for adding new features here and there; maybe you envision a wider system. And then, maybe, you just want to be in the navigator's seat and decide *where* to go, not only *how* to get there.

Many alternative design elements can be implemented by modifying and extending the software that you have written in the various projects. For example, the assembly language, the Jack language, and the operating system can be modified and extended at will, by changing their specifications and rewriting portions of your respective assembler, compiler, and OS implementations. Other changes would likely require modification of the software *supplied by us*. For example, if you change the VM specification or the hardware specification, then you would probably want to change the respective emulators as well. Or if you want to add a new input or output device to the Hack computer, you would probably need to model them as built-in chips in the hardware simulator.

In order to allow complete flexibility of modifications and extensions, we are making all the source code of the software associated with the book publicly available. All our code is 100 percent Java, expect for the batch files used for starting the software on the Windows and Linux platforms. The software and its documentation are available from the book's Web site at http://www.idc.ac.il/tecs. You are welcome to modify and extend all our tools as you deem desirable for your latest idea—and then share them with others, if you want. We hope that our code is written and documented well enough to make modification a satisfying experience. In particular, we wish to mention that the supplied hardware simulator has a simple and well-documented interface for adding new "built-in" chips. This interface can be used for extending the simulated hardware platform with, say, disk storage or communications devices.

While we cannot even start to imagine what *your* design improvements may be, we can briefly sketch some of the ones *we* were thinking of.

13.1   Hardware Realizations

Every hardware module presented in the book was software-based and HDL-simulated. This, in fact, is how hardware is actually designed. However, at some point the HDL designs are committed to silicon, becoming "real computers." Wouldn't it be nice to make Hack or Jack also run on some "real platform," made from some "real stuff"? Several different approaches may be taken towards this goal. On one extreme, you can attempt to nearly directly fabricate a real chip using the existing HDL design of Hack, and then deal with implementation issues related to the RAM, ROM, and I/O devices. Another extreme approach may be to attempt emulation (of either Hack, the VM, or even the Jack platform) on some existing hardware device like a cell phone or a PDA. It seems that any such project would want to reduce the size of the Hack screen as to keep the cost of the hardware resources reasonable.

13.2   Hardware Improvements

Although Hack is a *stored program computer*, the program that it runs must be pre-stored in its ROM device. In the present Hack architecture, there is no way of loading another program into the computer under user control, except for simulating the replacement of the entire physical ROM chip. Adding a "load program" capability in a balanced way would likely involve changes at several levels of the hierarchy. The Hack hardware can be modified to allow loaded programs to reside in a writable RAM rather than in the existing ROM. Some type of permanent storage (e.g., a disk-on-chip) can probably be added to the hardware, to allow storage of programs. The operating system can be extended to handle this permanent storage device, as well as new logic for loading and running programs. At this point some kind of an OS user interface ("shell" or "DOS window") would come in handy.

13.3   High-Level Languages

Like all professionals, programmers have strong feelings about their tools—the programming languages they use—and like to personalize them. And indeed, the Jack language, which leaves much to be desired, can be significantly improved or completely replaced (e.g., how about *Scheme*?). Some changes are simple, some are more involved, and some would likely require modifying the VM specification (e.g., adding real inheritance).

13.4   Optimizations

The book has almost completely sidestepped optimization issues (except for chapter 12, which introduced some efficiency measures). Optimization is a great playfield for every hacker. You can start with local optimizations in the existing compiler or hardware (or, in our platform, the best bang for the buck will probably come from optimizing the VM translator). Ambitious optimizations on a more global scale will involve changing specifications of interfaces such as the machine language or the VM language.

13.5   Communications

Wouldn't it be nice to connect the Hack computer to the Internet? This could probably be done by adding a built-in communication chip to the hardware and writing some OS code to deal with it and to handle higher-level communication protocols. Some other programs would need to "talk" with the simulated communication chip, providing an interface to the Internet. For example, an HTTP-speaking Web browser in Jack seems like a feasible and worthy project.

These are some of our design itches—what are yours?

Appendix A: Hardware Description Language (HDL)

Intelligence is the faculty of making artificial objects, especially tools to make tools.
—Henry Bergson (1859–1941)

A *Hardware Description Language* (HDL) is a formalism for defining and testing *chips*: objects whose interfaces consist of input and output pins that carry Boolean signals, and whose bodies are composed of interconnected collections of other, lower-level, chips. This appendix describes a typical HDL, as understood by the hardware simulator supplied with the book. Chapter 1 (in particular, section 1.1) provides essential background without which this appendix does not make much sense.

How to Use This Appendix   This is a technical reference, and thus there is no need to read it from beginning to end. Instead, we recommended focusing on selected sections, as needed. Also, HDL is an intuitive and self-explanatory language, and the best way to learn it is to play with some HDL programs using the supplied hardware simulator. Therefore, we recommend to start experimenting with HDL programs as soon as you can, beginning with the following example.

A.1   Example

Figure A.1 specifies a chip that accepts two three-bit numbers and outputs whether they are equal or not. The chip logic uses Xor gates to compare the three bit-pairs, and outputs true if all the comparisons agree. Each internal part Xxx invoked by an HDL program refers to a stand-alone chip defined in a separate `Xxx.hdl` program. Thus the chip designer who wrote the `EQ3.hdl` program assumed the availability of three other lower-level programs: `Xor.hdl`, `Or.hdl`, and `Not.hdl`. Importantly,

```
/** Checks if two 3-bit input buses are equal */
CHIP EQ3 {
    IN  a[3], b[3];
    OUT out;  // True iff a=b
    PARTS:
    Xor(a=a[0], b=b[0], out=c0);
    Xor(a=a[1], b=b[1], out=c1);
    Xor(a=a[2], b=b[2], out=c2);
    Or(a=c0, b=c1, out=c01);
    Or(a=c01, b=c2, out=neq);
    Not(in=neq, out=out);
}
```

Figure A.1   HDL program example.

though, the designer need not worry about *how* these chips are implemented. When building a new chip in HDL, the internal parts that participate in the design are always viewed as black boxes, allowing the designer to focus only on their proper arrangement in the current chip architecture.

Thanks to this modularity, all HDL programs, including those that describe high-level chips, can be kept short and readable. For example, a complex chip like RAM16K can be implemented using a few internal parts (e.g., RAM4K chips), each described in a single HDL line. When fully evaluated by the hardware simulator all the way down the recursive chip hierarchy, these internal parts are expanded into many thousands of interconnected elementary logic gates. Yet the chip designer need not be concerned by this complexity, and can focus instead only on the chip's top-most architecture.

A.2   Conventions

File extension: Each chip is defined in a separate text file. A chip whose name is Xxx is defined in file `Xxx.hdl`.

Chip structure: A chip definition consists of a *header* and a *body*. The header specifies the chip *interface*, and the body its *implementation*. The header acts as the chip's API, or public documentation. The body should not interest people who use the chip as an internal part in other chip definitions.

Syntax conventions: HDL is case sensitive. HDL keywords are written in uppercase letters.

Identifier naming: Names of chips and pins may be any sequence of letters and digits not starting with a digit. By convention, chip and pin names start with a capital letter and a lowercase letter, respectively. For readability, such names can include uppercase letters.

White space: Space characters, newline characters, and comments are ignored.

Comments: The following comment formats are supported:

```
//   Comment to end of line
/*   Comment until closing */
/** API documentation comment */
```

A.3   Loading Chips into the Hardware Simulator

HDL programs (chip descriptions) are loaded into the hardware simulator in three different ways. First, the user can open an HDL file interactively, via a "load file" menu or GUI icon. Second, a test script (discussed here) can include a `load Xxx.hdl` command, which has the same effect. Finally, whenever an HDL program is loaded and parsed, every chip name Xxx listed in it as an internal part causes the simulator to load the respective `Xxx.hdl` file, all the way down the recursive chip hierarchy. In every one of these cases, the simulator goes through the following logic:

if `Xxx.hdl` exists in the current directory
   then load it (and all its descendents) into the simulator
else
  if `Xxx.hdl` exists in the simulator's `builtIn` chips directory
    then load it (and all its descendents) into the simulator
  else
      issue an error message.

The simulator's `builtIn` directory contains executable versions of all the chips specified in the book, except for the highest-level chips (CPU, Memory, and Computer). Hence, one may construct and test every chip mentioned in the book before all, or even any, of its lower-level chip parts have been implemented: The simulator will automatically invoke their built-in versions instead. Likewise, if a lower-level chip Xxx has been implemented by the user in HDL, the user can still force the simulator to use its built-in version instead, by simply moving the Xxx.hdl file out from the current directory. Finally, in some cases the user (rather than the simulator) may want to load a built-in chip directly, for example, for experimentation. To do so, simply navigate to the tools/builtIn directory—a standard part of the hardware simulator environment—and select the desired chip from there.

A.4   Chip Header (Interface)

The header of an HDL program has the following format:

CHIP *chip name* {
   IN *input pin name, input pin name, . . . ;*
   OUT *output pin name, output pin name, . . . ;*
   // Here comes the body.
}

- *CHIP declaration:*   The CHIP keyword is followed by the chip name. The rest of the HDL code appears between curly brackets.

- *Input pins:*   The IN keyword is followed by a comma-separated list of input pin names. The list is terminated with a semicolon.

- *Output pins:*   The OUT keyword is followed by a comma-separated list of output pin names. The list is terminated with a semicolon.

Input and output pins are assumed by default to be single-bit wide. A multi-bit *bus* can be declared using the notation *pin name*[w] (e.g., a[3] in EQ3.hdl). This specifies that the pin is a bus of width w. The individual bits in a bus are indexed $0 \ldots w - 1$, from right to left (i.e., index 0 refers to the least significant bit).

A.5   Chip Body (Implementation)

A.5.1   Parts

A typical chip consists of several lower-level chips, connected to each other and to the chip input/output pins in a certain "logic" (connectivity pattern) designed to deliver the chip functionality. This logic, written by the HDL programmer, is described in the chip body using the format:

```
PARTS:
```
internal chip part;
internal chip part;
...
internal chip part;

Where each *internal chip part* statement describes one internal chip with all its *connections*, using the syntax:

chip name (connection, ..., connection);

Where each *connection* is described using the syntax:

part's pin names = chip's pin name

(Throughout this appendix, the presently defined chip is called *chip*, and the lower-level chips listed in the PARTS section are called *parts*).

A.5.2 Pins and Connections

Each *connection* describes how one pin of a part is connected to another pin in the chip definition. In the simplest case, the programmer connects a part's pin to an input or output pin of the chip. In other cases, a part's pin is connected to another pin of another part. This internal connection requires the introduction of an *internal pin*, as follows:

Internal Pins   In order to connect an output pin of one part to the input pins of other parts, the HDL programmer can create and use an *internal pin*, say v, as follows:

```
Part1 (..., out=v);        // out of Part1 is piped into v
Part2 (in=v, ...);         // v is piped into in of Part2
Part3 (a=v, b=v, ...);     // v is piped into both a and b of Part3
```

Internal pins (like v) are created as needed when they are specified the first time in the HDL program, and require no special declaration. Each internal pin has fan-in 1 and unlimited fan-out, meaning that it can be fed from a single source only, yet it can feed (through multiple connections) many other parts. In the preceding example, the internal pin v simultaneously feeds both Part2 (through in) and Part3 (though a and b).

Input Pins   Each input pin of a part may be fed by one of the following sources:

- an input pin of the chip
- an internal pin
- one of the constants `true` and `false`, representing 1 and 0, respectively

Each input pin has fan-in 1, meaning that it can be fed by one source only. Thus `Part (in1=v,in2=v,...)` is a valid statement, whereas `Part (in1=v,in1=u, ...)` is not.

Output Pins   Each output pin of a part may feed one of the following destinations:

- an output pin of the chip
- an internal pin

A.5.3   Buses

Each pin used in a connection—whether input, output, or internal—may be a *multi-bit bus*. The widths (number of bits) of input and output pins are defined in the chip header. The widths of internal pins are deduced implicitly, from their connections.

In order to connect individual elements of a multi-bit bus input or output pin, the pin name (say x) may be subscripted using the syntax `x[i]` or `x[i..j]=v`, where v is an internal pin. This means that only the bits indexed i to j (inclusive) of pin x are connected to the specified internal pin. An internal pin (like v above) may not be subscripted, and its width is deduced implicitly from the width of the bus pin to which it is connected the first time it is mentioned in the HDL program.

The constants `true` and `false` may also be used as buses, in which case the required width is deduced implicitly from the context of the connection.

Example

```
CHIP Foo {
    IN in[8]     // 8-bit input
    OUT out[8]   // 8-bit output
    // Foo's body (irrelevant to the example)
}
```

Suppose now that `Foo` is invoked by another chip using the part statement:

```
Foo(in[2..4]=v, in[6..7]=true, out[0..3]=x, out[2..6]=y)
```

where v is a previously declared 3-bit internal pin, bound to some value. In that case, the connections in[2..4]=v and in[6..7]=true will bind the in bus of the Foo chip to the following values:

in:	7	6	5	4	3	2	1	0	(Bit)
	1	1	?	v[2]	v[1]	v[0]	?	?	(Contents)

Now, let us assume that the logic of the Foo chip returns the following output:

out:	7	6	5	4	3	2	1	0
	1	1	0	1	0	0	1	1

In that case, the connections out[0..3]=x and out[2..6]=y will yield:

x:	3	2	1	0
	0	0	1	1

y:	4	3	2	1	0
	1	0	1	0	0

A.6   Built-In Chips

The hardware simulator features a library of built-in chips that can be used as internal parts by other chips. Built-in chips are implemented in code written in a programming language like Java, operating behind an HDL interface. Thus, a built-in chip has a standard HDL header (interface), but its HDL body (implementation) declares it as built-in. Figure A.2 gives a typical example.

The identifier following the keyword BUILTIN is the name of the program unit that implements the chip logic. The present version of the hardware simulator is built in Java, and all the built-in chips are implemented as compiled Java classes. Hence, the HDL body of a built-in chip has the following format:

BUILTIN *Java class name;*

where *Java class name* is the name of the Java class that delivers the chip functionality. Normally, this class will have the same name as that of the chip, for example Mux.class. All the built-in chips (compiled Java class files) are stored in a directory called tools/builtIn, which is a standard part of the simulator's environment.

Built-in chips provide three special services:

■ *Foundation:* Some chips are the atoms from which all other chips are built. In particular, we use Nand gates and flip-flop gates as the building blocks of all

```
/** 16-bit Multiplexor.
If sel = 0 then out = a else out = b.
This chip has a built-in implementation delivered by an external
Java class. */
CHIP Mux16 {
    IN a[16], b[16], sel;
    OUT out[16];
    BUILTIN Mux;  // Reference to builtIn/Mux.class, that
                  // implements both the Mux.hdl and the
                  // Mux16.hdl built-in chips.

}
```

Figure A.2   HDL definition of a built-in chip.

combinational and sequential chips, respectively. Thus the hardware simulator features built-in versions of Nand.hdl and DFF.hdl.

■ *Certification and efficiency:*   One way to modularize the development of a complex chip is to start by implementing built-in versions of its underlying chip parts. This enables the designer to build and test the chip logic while ignoring the logic of its lower-level parts—the simulator will automatically invoke their built-in implementations. Additionally, it makes sense to use built-in versions even for chips that were already constructed in HDL, since the former are typically much faster and more space-efficient than the latter (simulation-wise). For example, when you load RAM4k.hdl into the simulator, the simulator creates a memory-resident data structure consisting of thousands of lower-level chips, all the way down to the flip-flop gates at the bottom of the recursive chip hierarchy. Clearly, there is no need to repeat this drill-down simulation each time RAM4K is used as part in higher-level chips. ***Best practice tip:*** To boost performance and minimize errors, always use built-in versions of chips whenever they are available.

■ *Visualization:*   Some high-level chips (e.g., memory units) are easier to understand and debug if their operation can be inspected visually. To facilitate this service, built-in chips can be endowed (by their implementer) with GUI side effects. This GUI is displayed whenever the chip is loaded into the simulator or invoked as a lower-level part by the loaded chip. Except for these visual side effects, GUI-empowered chips behave, and can be used, just like any other chip. Section A.8 provides more details about GUI-empowered chips.

A.7   Sequential Chips

Computer chips are either *combinational* or *sequential* (also called *clocked*). The operation of combinational chips is instantaneous. When a user or a test script changes the values of one or more of the input pins of a combinational chip and reevaluates it, the simulator responds by immediately setting the chip output pins to a new set of values, as computed by the chip logic. In contrast, the operation of sequential chips is clock-regulated. When the inputs of a sequential chip change, the outputs of the chip may change only at the beginning of the next time unit, as effected by the simulated clock.

In fact, sequential chips (e.g., those implementing counters) may change their output values when the time changes even if none of their inputs changed. In contrast, combinational chips never change their values just because of the progression of time.

A.7.1   The Clock

The simulator models the progression of time by supporting two operations called *tick* and *tock*. These operations can be used to simulate a series of *time units*, each consisting of two phases: a *tick* ends the first phase of a time unit and starts its second phase, and a *tock* signals the first phase of the next time unit. The *real time* that elapsed during this period is irrelevant for simulation purposes, since we have full control over the clock. In other words, either the simulator's user or a test script can issue *ticks* and *tocks* at will, causing the clock to generate series of simulated time units.

The two-phased time units regulate the operations of *all* the sequential chip parts in the simulated chip architecture, as follows. During the first phase of the time unit (*tick*), the inputs of each sequential chip in the architecture are read and affect the chip's internal state, according to the chip logic. During the second phase of the time unit (*tock*), the outputs of the chip are set to the new values. Hence, if we look at a sequential chip "from the outside," we see that its output pins stabilize to new values only at *tocks*—between consecutive time units.

There are two ways to control the simulated clock: manual and script-based. First, the simulator's GUI features a clock-shaped button. One click on this button (a *tick*) ends the first phase of the clock cycle, and a subsequent click (a *tock*) ends the second phase of the cycle, bringing on the first phase of the next cycle, and so on. Alternatively, one can run the clock from a test script, for example, using the command `repeat n {tick, tock, output;}`. This particular example instructs the simulator to advance the clock *n* time units, and to print some values in the process. Test scripts and commands like `repeat` and `output` are described in detail in appendix B.

A.7.2   Clocked Chips and Pins

A built-in chip can declare its dependence on the clock explicitly, using the statement:

CLOCKED *pin, pin, . . . , pin;*

where each *pin* is one of the input or output pins declared in the chip header. The inclusion of an *input pin x* in the CLOCKED list instructs the simulator that changes to *x* should not affect any of the chip's output pins until the beginning of the next time unit. The inclusion of an *output pin x* in the CLOCKED list instructs the simulator that changes in any of the chip's input pins should not affect *x* until the beginning of the next time unit.

Note that it is quite possible that only some of the input or output pins of a chip are declared as clocked. In that case, changes in the nonclocked input pins may affect the nonclocked output pins in a combinational manner, namely, independent of the clock. In fact, it is also possible to have the CLOCKED keyword with an empty list of pins, signifying that even though the chip may change its internal state depending on the clock, changes to any of its input pins may cause immediate changes to any of its output pins.

The "Clocked" Property of Chips   How does the simulator know that a given chip is clocked? If the chip is built-in, then its HDL code may include the keyword CLOCKED. If the chip is not built-in, then it is said to be clocked when one or more of its lower-level chip parts are clocked. This "clocked" property is checked recursively, all the way down the chip hierarchy, where a built-in chip may be explicitly clocked. If such a chip is found, it renders every chip that depends on it (up the hierarchy) implicitly clocked. It follows that nothing in the HDL code of a given chip suggests that it may be clocked—the only way to know for sure is to read the chip documentation. For example, let us consider how the built-in DFF chip (figure A.3) impacts the "clockedness" of some of other chips presented in the book.

Every sequential chip in our computer architecture depends in one way or another on (typically numerous) DFF chips. For example, the RAM64 chip is made of eight RAM8 chips. Each one of these chips is made of eight lower-level Register chips. Each one of these registers is made of sixteen Bit chips. And each one of these Bit

```
/** D-Flip-Flop.
If load[t-1]=1 then out[t]=in[t-1] else out does not change. */
CHIP DFF {
  IN in;
  OUT out;
  BUILTIN DFF;        // Implemented by builtIn/DFF.class.
  CLOCKED in, out;    // Explicitly clocked.
}
```

Figure A.3   HDL definition of a clocked chip.

chips contains a DFF part. It follows that Bit, Register, RAM8, RAM64 and all the memory units above them are also clocked chips.

It's important to remember that a sequential chip may well contain combinational logic that is not affected by the clock. For example, the structure of every sequential RAM chip includes combinational circuits that manage its addressing logic (described in chapter 3).

A.7.3   Feedback Loops

We say that the use of a chip entails a feedback loop when the output of one of its parts affects the input of the same part, either directly or through some (possibly long) path of dependencies. For example, consider the following two examples of direct feedback dependencies:

```
Not (in=loop1, out=loop1)    // Invalid
DFF (in=loop2, out=loop2)    // Valid
```

In each example, an internal pin (`loop1` or `loop2`) attempts to feed the chip's input from its output, creating a cycle. The difference between the two examples is that `Not` is a *combinational* chip whereas DFF is *clocked*. In the Not example, `loop1` creates an instantaneous and uncontrolled dependency between `in` and `out`, sometimes called *data race*. In the DFF case, the `in-out` dependency created by `loop2` is delayed by the clocked logic of the DFF, and thus `out(t)` is not a function of `in(t)` but rather of `in(t-1)`. In general, we have the following:

Valid/Invalid Feedback Loops   When the simulator loads a chip, it checks recursively if its various connections entail feedback loops. For each loop, the simulator checks if the loop goes through a clocked pin, somewhere along the loop. If so, the loop is allowed. Otherwise, the simulator stops processing and issues an error message. This is done in order to avoid uncontrolled data races.

A.8   Visualizing Chip Operations

Built-in chips may be "GUI-empowered." These chips feature visual side effects, designed to animate chip operations. A GUI-empowered chip can come to play in a simulation in two different ways, just like any other chip. First, the user can load it directly into the simulator. Second, and more typically, whenever a GUI-empowered chip is used as a part in the simulated chip, the simulator invokes it automatically. In both cases, the simulator displays the chip's graphical image on the screen. Using this image, which is typically an interactive GUI component, one may inspect the current contents of the chip as well as change its internal state, when this operation is supported by the built-in chip implementation. The current version of this simulator features the following set of GUI-empowered chips:

ALU: Displays the Hack ALU's inputs and output as well as the presently computed function.

Registers (There are three of them: ARegister—address register, DRegister—data register, and PC—program counter):   Displays the contents of the register and allows modifying its contents.

Memory chips (ROM32K and various RAM chips):   Displays a scrollable array-like image that shows the contents of all the memory locations and allows their modification. If the contents of a memory location changes during the simulation, the respective entry in the GUI changes as well. In the case of the ROM32K chip (which serves as the instruction memory of our computer platform), the GUI also features a button that enables loading a machine language program from an external text file.

Screen chip: If the HDL code of a loaded chip invokes the built-in Screen chip, the hardware simulator displays a 256 rows by 512 columns window that simulates the physical screen. When the RAM-resident memory map of the screen changes during the simulation, the respective pixels in the screen GUI change as well, via a "refresh logic" embedded in the simulator implementation.

Keyboard chip: If the HDL code of a loaded chip invokes the built-in Keyboard chip, the simulator displays a clickable keyboard icon. Clicking this button connects the real keyboard of your computer to the simulated chip. From this point on, every

```
// Demo of GUI-empowered chips.
// The logic of this chip is meaningless, and is used merely to
// force the simulator to display the GUI effects of some other
// chips.
CHIP GUIDemo {
   IN in[16], load, address[15];
   OUT out[16];
   PARTS:
   RAM16K(in=in, load=load, address=address[0..13], out=a);
   Screen(in=in, load=load, address=address[0..12], out=b);
   Keyboard(out=c);
}
```

Figure A.4   HDL definition of a GUI-empowered chip.

key pressed on the real keyboard is intercepted by the simulated chip, and its binary code is displayed in the keyboard's RAM-resident memory map. If the user moves the mouse focus to another area in the simulator GUI, the control of the keyboard is restored to the real computer. Figure A.4 illustrates many of the features just described.

The chip logic in figure A.4 feeds the 16-bit in value into two destinations: register number *address* in the RAM16K chip and register number *address* in the Screen chip (presumably, the HDL programmer who wrote this code has figured out the widths of these address pins from the documentation of these chips). In addition, the chip logic routes the value of the currently pressed keyboard key to the internal pin c. These meaningless operations are designed for one purpose only: to illustrate how the simulator deals with built-in GUI-empowered chips. The actual impact is shown in figure A.5.

A.9   Supplied and New Built-In Chips

The built-in chips supplied with the hardware simulator are listed in figure A.6. These Java-based chip implementations were designed to support the construction and simulation of the Hack computer platform (although some of them can be used to support other 16-bit platforms). Users who wish to develop hardware platforms

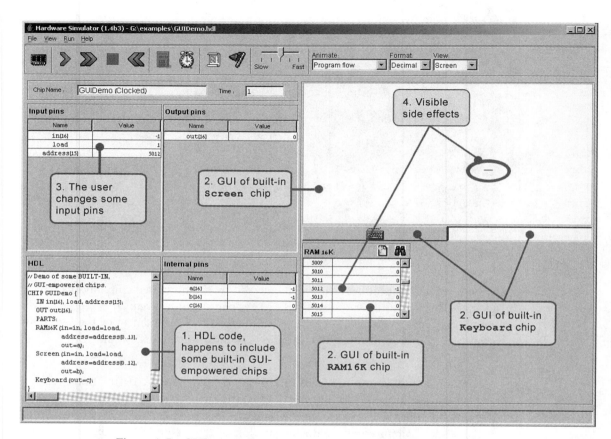

Figure A.5 GUI-empowered chips. Since the loaded HDL program uses GUI-empowered chips as internal parts (step 1), the simulator draws their respective GUI images (step 2). When the user changes the values of the chip input pins (step 3), the simulator reflects these changes in the respective GUIs (step 4). The circled horizontal line is the visual side effect of storing −1 in memory location 5012. Since the 16-bit 2's complement binary code of −1 is 1111111111111111, the computer draws 16 pixels starting at the 320th column of row 156, which happen to be the screen coordinates associated with address 5012 of the screen memory map (the exact memory-to-screen mapping is given in chapter 4).

Chip name	Specified in chapter	Has GUI	Comment
Nand	1		Foundation of all combinational chips
Not	1		
And	1		
Or	1		
Xor	1		
Mux	1		
DMux	1		
Not16	1		
And16	1		
Or16	1		
Mux16	1		
Or8way	1		
Mux4way16	1		
Mux8way16	1		
DMux4way	1		
DMux8way	1		
HalfAdder	2		
FullAdder	2		
Add16	2		
ALU	2	☑	
Inc16	2		
DFF	3		Foundation of all sequential chips
Bit	3		
Register	3		
ARegister	3	☑	Identical operation to Register, with GUI
DRegister	3	☑	Identical operation to Register, with GUI
RAM8	3	☑	
RAM64	3	☑	
RAM512	3	☑	
RAM4K	3	☑	
RAM16K	3	☑	
PC	3	☑	Program counter
ROM32K	5	☑	GUI allows loading a program from a text file
Screen	5	☑	GUI connects to a simulated screen
Keyboard	5	☑	GUI connects to the actual keyboard

Figure A.6   All the built-in chips supplied with the present version of the hardware simulator. A built-in chip has an HDL interface but is implemented as an executable Java class.

other than Hack would probably benefit from the simulator's ability to accommodate new built-in chip definitions.

Developing New Built-In Chips   The hardware simulator can execute any desired chip logic written in HDL; the ability to execute new built-in chips (in addition to those listed in figure A.6) written in Java is also possible, using a chip-extension API. Built-in chip implementations can be designed by users in Java to add new hardware components, introduce GUI effects, speed-up execution, and facilitate behavioral simulation of chips that are not yet developed in HDL (an important capability when designing new hardware platforms and related hardware construction projects). For more information about developing new built-in chips, see chapter 13.

Appendix B: Test Scripting Language

Mistakes are the portals of discovery.
—James Joyce (1882–1941)

Testing is a critically important element of systems development, and one that typically gets little attention in computer science education. In this book we take testing very seriously. In fact, we believe that before one sets out to develop a new hardware or software module *P*, one should first develop a module *T* designed to test it. Further, *T* should then become part of *P*'s official development's contract.

As a matter of best practice, the ultimate test of a newly designed module should be formulated not by the module's developer, but rather by the architect who specified the module's interface. Therefore, for every chip or software system specified in the book, we supply an official test program, written by us. Although you are welcome to test your work in any way you see fit, the contract is such that eventually, *your* implementation must pass *our* tests.

In order to streamline the definition and execution of the numerous tests scattered all over the book projects, we designed a uniform *test scripting language*. This language works almost the same across all the simulators supplied with the book:

- *Hardware simulator:*   used to simulate and test chips written in HDL
- *CPU emulator:*   used to simulate and test machine language programs
- *VM emulator:*   used to simulate and test programs written in the VM language

Every one of these simulators features a rich GUI that enables the user to test the loaded chip or program interactively, using graphical icons, or batch-style, using a test script. A *test script* is a series of commands that (a) load a hardware or software module into the relevant simulator, and (b) subject the module to a series of preplanned (rather than ad hoc) testing scenarios. In addition, the test scripts feature commands for printing the test results and comparing them to desired results, as defined in supplied compare files. In sum, a test script enables a systematic, replicable, and documented testing of the underlying code—an invaluable requirement in any hardware or software development project.

Important   We don't expect students to write test scripts. *The test scripts necessary to test all the hardware and software modules mentioned in the book are supplied by us and available on the book's Web site.* Therefore, the chief purpose of this appendix is to explain the syntax and logic of the supplied test scripts, as needed.

B.1   File Format and Usage

The act of testing a hardware or software module using any one of the supplied simulators involves four types of files:

Xxx.yyy: where Xxx is the module name and yyy is either `hdl`, `hack`, `asm`, or `vm`, standing respectively for a chip definition written in HDL, a program written in the Hack machine language, a program written in the Hack assembly language, or a program written in the VM virtual machine language;

Xxx.tst: this *test script* walks the simulator through a series of steps designed to test the code stored in Xxx.yyy;

Xxx.out: this optional *output file* keeps a printed record of the actual simulation results;

Xxx.cmp: this optional *compare file* contains a presupplied record of the desired simulation results.

All these files should be kept in the same directory, which can be conveniently named xxx. In all simulators, the "current directory" refers to the directory from which the last file has been opened in the simulator environment.

White space: Space characters, newline characters, and comments in test scripts (Xxx.tst files) are ignored. Test scripts are not case sensitive, except for file and directory names.

Comments: The following comment formats can appear in test scripts:

```
//   Comment to end of line
/*   Comment until closing */
/** API documentation comment */
```

Usage: In all the projects that appear in the book, the files `Xxx.tst`, `Xxx.out`, and `Xxx.cmp` are supplied by us. These files are designed to test `Xxx.yyy`, whose development is the essence of the project. In some cases, we also supply a skeletal version of `Xxx.yyy`, for example, an HDL interface with a missing implementation part. All the files in all the projects are plain text files that can be viewed and edited using plain text editors.

Typically, one starts a simulation session by loading the supplied `Xxx.tst` script file into the relevant simulator. Typically, the first commands in the script instruct the simulator to load the code stored in `Xxx.yyy` and then, optionally, initialize an output file and a compare file. The remaining commands in the script run the actual tests, as we elaborate below.

B.2   Testing Chips on the Hardware Simulator

The hardware simulator supplied with the book is designed for testing and simulating chip definitions written in the Hardware Description Language (HDL) described in appendix A. Chapter 1 provides essential background on chip development and testing, and thus it is recommended to read it first.

B.2.1   Example

The script shown in figure B.1 is designed to test the EQ3 chip defined in figure A.1. A test script normally starts with some initialization commands, followed by a series of *simulation steps*, each ending with a semicolon. A simulation step typically instructs the simulator to bind the chip's input pins to some test values, evaluate the chip logic, and write selected variable values into a designated output file. Figure B.2 illustrates the EQ3.tst script in action.

B.2.2   Data Types and Variables

Data Types Test scripts support two data types: integers and strings. Integer constants can be expressed in hexadecimal (`%X` prefix), binary (`%B` prefix), or decimal (`%D` prefix) format, which is the default. These values are always translated into their equivalent 2's complement binary values. For example, the commands `set a1 %B1111111111111111`, `set a2 %XFFFF`, `set a3 %D-1`, `set a4 -1` will set the four variables to the same value: a series of sixteen 1's, representing "minus one" in

```
/* EQ3.tst: tests the EQ3.hdl program. The EQ3 chip should
   return true if its two 3-bit inputs are equal and false
   otherwise. */
load EQ3.hdl,          // Load the HDL program into the simulator
output-file EQ3.out,   // Write script outputs to this file
compare-to EQ3.cmp,    // Compare script outputs to this file
output-list a b out;   // Each subsequent output command should
                       // print the values of the variables
                       // a, b, and out
set a %B000, set b %B000, eval, output;
set a %B111, set b %B111, eval, output;
set a %B111, set b %B000, eval, output;
set a %B000, set b %B111, eval, output;
set a %B001, set b %B000, eval, output;
// Since the chip has two 3-bit inputs,
// an exhaustive test requires 2^3*2^3=64 such scenarios.
```

Figure B.1   Testing a chip on the hardware simulator.

decimal. String values (%s prefix) are used strictly for printing purposes and cannot be assigned to variables. String constants must be enclosed by " ".

The simulator clock (used in testing sequential chips only) emits a series of values denoted 0, 0+, 1, 1+, 2, 2+, 3, 3+, and so forth. The progression of these *clock cycles* (also called *time units*) is controlled by two script commands called tick and tock. A tick moves the clock value from t to $t+$, and a tock from $t+$ to $t+1$, bringing upon the next time unit. The current time unit is stored in a system variable called time.

Script commands can access three types of variables: pins, variables of built-in chips, and the system variable time.

Pins: Input, output, and internal pins of the simulated chip. For example, the command set in 0 sets the value of the pin whose name is in to 0.

Variables of built-in chips: Exposed by the chip's external implementation. See section B.2.4 for more details.

Time: The number of time units that elapsed since the simulation started running (read-only).

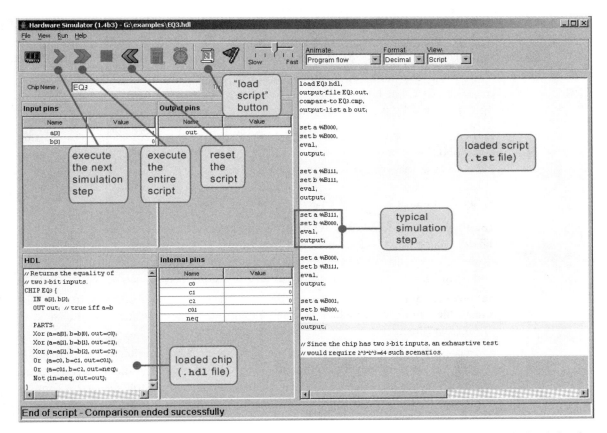

Figure B.2 Typical hardware simulation session, shown at the script's end. The loaded script is identical to EQ3.tst from figure B.1, except that some white space was added to improve readability.

B.2.3 Script Commands

Command Syntax A script is a sequence of commands. Each command is terminated by a comma, a semicolon, or an exclamation mark. These terminators have the following semantics:

- Comma (**,**): terminates a script command.

- Semicolon (**;**): terminates a script command and a simulation step. A simulation step consists of one or more script commands. When the user instructs the simulator to "single-step" via the simulator's GUI, the simulator executes the script from the current command until a semicolon is reached, at which point the simulation is paused.

- Exclamation mark (!): terminates a script command and stops the script execution. The user can later resume the script execution from that point onward. This option is typically used to facilitate interactive debugging.

It is convenient to organize the script commands in two conceptual sections. "Set up commands" are used to load files and initialize global settings. "Simulation commands" walk the simulator through a series of tests.

Setup Commands

load Xxx.hdl: Loads the HDL program stored in Xxx.hdl into the simulator. The file name must include the .hdl extension and must not include a path specification. The simulator will try to load the file from the current directory, and, failing that, from the simulator's builtIn directory, as described in section A.3.

output-file Xxx.out: Instructs the simulator to write further output to the named file, which must include an .out extension. The output file will be created in the current directory.

output-list $v1, v2, \dots$:   Instructs the simulator what to write to the output file in every subsequent output command in this script (until the next output-list command, if any). Each value in the list is a variable name followed by a formatting specification. The command also produces a single header line consisting of the variable names. Each item v in the output-list has the syntax *variable format padL.len.padR*. This directive instructs the simulator to write *padL* spaces, then the current *variable* value in the specified *format* using *len* columns, then *padR* spaces, then the divider symbol "|". *Format* can be either %B (binary), %X (hexa), %D (decimal) or %S (string). The default format specification is %B1.1.1.

For example, the CPU.hdl chip of the Hack platform has an input pin named reset, an output pin named pc (among others), and a chip part named DRegister (among others). If we want to track the values of these variables during the chip's execution, we can use something like the following command:

```
Output-list   time%S1.5.1            // System variable
              reset%B2.1.2           // Input pin of the chip
              pc%D2.3.1              // Output pin of the chip
              DRegister[] %X3.4.4    // State of this built-in part
```

(State variables of built-in chips are explained here.) This command may produce the following output (after two subsequent output commands):

```
| time  |reset|  pc |DRegister[]|
|   20+ |  0  | 21  |    FFFF   |
|   21  |  0  | 22  |    FFFF   |
```

compare-to Xxx.cmp: Instructs the simulator that each subsequent output line should be compared to its corresponding line in the specified comparison file (which must include the .cmp extension). If any two lines are not the same, the simulator displays an error message and halts the script execution. The compare file is assumed to be present in the current directory.

Simulation Commands

set *variable value*:   Assigns the *value* to the *variable*. The variable is either a pin or an internal variable of the simulated chip or one of its chip parts. The widths of the *value* and the *variable* must be compatible. For example, if x is a 16-bit pin and y is a 1-bit pin, then set x 153 is valid whereas set y 153 will yield an error and halt the simulation.

eval: Instructs the simulator to apply the chip logic to the current values of the input pins and compute the resulting output values.

output: This command causes the simulator to go through the following logic:

1.   Get the current values of all the variables listed in the last output-list command.

2.   Create an output line using the format specified in the last output-list command.

3.   Write the output line to the output file.

4.   (if a compare file has been previously declared via the compare-to command): If the output line differs from the current line of the compare file, display an error message and stop the script's execution.

5.   Advance the line cursors of the output file and the compare file.

tick: Ends the first phase of the current time unit (clock cycle).

tock: Ends the second phase of the current time unit and embarks on the first phase of the next time unit.

repeat *num* {*commands*}:   Instructs the simulator to repeat the *commands* enclosed by the curly brackets *num* times. If *num* is omitted, the simulator repeats the *commands* until the simulation has been stopped for some reason.

while *Boolean-condition* **{***commands***}**:   Instructs the simulator to repeat the *com-mands* enclosed in the curly brackets as long as the *Boolean-condition* is true. The condition is of the form *x op y* where *x* and *y* are either constants or variable names and *op* is one of the following: =, >, <, >=, <=, <>. If *x* and *y* are strings, *op* can be either = or <>.

echo *text*:   Instructs the simulator to display the *text* string in the status line (which is part of the simulator GUI). The text must be enclosed by " ".

clear-echo: Instructs the simulator to clear the status line.

breakpoint *variable value*:   Instructs the simulator to compare the value of the specified *variable* to the specified *value*. The comparison is performed after the execution of each script command. If the *variable* contains the specified *value*, the execution halts and a message is displayed. Otherwise, the execution continues normally.

clear-breakpoints: Clears all the previously defined breakpoints.

built-in-chip *method argument(s)*:   External implementations of built-in chips can expose methods that perform chip-specific operations. The syntax of the allowable method calls varies from one built-in chip to another and is documented next.

B.2.4   Variables and Methods of Built-In Chips

The logic of a chip can be implemented by either an HDL program or by a high-level programming language, in which case the chip is said to be "built-in" and "exter-nally implemented." External implementations of built-in chips can facilitate access to the chip's state via the syntax *chipName[varName]*, where *varName* is an imple-mentation-specific variable that should be documented in the chip API. The APIs of all the built-in chips supplied with the book (as part of the Hack computer platform) are shown in figure B.3.

For example, consider the command set RAM16K[1017] 15. If RAM16K is the currently simulated chip or an internal part of the currently simulated chip, this command will set its memory location number 1017 to the 2's complement binary value of 15. Further, since the built-in RAM16K chip happens to have GUI side effects, the new value will also be displayed in the chip's visual image.

If a built-in chip maintains a single-valued internal state, the current value of the state can be accessed through the notation *chipName[ ]*. If the internal state is a vector, the notation *chipName[i]* is used. For example, when simulating the built-in Register chip, one can write script commands like set Register[ ] 135. This com-mand sets the internal state of the chip to the 2's complement binary value of 135; in

Chip name	Exposed variables	Data type/range	Methods
Register	Register[ ]	16-bit (-32768...32767)	
ARegister	ARegister[ ]	16-bit	
DRegister	DRegister[ ]	16-bit	
PC	PC[ ]	15-bit (0..32767)	
RAM8	RAM8[0..7]	Each entry is 16-bit	
RAM64	RAM64[0..63]	"	
RAM512	RAM512[0..511]	"	
RAM4K	RAM4K[0..4095]	"	
RAM16K	RAM16K[0..16383]	"	
ROM32K	ROM32K[0..32767]	"	load Xxx.hack/Xxx.asm
Screen	Screen[0..16383]	"	
Keyboard	Keyboard[ ]	16-bit, read-only	

Figure B.3   API of all the built-in chips supplied with the book.

the next time unit, the Register chip will commit to this value and its output will start emitting it.

Built-in chips can also expose implementation-specific *methods* that extend the simulator's commands repertoire. For example, in the Hack computer, programs reside in an instruction memory unit implemented by a chip named ROM32K. Before one runs a machine language program on this computer, one must first load a program into this chip. In order to facilitate this service, our built-in implementation of ROM32K features a load *file name* method, referring to a text file that, hopefully, contains machine language instructions. This chip-specific method can be accessed by a test script via commands like ROM32K load Myprog.hack. In the chip set supplied with the book, this is the only method supported by any of the built-in chips.

B.2.5   Ending Example

We end this section with a relatively complex test script, designed to test the topmost Computer chip of the Hack platform. One way to test the Computer chip is to load a machine language program into it and monitor selected values as the computer executes the program, one instruction at a time. For example, we wrote a program that (hopefully) computes the maximum of RAM[0] and RAM[1] and writes the result to RAM[2]. The machine language version of this program is stored in the text file Max.hack. Note that at the very low level in which we operate, if such a program does not run properly it may be either because the program is buggy, or the hardware is buggy (and, for completeness, it may also be that the test script or the hardware simulator are buggy). For simplicity, let us assume that everything is error-free, except, possibly, for the tested Computer chip.

To test the Computer chip using the `Max.hack` program, we wrote a test script called `ComputerMax.tst`. This script loads `Computer.hdl` into the hardware simulator and then loads the `Max.hack` program into its ROM32K chip part. A reasonable way to check if the chip works properly is as follows: put some values in RAM[0] and RAM[1], reset the computer, run the clock, and inspect RAM[2]. This, in a nutshell, is what the script in figure B.4 is designed to do.

How can we tell that fourteen clock cycles are sufficient for executing this program? This can be found by trial and error, starting with a large value and watching the computer's outputs stabilizing after a while, or by analyzing the run-time behavior of the currently loaded program.

B.2.6   Default Script

The simulator's GUI buttons (single step, run, stop, reset) don't control the loaded chip. Rather, they control the progression of the loaded script, which controls the loaded chip's operation. Thus, there is a question of what to do if the user has loaded a chip directly into the simulator without loading a script first. In such cases, the simulator uses the following default script:

```
// Default script of the hardware simulator
repeat {
  tick,
  tock;
}
```

B.3   Testing Machine Language Programs on the CPU Emulator

The CPU emulator supplied with the book is designed for testing and simulating the execution of binary programs on the Hack computer platform described in chapter 5. The tested programs can be written in either the native Hack code or the assembly language described in chapter 4. In the latter case, the simulator translates the loaded code into binary on the fly, as part of the "load program" operation.

```
/* ComputerMax.tst script.
   The max.hack program should compute the maximum of
   RAM[0] and RAM[1] and write the result in RAM[2]. */

// Load the Computer chip and set up for the simulation
load Computer.hdl,
output-file Computer.out,
compare-to ComputerMax.cmp,
output-list RAM16K[0] RAM16K[1] RAM16K[2];

// Load the Max.hack program into the ROM32K chip part
ROM32K load Max.hack,
// Set the first 2 cells of the RAM16K chip part to some test values
set RAM16K[0] 3,
set RAM16K[1] 5,
output;
// Run the clock enough cycles to complete the program's execution
repeat 14 {
    tick, tock,
    output;
}

// Reset the Computer
set reset 1,
tick,          // Run the clock in order to commit the Program
tock,          // Counter (PC, a sequential chip) to the new reset value
output;
// Now re-run the program with different test values.
set reset 0,   // "De-reset" the computer (committed in next tick-tock)
set RAM16K[0] 23456,
set RAM16K[1] 12345,
output;
repeat 14 {
    tick, tock,
    output;
}
```

Figure B.4   Testing the topmost Computer chip.

As a convention, a script that tests a machine language program `Xxx.hack` or `Xxx.asm` is called `Xxx.tst`. As usual, the simulation involves four files: the test script itself (`Xxx.tst`), the tested program (`Xxx.hack` or `Xxx.asm`), an optional output file (`Xxx.out`) and an optional compare file (`Xxx.cmp`). All these files must reside in the same directory. This directory can be conveniently named `xxx`. For more information about file structure and recommended usage, see section B.1.

B.3.1   Example

Consider the multiplication program `Mult.hack`, designed to effect $RAM[2] = RAM[0]*RAM[1]$. A reasonable way to test this program is to put some values in $RAM[0]$ and $RAM[1]$, run the program, and inspect $RAM[2]$. This logic is carried out in figure B.5.

```
// Load the program and set up for the simulation
load Mult.hack,
output-file Mult.out,
compare-to Mult.cmp,
output-list RAM[2]%D2.6.2;

// Set the first 2 cells of the RAM to some test values
set RAM[0] 2,
set RAM[1] 5;
// Run the clock enough cycles to complete the program's execution
repeat 20 {
  ticktock;
}
output;

// Re-run the same program with different test values
set PC 0,
set RAM[0] 8,
set RAM[1] 7;
repeat 50 {    // Mult.hack is based on repetitive addition, so
  ticktock;    // greater multiplicands require more clock cycles
}
output;
```

Figure B.5   Testing a machine language program on the CPU emulator.

B.3.2   Variables

The CPU emulator, which is hardware-specific, recognizes a set of variables related to internal components of the Hack platform. In particular, scripting commands running on the CPU emulator can access the following elements:

A: value of the address register (unsigned 15-bit);

D: value of the data register (16-bit);

PC: value of the Program Counter register (unsigned 15-bit);

RAM[i]:   value of RAM location *i* (16-bit);

time: Number of time units (also called clock cycles, or *ticktocks*) that elapsed since the simulation started (read-only).

B.3.3   Commands

The CPU emulator supports all the commands described in section B.2.3, except for the following changes:

load *program*:   Here *program* is either Xxx.hack or Xxx.asm. This command loads a machine language program (to be tested) into the simulated instruction memory. If the program is written in assembly, it is translated into binary on the fly.

eval: Not applicable;

built-in-chip *method argument(s)*:   Not applicable;

ticktock: This command is used instead of tick and tock. Each ticktock advances the clock one time unit (cycle).

B.3.4   Default Script

The CPU emulator's GUI buttons (single step, run, stop, reset) don't control the loaded program. Rather, they control the progression of the loaded script, which controls the program's operation. Thus, there is a question of what to do if the user has loaded a program directly into the CPU emulator without loading a script first. In such cases, the emulator uses the following default script:

```
// Default script of the CPU emulator
repeat {
  ticktock;
}
```

B.4   Testing VM Programs on the VM Emulator

Chapters 7–8 describe a virtual machine model and specify a VM implementation on the Hack platform. The VM emulator supplied with the book is an alternative VM implementation that uses Java to run VM programs, visualize their operations, and display the states of the effected virtual memory segments.

Recall that a VM program consists of one or more `.vm` files. Thus, the simulation of a VM program involves four elements: the test script (`Xxx.tst`), the tested program (a single `Xxx.vm` file or an `Xxx` directory containing one or more `.vm` files), an optional output file (`Xxx.out`) and an optional compare file (`Xxx.cmp`). All these files must reside in the same directory, which can be conveniently named `xxx`. For more information about file structure and recommended usage, see section B.1. Chapter 7 provides essential information about the virtual machine architecture, without which the discussion below will not make much sense.

Startup Code   A VM program is normally assumed to contain at least two functions: `Main.main` and `Sys.init`. When the VM translator translates a VM program, it generates machine language code that sets the stack pointer to 256 and then calls the `Sys.init` function, which then calls `Main.main`. In a similar fashion, when the VM emulator is instructed to execute a VM program (collection of one or more VM functions), it is programmed to start running the `Sys.init` function, which is assumed to exist somewhere in the loaded VM code. If a `Sys.init` function is not found, the emulator is programmed to start executing the first command in the loaded VM code.

The latter convention was added to the emulator in order to assist the gradual development of the VM implementation, which spans two chapters in the book. In chapter 7, we build only the part of the VM implementation that deals with `pop`, `push`, and arithmetic commands, without getting into subroutine calling commands. Thus, the test programs associated with Project 7 consist of "raw" VM commands without the typical `function/return` wrapping. Since we wish to allow informal experimentation with such commands, we gave the VM emulator the ability to execute "raw" VM code which is neither properly initialized nor properly packaged in a function structure.

Virtual Memory Segments   In the process of simulating the virtual machine's operations, the VM emulator manages the virtual memory segments of the Hack VM (`argument`, `local`, etc.). These segments must be allocated to the host RAM—a task that the emulator normally carries out as a side effect of simulating the execution of `call`, `function`, and `return` commands. This means that when simulating "raw" VM code that contains no subroutine calling commands, we must force the VM emulator to explicitly anchor the virtual segments in the RAM—at least those segments mentioned in the current code. Conveniently, this initialization can be accomplished by script commands that manipulate the pointers controlling the base RAM addresses of the virtual segments. Using these script commands, we can effectively put the virtual segments in selected areas in the host RAM.

B.4.1   Example

The `FibonacciSeries.vm` file contains a series of VM commands that compute the first n elements of the Fibonacci series. The code is designed to operate on two arguments: the value of n and the starting memory address in which the computed elements should be stored. The script in figure B.6 is designed to test this program using the actual arguments 6 and 4000.

B.4.2   Variables

Scripting commands running on the VM emulator can access the following elements:

Contents of Virtual Memory Segments

`local[i]`:   value of the i-th element of the `local` segment;

`argument[i]`:   value of the i-th element of the `argument` segment;

`this[i]`:   value of the i-th element of the `this` segment;

`that[i]`:   value of the i-th element of the `that` segment;

`temp[i]`:   value of the i-th element of the `temp` segment.

Pointers to Virtual Memory Segments

`local`:   base address of the `local` segment in the RAM;

`argument`:   base address of the `argument` segment in the RAM;

`this`:   base address of the `this` segment in the RAM;

`that`:   base address of the `that` segment in the RAM.

```
/* The FibonacciSeries.vm file contains a series of VM commands
   that compute the first n Fibonacci numbers. The program's
   code contains no function/call/return commands, and thus the
   VM emulator must be forced to initialize the virtual memory
   segments used by the code explicitly.
*/
// Load the program and set up for the simulation
load FibonacciSeries.vm,
output-file FibonacciSeries.out,
compare-to FibonacciSeries.cmp,
output-list RAM[4000]%D1.6.2 RAM[4001]%D1.6.2 RAM[4002]%D1.6.2
            RAM[4003]%D1.6.2 RAM[4004]%D1.6.2 RAM[4005]%D1.6.2;
// Initialize the stack and the argument and local segments.
set SP 256,              // Stack pointer (stack begins in RAM[256])
set local 300,           // Base the local segment in some RAM location
set argument 400;        // Base the argument segment in some RAM loc.
// Set the arguments to two test values
set argument[0] 6,       // n=6
set argument[1] 4000;    // Put the series at RAM[4000] and onward
// Execute enough VM steps to complete the program's execution
repeat 140 {
  vmstep;
}
output;
```

Figure B.6   Testing a VM program on the VM emulator.

Implementation-Specific Variables

RAM[i]:   value of the i-th RAM location;

SP: value of the stack pointer;

currentFunction: name of the currently executing function (read only).

line: contains a string of the form: *current-function-name.line-index-in-function* (read only).

For example, when execution reaches the third line of the function Sys.init, the line variable contains "Sys.init.3". This is a useful means for setting breakpoints in selected locations in the loaded VM program.

B.4.3   Commands

The VM emulator supports all the commands described in section B.2.3, except for the following changes:

load *source*:   Here *source* is either `Xxx.vm`, the name of a file containing one or more VM functions, or a series of "raw" VM commands, or `Xxx`, the name of a directory containing one or more `.vm` files (in which case all of them are loaded).

If the `.vm` files are located in the current directory, the *source* argument can be omitted.

tick/tock: Not applicable.

vmstep: Simulates the execution of a single VM command from the VM program, and advances to the next command in the code.

B.4.4   Default Script

The VM emulator's GUI buttons (single step, run, stop, reset) don't control the loaded VM code. Rather, they control the progression of the loaded script, which controls the code's operation. Thus, there is a question of what to do if the user has loaded a program directly into the VM emulator without loading a script first. In such cases, the emulator uses the following default script:

```
// Default script of the VM emulator
repeat {
  vmstep;
}
```

Index